DAPHNE M. HURFORD

TO READ
OR
NOT
TO READ

Answers to All Your Questions
About Dyslexia

A LISA DREW BOOK

SCRIBNER

A LISA DREW BOOK/SCRIBNER
1230 Avenue of the Americas
New York, NY 10020

Set in New Caledonia
Designed by Brooke Zimmer
Manufactured in the United States of America

1 3 5 7 9 10 8 6 4 2

Library of Congress Cataloging-in-Publication Data

Hurford, Daphne.
To read or not to read: answers to all your questions about
dyslexia/Daphne M. Hurford.
p. cm.
"A Lisa Drew Book."
Includes index.
1. Dyslexia—Popular works. I. Title.
RC394.W6H866   1998
616.85'53—dc21   98-11512
✓   CIP

ISBN 0-684-83950-4

For Sandy,
AND IN MEMORY OF
Nancy Brown Gislason

Contents

Introduction

From the moment I left journalism and began work as a learning specialist, my plan was to merge my two careers at some point and write about those with reading difficulties. What made me actually sit down and do so was the realization that in spite of the enormous progress made in terms of what we know about learning to read and the problems so many people have doing so, we have a long way to go before there is a true understanding and acceptance of dyslexia and dyslexics by the general public. Ignorance and prejudice still abound, and shame still fills the hearts of children who are convinced it is their fault that reading and writing are so difficult, of parents who feel guilty about passing on their own weaknesses to their offspring, and of adults who hide from either professional or personal fulfillment because of their dyslexia.

Nothing banishes shame as well as understanding does, and it is my hope that this book will contribute to the understanding of reading problems, to learning what to do about them, and to defeating the humiliation that so often accompanies them. The stories I tell are about valiant children, adolescents, and adults who have had their own confrontations with shame and who have bested it by learning to understand themselves and their disorder, their "difficulty with words," their dyslexia. They are all real people with real stories; through them it is possible to learn about the origins of dyslexia and its manifestations, also how to identify and conquer it and lose all sense of shame and guilt, of being less than others.

I knew my idea was right when I offered the possibility of a pseudonym to Cyprian, a teenager I work with, in case he wanted to protect his privacy. To the contrary, he felt totally at ease with his dyslexia and with having people read about him; he said he would prefer to be called Cyp to Cyprian, and added that he hoped his teachers would read the book and then "maybe they'd understand more."

Part One

The
Many Faces
of Dyslexia

CHAPTER ONE

Dyslexia Doesn't Discriminate

From Einstein to Churchill to the Boy Next Door

NOT LONG AGO, in a writing class I was teaching to some middle school girls, Albert Einstein's name came up. One of the students began talking about an article she had read about his personal life, and I asked, "Did you know Einstein was dyslexic?" Two girls, who themselves were so afflicted but had not known about the math genius's problems, immediately pumped the air with their arms and spat out a determined "YES!" thrilled to welcome him as a member of their club. A third, a beautiful and gentle child who clearly was also dyslexic but who had never been diagnosed, turned to me and queried, "You mean like Helen Keller?" "No," I said slowly, "not really . . . remember, Helen Keller couldn't see, hear, or speak." She rolled her eyes, smiled an embarrassed smile, and said, "Oh, of course. I knew that."

And she did. This was not a stupid, silly girl. She was very intelligent; I had seen ample evidence of her ability to think well and deeply. I had also heard her sound, and seen her write, as though she were a complete ditz. She simply couldn't find the right words when she needed them; she searched around her brain's storage compartments and found similar categories but imprecise, incorrect substitutes.

When she tried to explain her interpretation of something she had read, she stammered and repeated, and waved her hands, and apologized profusely before she even began. Rarely could she express clearly and concisely what was on her mind, in spite of the fact that sometimes her thoughts were more penetrating and interesting than the other students'.

The same problem, of course, appeared in her writing. To turn in a paper that had any sense of order and clear exposition, she had to make an outline, take notes, write, rewrite, alter her outline, rewrite again, and then have someone go over it with her. She had made her difficulty a part of her style; an attractive and elegant young lady, she handled it with a fey kind of charm. But it was easy to see how confusing and frustrating it was for her, and how she thought less of herself for being always restricted by weak word retrieval. She didn't know why she had such difficulty; she and her family had never come to grips with getting her a proper diagnosis so that she could understand how her own brain worked and what she needed to do to get it to give optimal performance. She would have been much better off, of course, if denial were not a part of her life. Instead, she and her friends all thought she was a bit of a ditz, and she acted accordingly. Hers is one of the many faces of dyslexia.

One of the observations of scientists researching reading difficulties is that it is possible that the neurons in the developing dyslexic brain don't march exactly to their assigned places as they do in nondyslexic brains, that they over- or undershoot their marks, that they don't stop at the outer layer of the cortex but sometimes march right on through, that they are scattered more than they are lined up like well-trained, obedient soldiers. Watching someone think and express herself in such a random fashion, her thoughts racing hither and thither, unable to land on exactly what she wants, makes this concept come vividly alive and all too real. Dyslexics often talk all around a subject, describe in great detail the word that they cannot put their mental fingers on, add details as though they were plucking them frantically from the stratosphere. Rebecca Tomasini, a graduate of Smith College and the University of London, says she can practically feel the bouncing around of neurons when she is trying to write a paper or have a conversation. She is sure this is the way her brain is organized. "It's kind of like the way crystals form," she says. The specific eludes her, dancing just out of reach; she must pursue it through the soup of the general and the irrelevant, the almost-on-target, the close-but-no-cigar, until she can finally capture it and wrestle it to her paper or voice. "I'm not a linear thinker," comments Rebecca. "There's too much going through my head at once. I have to go through many different things before I get to the main point. Huge bursts of things come at once, so it takes me a long time to get from A to B. I've learned to be patient with myself. When I write, I can't sit down and type because my hands can't keep up with my head. I have to use my verbal skills and talk into a tape recorder, then type it. That's probably why I hate writing letters; they seem so empty. It's really hard to make a piece of writing as packed as my head is." Rebecca is far from alone. What she has to deal with is a fact of life for many, many dyslexics. Time is their best friend; they need time literally to gather their thoughts, to put them in some sort of order before releasing them to the world at large.

Rebecca's difficulties describe exactly what dyslexia *is* and what the word means: *dys-*, "difficult," plus *lexis*, "word"—difficulty with words. It's a broad definition, and, of course, there is more to it than that, much more, but what it means is difficulty . . . difficulty reading words, writing words, remembering words, and sometimes even pronouncing words. The difficulty is most dramatically seen at the single-word level. It is much harder for dyslexics to read lists of words than to read connected text, because there is no meaning involved in a list; they cannot use their intelligence to figure out the words from what the rest of the sentence or paragraph says. And intelligent is something that dyslexics *are;* one must be of at least average intelligence to be diagnosed dyslexic. Dyslexics *are* also hardworking—at least until they get completely discouraged. Their difficulties are in spite of their efforts, not because of them.

Another of the many faces of dyslexia belongs to Ralph. I went to school with him back in the late fifties, before much was known about dyslexics. I didn't know Ralph in grammar school, but I know he was slow to "catch on" to reading about Spot and how he ran. By the time I knew him, in junior high school, he was considered a very slow reader and a bit slower in general than the others of us in our suburban public school. He was quiet, he was very sweet, and he dressed in what we considered, in those incredibly innocent times, as rather "hoody" clothes—boots, jeans, a shirt or sweater, and a black leather jacket, what would now be considered chic. His body language told more about him than we were then able to read: hunched over as if to protect himself, he walked on the periphery of any group, not quite outside and not quite inside. His eyes were usually downcast. He was the star of our mechanical engineering and shop classes, where we all spent most of the class time working with our hands, but he was neither a good athlete nor an academic achiever, the two successes respected by all.

Ralph rarely volunteered an answer, and when called upon anyhow, he had great difficulty coming up with the correct response as quickly as he needed to, to keep the teacher's interest. Yet, if we ever talked about the subject outside of class, when there was time and no pressure, he often had the most original, thoughtful, perceptive comments to make about what we were studying. But Ralph hid his light under a barrel, as the old expression goes. He never sat in the front of the class—where, of course, he should have been, but where he feared he would be more obvious. He came to class always at the last minute and slumped down in his seat. He started off alert and as ready as any of us, notebook and sharpened pencils at the ready. He would somehow have struggled through the reading the night before, and he was genuinely interested in many subjects, particularly American history; he was fascinated by the Civil War, for instance.

Then the teacher would start to talk. And talk. And talk. And talk some more. A few snippets of facts and dates appeared sporadically on the board, but basically we were supposed to listen and take notes. There is no more complicated cognitive function than listening to new material, digesting it, writing down key phrases and points, and simultaneously keeping up with a lecture. If Dante were to describe a list of levels of a hell designed especially for dyslexics, one of the most torturous would be the one where the daily task was listening to a lecture and taking notes. Back at Rye High School, you could almost hear Ralph's brain trying to keep up at the beginning of a lecture that was racing far ahead of his ability to process and make sense of the words, and you could also almost hear his gears grind to a halt when, halfway through, he would give up his heroic attempt and begin to look out the window and to doodle, making the intricate, elegant, complex drawings that

filled the pages of his history notebook where class notes should have
been.

Ralph was bright, and he was interested; his enthusiasm for the
material and availability for instruction should have made him a student any teacher would be eager to teach. But he was also dyslexic in a
place and time unfriendly to and uninformed about his plight. To
his teachers, Ralph was uncaring; he didn't pay attention, didn't try.
They decided he just didn't have it in him to master this material. If
Ralph had just acted out a bit more, been a behavior problem, he might
have found someone who insisted on doing something about him and
who might have decided he should be evaluated. On the very off
chance that he might have found someone who knew what to look for
in those pre-enlightened days, I feel sure—in my informed hindsight—
his dyslexia would have been discovered. I don't know where he is now,
but I did see him at our tenth high school reunion. He looked great;
being out of school for a decade agreed with him enormously. His
grades throughout high school had not been good enough to get him
the scholarship to college that he needed, so he went into the army. He
was lucky. He didn't have to go to Vietnam; he got some training and
some self-confidence, and then he went to college on the GI bill and
studied electrical engineering. Once freed from the strictures and pain
of a daily routine of try and fail, try and fail, Ralph found a place for
himself in society; he had a job that interested him and a wife who
loved him. He had *Liebe,* and he had *Arbeit*: love and work, the two
elements Freud felt most vital to mental health. Ralph came to the
reunion to share his happier life with the rest of us, to let us see how
much kinder the larger world was to him than the school world, but the
mere mention of the names of some of our former teachers still made
him shudder.

At the same time that Ralph was struggling away in a New York
City suburb, a young black boy named Cassius Clay was suffering
the same sort of plight in Louisville, Kentucky—except that he never
became shy and introverted the way Ralph did. No, Clay was an outgoing, supremely handsome, brash, charming kid. Still, his teachers at the
Virginia Street School despaired as his grades slipped lower and lower.
But Clay had a lucky experience that Ralph was denied; his brand-new
bicycle was stolen. After he discovered his red and white Schwinn miss-

ing, the twelve-year-old Clay searched out a white policeman named Joe Martin and told him furiously what had happened and what he was going to do about it. Martin, a known trainer of young boxers in the Louisville area, told the livid Clay that if he had any intention of fighting, he ought to learn how to do it right, and he said he would teach him.

At first Clay was no prodigy in the ring; Martin says he was no better than any number of boys he had trained. But he was a worker. He had found something he liked and could do, and he wanted to get better and better. All through his teens, Clay trained six days a week, many hours a day, year in, year out. While Ralph was struggling to pass at school, Cassius Clay actually dropped out for a while, but boxing gave him a focus, and boxing sent him back to school. "Boxing kept me out of trouble," he said many times. Cassius Clay barely graduated from high school, and his standardized test scores were always very low. From the time he was a little boy, he had severe trouble figuring out what the words were on a page, and he was a very slow reader even as an adult. Still, it was only many years later—long after he had won the Golden Gloves championship, won a gold medal at the Olympics, and become heavyweight champion Muhammad Ali, the most recognizable person in the world—and only after two of his own children were diagnosed as dyslexic, that people finally realized what his trouble was all along. His is another of the many faces of dyslexia.

Long before, and unfortunately also after, Ralph and Muhammad Ali, countless dyslexics spent most or all of their lives not knowing what was going on with them, feeling only that they were stupid and inept and different. Many actors and performers are dyslexic—motivated by the appeal of putting one's own struggles aside and of taking on new and varying personas, and by the fact that there is real power for those who have "difficulty with words" in being supplied with and knowing exactly the right words to say and in sounding really smart. It's also a way of getting positive attention. Tom Cruise and Whoopi Goldberg are famous examples of dyslexic actors—who often have to use tapes to learn their lines because it's so hard to memorize them from a piece of paper. Henry Winkler (the Fonz) is dyslexic; so is Harry Belafonte, and so was George Burns, though his wife, Gracie Allen, was the one you might have thought had trouble reading. The singer/actress Cher is eloquent when she talks about her own dyslexia, about the pain of high school and of feeling like a failure day in and day out.

An odd contradiction about dyslexics is that sometimes they are clumsy, lead footed, and not very good at sports, and sometimes their kinesthetic senses are so refined that they can achieve great feats in athletics or dance. Pitcher Nolan Ryan is dyslexic, as is Olympic gold–winning decathlete Bruce Jenner. There are ballet dancers who are so smart kinesthetically that they can do almost anything with their bodies. Yet, there was one I knew who lost a job with a top ballet company because of the memory difficulties that often accompany dyslexia; it was impossible to learn all the steps of so many ballets and keep them in the correct sequence.

I interviewed Greg Louganis, three-time Olympic diving champion, several times when he was competing and I was at *Life* magazine. He was already an Olympic winner when we first met, and his good looks and flashing smile added to his star appeal, but Greg showed not one iota of conceit about either his accomplishments or his looks. He was gentle and soft-spoken, cooperative and forthcoming. This was before either one of us knew anything about dyslexia; nonetheless, he was also dyslexic. Louganis, whose diving was always the epitome of grace and control and elegance, couldn't read at all as a child, except for one-syllable words and sentences made up of one-syllable words. Anything longer scrambled his brain, and no one knew enough to try to help him unscramble it. His school years were torturous; he spent most of his time trying to figure out how to avoid being called on to read; after many assorted schemes, he found that sitting in the very first row got him off the hook. (This is a bit of good advice for those who think they can languish unnoticed in the back of the room.) Still, he was called "retard" and other names so many times by his classmates that at the age of twelve he made his first of three suicide attempts, and when he went to the University of Miami on a sports scholarship, he described his academic efforts as his attempts to "keep from drowning," an interesting choice of metaphor from one so used to feeling safe in the water.

Diving was always the refuge of Louganis, the refuge from everything else that assailed him, and it was through diving that he made up for his academic difficulties and the problems he had with his parents, particularly his father, because of them. Louganis was always gifted athletically, and his innate awareness of himself in space and his exquisite timing made his diving career almost inevitable. He started off as an acrobat, though, at the tender age of eighteen months. His mother regularly took him with her when she picked up his older sister at her acrobatics class, and soon the handsome little Polynesian boy was doing everything the older kids could do. He won many competitions as an acrobat and had some trophies that were almost bigger than he was before he started diving. Once he began to dive, however, there was an unexpected complication due to his dyslexia, which Louganis described in his 1995 autobiography, *Breaking the Surface*. In diving, the goal is to enter the pool headfirst; in acrobatics, the goal is to land on the floor feetfirst. When Louganis was training for both, his brain would jumble directions, and he would end an acrobatic move as though he were diving, finishing on his face with a bloody nose. Another of the many countenances of dyslexia, this one rather battered and bruised.

It's no surprise when an artist is defined as dyslexic; we are used to expecting those who have strong visual gifts to be less gifted in the area of language. Auguste Rodin was believed to have been reading disabled; there is some thought that even the great Leonardo da Vinci was dyslexic. He was left-handed; he, who seemed to be able to solve any scientific or artistic dilemma, had great difficulty with reading and writing words; and he always wrote from right to left, a mirror image of what we consider "normal" writing. This may have been a protective device, a sort of code to keep his ideas secret, but he may also have done so involuntarily. Among writers, Joyce, Yeats, and Hans Christian Andersen were dyslexic. So is playwright Wendy Wasserstein; she has said that she thinks that is why she writes plays, with dialogue and conversation, instead of novels.

In the world of medicine, where there are many with profound spelling disabilities, it seems that more dyslexic doctors go into surgery than into any other branch. There are also dyslexics peppered throughout government offices. I recently heard a funny story about how a little town in Alabama got its unusual name. Arab (pronounced Ay-rab) has nothing to do with Arabs, Arabia, or the Middle East. The man who founded it sent in three possible names to the proper offices in Washington, D.C., for approval. One was the name of his son, Arad (pronounced Ay-rad), and whoever entered the name of the town onto all the proper documents and sent back the official notification of the name replaced the d with a b. Maybe Arab should become the dyslexia capital of America.

Charles Schwab, of discount brokerage fame, was an unidentified dyslexic who went through Stanford University reading at what he always felt was half the speed of the other students. To survive, he made full use of *Classic Comics* and *Cliff Notes;* he knew he learned much better when there was some sort of picture or visual clue to help him understand what the words were saying. Some dyslexics have the same kind of difficulty with numbers that they do with letters and words; others find math to be an area of strength for them. Charles Schwab fit the latter category; figures always made sense to him. He has also always felt he is a better, more creative, and clearer thinker than those whose thoughts are linear, who need and can accurately use sequencing. When Schwab was finally diagnosed at the same time as his eight-year-old son, he was greatly relieved to learn there was an explanation for his strengths and weaknesses, and he quickly became an advocate of those similarly designed. Schwab has founded the Parents' Educational Resource Center to help parents help their children, and his motto is, he says, "Dyslexics of the World—Untie!"

Nelson Rockefeller was the first famous dyslexic to "go public" with his difficulties. Of course, he was not identified as such as a child, and he had the same struggles in school as Ralph and Ali and Charles Schwab, but he triumphed over his problems and tried to help others do so, too. As an adult, Rockefeller often inspired dyslexic students with stories of his own struggles. He spoke about how he always had to work harder and longer than others; he urged children to accept the fact of their disability, to be brave and not to try to hide it or make excuses for themselves. Accept it as a challenge, and never, ever quit was the message he relayed, and he offered himself as an example of what dyslexics could achieve. And what an example! It would be hard to top the list of accomplishments of Nelson Aldrich Rockefeller. There were failures and setbacks for Rockefeller, too, of course, but, still, he oversaw much of the building of Rockefeller Center and of the Museum of Modern Art; he served as president of MOMA, as governor of New York, as assistant secretary of state for Latin America, and, briefly, as vice president of the United States.

In spite of his wealth and position, "Rocky" had to struggle throughout his school years to get out from under something he didn't understand, something that was always in his way, that made him feel stupid . . . his dyslexia. Always he was made to feel that his poor grades were his own fault, that if he just settled down, he would do better. And always he was trying to do better, longing to be as good and capable as the others, as his brothers and his classmates. He had an ambition that was most unusual for one born into his lofty family, a hunger to achieve that was rarely satisfied. No wonder he was so often described as someone who was out there fighting, not with his fists like Ali, but fighting nonetheless, the way those born poor or disadvantaged have always had to fight to overcome their backgrounds, or the way those born learning disabled have always had to fight to overcome their difficulties. In *Worlds to Conquer*, Rockefeller biographer Cary Reich quotes Thomas Braden, who knew Rockefeller for many years: "It's hard to believe that a guy with all the natural advantages Nelson had would be remembered as someone who overcame obstacles, but that's how I remember him. That was his strength, the thing I always admired."

The third of six children and the second son born to a father who would unfortunately always be known as Junior (that is, John D., Jr.), Nelson Rockefeller was curious and active, high-spirited and self-confident as a youngster, though uninterested in the quieter pursuits of reading and writing. At least, they thought he was uninterested. Looking back, of course, why should he care about something that was so hard, that offered only pain and no pleasure? When he was just seven years old, his nurse, Florence Scales, wrote to his mother, "Nelson is having great struggles with his reading." Mrs. Rockefeller seemed intuitively to know something about the genetic nature of dyslexia; she might even have known firsthand. Her son Nelson resembled her physically much more than he did his father, and she worried that the atrocious spelling that stayed with him throughout his life was something he had inherited from her and her father as well. Most likely she was entirely correct; the Aldrich side of the family was probably the genetic source of his dyslexia. Rockefeller's struggles with reading continued throughout grammar school, with the accompanying negative effect on his studies in general, and when it came time for him to go to prep school, Junior decided that he would send Nelson not to St. Paul's or Groton, not even to the traditional (and Rockefeller-funded) Browning School, where his older brother was a student, but to the (also Rockefeller-funded) Lincoln School.

Lincoln was brand-new, progressive, experimental, a sort of laboratory created by Teachers College, Columbia University, meant to put into practice the latest theories in education then being formulated by John Dewey and others at the graduate school. Junior may not have been familiar with dyslexia, and his reasons for sending Nelson to Lincoln had as much to do with his desire to have his son in school with a less elite, more egalitarian student body as with anything else, but his choice was an excellent one. He sent his son to a school that did not squash the boy's spirit over his difficulties, but encouraged his intellectual curiosity and took advantage of his nonacademic strengths.

Lincoln was an exciting, creative school. Math and science and English and history merged into one great subject, and everything related to everything else. There was no rote learning—that memorizing and spitting back to the teacher that is such a nightmare for dyslexics—and Greek and Latin were *out. In* were varying forms of measuring a student's progress besides tests and exams, all kinds of hands-on scientific inquiry, the trying on of all sorts of methods and materials, and a daily opportunity for each student to think and learn for himself and not just absorb what those in charge felt was appropriate. Also *in*, apparently, was a great deal of horsing around. It was a school that lived up to the lively nature of Nelson Rockefeller, and he lived up to it—mostly. He was a star athlete; he performed in all the school dramas and musicals; he was popular with students and faculty alike. *But.* The *but*, of course, was academics. Rockefeller's grades were low in spite of the nurturing of Lincoln and in spite of regular after-school tutoring. The kind of tutoring available to him back then was not what a dyslexic would receive today, remediation that actively addresses the difficulties in the way that the student can learn; what Rockefeller probably received was help with his homework and, if he had extra work, more of what he was taught in school, where he could not learn it.

Lincoln was great in most ways, but it was unable to do much to help Nelson Rockefeller understand his learning disability. No one at Lincoln really knew anything about what to do for his dyslexia—it wasn't until several years later that Rockefeller met Dr. Samuel Orton, the man who defined dyslexia, and received the diagnosis that finally let him understand that there was a reason he had such difficulty reading, that he was not merely stupid, that his IQ might in fact have seemed lower than it should have because of his dyslexia. Meantime, he struggled academically, even at Lincoln. By the time he was a teenager, his father was convinced it was all his son's fault, that he simply didn't put in enough time studying, a familiar refrain. So Rockefeller forswore listening to the radio and playing his phonograph on weekdays to increase his study time, and he kept a daily log of his hours spent with the books, but that did not assuage his father or improve his grades. Things reached a crisis point—as they do with so many dyslexics— when he tried to learn a foreign language, Spanish. He couldn't pass it during the school year, and he was still unable to pass it after a full summer of individual work.

By the time he was in eleventh grade, Rockefeller had to reevaluate his plans for the future. Without a second language, his dream of going to Princeton was completely unobtainable, as unobtainable as was the mastery of a second language. But he was never one to be defeated. He couldn't go to Princeton, but if he found a school that would accept him without the language, he could spare himself the torture of trying to learn one, failing, trying again, and failing again. Ever resourceful and adaptable, Rockefeller decided to drop Spanish, to put all his effort into improving his grades in the subjects where he had a chance to do so, and to go to Dartmouth. In the words of a real fighter, Rockefeller said years later of his senior year at Lincoln, "I was told that if I worked harder, I could make it. And that was absolutely true." Still, Rockefeller had to fight his dyslexia his whole life; he was born too soon to have had the benefit of the early training that today helps so many achieve the stronger reading and writing skills that enable them to rely on themselves, to put their difficulties behind them, to build a structured peace with the way their brains work. Rockefeller was a born politician, brimming with charm, quick on his feet, and quick with his wits, but he could never take for granted what so many politicians can: a quick glance at notes or a TelePrompTer to reassure them of some facts, and they're off! Long after the Lincoln School, long after Dartmouth, even after he had become a highly successful public figure, Rockefeller said to his head speechwriter, "I have a terrible time. I can't see a whole word. I have to go through it syllable by syllable. If I just glance at something, I get it mixed up. I have no confidence in reading."

Another famous overachiever who was thought to be dyslexic was Winston Churchill. Author William Manchester states definitively in *The Last Lion* that the prime minister was not so afflicted, but when I read in Churchill's autobiography, *A Roving Commission/My Early Life*, about his school history and his own discussion of his experiences—letters written home at the time and comments written later— I came to the inescapable conclusion that he most certainly was. There were just too many indications of dyslexia to think any other way. School was the one place where he was more miserable than any other; school demanded of him all that he found difficult and placed little value on all he did with ease. He was always at the bottom of his class in spite of his intense intelligence; his behavior, which was mischievous and defiant, would be interpreted today as a clear sign of his frustration. He could not learn Latin or Greek, and examinations defeated him. He failed his entrance exam for Harrow (a British public school similar to a top American private prep school), being completely unable to answer even one question on the Latin paper, but he was accepted anyhow. Said the grateful Churchill of the headmaster's decision to enroll him, "It is very much to his [Dr. Welldon's] credit. It showed that he was a man capable of looking beneath the surface of things: a man not dependent upon paper manifestations. I have always had the greatest regard of him." After four and a half years of being at the very bottom of his class at Harrow, Churchill had to take the entrance exam to Sandhurst three separate times—and have a great deal of private instruction—before he passed it. This sounds like what so many dyslexics go through when they must take standardized tests such as SATs. Looking back at his years in school, Churchill mused, "I was on the whole considerably discouraged by my school days. Except in Fencing, in which I had won the Public School Championship, I had achieved no distinction. All my contemporaries and even younger boys seemed in every way better adapted to the conditions of our little world. They were far better both at the games and at the lessons. It is not pleasant to feel oneself so completely outclassed and left behind at the very beginning of the race."

Churchill's dyslexia did not keep him from literature; he became an avid reader—a copy of *Treasure Island* sent him by his cold and distant father was one of the first books that lured him into the world of literature—but reading did not come quickly and easily to him. He described with charm and humor his first reading instruction by his beloved nurse, Mrs. Everest, when he was just about the age American children go to kindergarten, but the fear and pain are clear as well. Said Churchill,

> It was at "The Little Lodge" I was first menaced with Education. The approach of a sinister figure described as "the governess" was announced. Her arrival was fixed for a certain day. In order to prepare for this day Mrs. Everest produced a book called *Reading Without Tears*. It certainly did not justify its title in my case. I was made aware that before the Governess arrived I must be able to read without tears. We toiled each day. My nurse pointed with a pen at the different letters. I thought it all very tiresome. Our preparations were by no means completed when the fateful hour struck and the Governess was due to arrive. I did what so many oppressed peoples have done in similar circumstances: I took to the woods.

And if reading was a daunting challenge at first, arithmetic was even worse. Said Churchill,

> We continued to toil every day, not only at letters but at words, and also at what was much worse, figures . . . the figures were tied into all sorts of tangles and did things to one another which it was extremely difficult to forecast with complete accuracy . . . and the Governess apparently attached enormous importance to the answers being exact. . . . They became a general worry and preoccupation. More especially was this true when we descended into a dismal bog called 'sums.' There appeared to be no limit to these. . . . Just as soon as I managed to tackle a particular class

of these afflictions, some other much more variegated type was thrust upon me.

(Sounds just like a clever ten-year-old student of mine for whom the mysteries of math make no sense and have no appeal whatever—except when they can be tied to dollars and cents.) Years later, when he was trying to get into Sandhurst, Churchill determined that he had to learn enough mathematics to pass the entrance exam. It was his only choice; math, English, and Latin tests were mandatory, and he needed a high enough total score to gain admittance. He knew he could pass English, but Latin was as impossible for the future world leader as it might be for any dyslexic. Assessing his chances of passing the exam, Churchill commented, "Latin I could not learn. . . . Mathematics was the only recourse available." He embarked on a fervid six-month course of study under the aegis of a highly respected Harrow master, and he learned enough math to pass the exam. Just. Immediately he determined he would never deal with the subject ever again, saying, "I hope the Mathematicians . . . are well rewarded. I promise never to blackleg their profession or take the bread out of their mouths."

Churchill wasn't able to use a dictionary very well, either, a task dyslexics can find difficult and onerous; he described the confusion of trying to locate the exact word among so many similarly spelled words as a Herculean task that exhausted him. Today this kind of "overloading" when presented with too much stimuli is well understood among those of us who work with dyslexics, but Churchill realized it intuitively. He also seemed to understand the value visual aids play in helping dyslexics digest spoken or written material. He described as some of his favorite experiences at Harrow the occasional lectures by an authority on a particular subject who showed pictures to accompany his talk. Said Churchill of these occasions, "I wonder they do not have these lectures more often. They might well have one every fortnight, and afterwards all the boys should be set to work to write first what they could remember about it, and secondly what they could think about it. Then the masters would soon begin to find out who could pick things up as they went along and make them into something new, and who were the dullards; and the classes of the school would soon get sorted out accordingly. Thus Harrow would not have stultified itself by keeping me at the bottom of the school, and I should have had a much jollier time." He was absolutely right about himself and also right on the mark about education in general. In this one observation, Churchill unknowingly described the kind of teaching that stimulates and can assist a dyslexic and allow him to show what he can do intellectually without hamstringing him with declensions and long divisions and lists of facts (provided, of course, that the student could dictate his thesis, as Churchill always did, and not have to handwrite it).

The few successes Churchill enjoyed in school were usually the result of some teacher's taking him under his wing and teaching him in a way that he could learn. Today the schools I consider really good give their students extra support in learning how to read and write the English language before they send them on to anything more than conversation in a second modern language. In addition to English, the best have systems called skills programs, which give students extra time to work on their creative and expository writing, and which help them with their vocabulary development, with their knowledge of grammar and syntax and their ability to manipulate the language, with their reading comprehension and their computer skills, and with their outlining, note taking, and other study skills. The best of these programs also use the kind of multisensory instruction that has been proved to be successful with dyslexics. In addition, things like color-coding various elements of a sentence or a story or an outline are used to help students who learn better with visual aids—as most dyslexics do. Churchill had at least some of the benefit of what we know today about teaching dyslexics back before the condition was even identified, almost a decade before Dr. W. Pringle Morgan was talking about "word blindness" in *The Lancet,* and more than a decade before the turn of the twentieth century. This is what Churchill had to say about his instruction in English:

> . . . by being so long in the lowest form I gained an immense advantage over the cleverer boys. They all went on to learn Latin and Greek and splendid things like that. But I was taught English. We were considered such dunces that we could learn only English. Mr. Somervell—a most delightful man, to whom my debt is great—was charged with the duty of teaching the stu-

pidest boys the most disregarded thing—namely, to write mere English. He knew how to do it. He taught it as no one else has ever taught it. Not only did we learn English parsing thoroughly but we also practiced continually English analysis. Mr. Somervell had a system of his own. He took a fairly long sentence and broke it up into its components by means of black, red, blue and green inks. Subject, verb, object: Relative clauses, Conditional Clauses, Conjunctive and Disjunctive Clauses! Each had its colour and its bracket. It was a kind of drill. We did it almost daily. As I remained in the Third Fourth three times as long as anyone else, I had three times as much of it. I learned it thoroughly. Thus I got into my bones the essential structure of the ordinary British sentence—which is a noble thing. And when in years after my schoolfellows who had won prizes and distinction for writing such beautiful Latin poetry and pithy Greek epigrams had to come down again to common English, to earn their living or make their way, I did not feel myself at any disadvantage. Naturally I am biassed in favour of boys learning English. I would make them all learn English: and then I would let the clever ones learn Latin as an honour, and Greek as a treat. But the only thing I would whip them for would be for not knowing English. I would whip them hard for that.

Another of the many faces of dyslexia.

One of the great difficulties of the dyslexic, one that Churchill had some problems with at school, is the feeling of being found out, of being a fraud. A friend of mine, a successful and well-known if not famous author, felt every time she started a new project that "this is the one . . . this is the one where they are going to find out I can't do it, that I don't know how to write, and that I've just been fooling them and myself all these years." She never got over this panic at the beginning of a new assignment, this feeling of being a fraud who is soon to be discovered. This is how dyslexics feel all the time, and about many things, and it's even worse for dyslexics who have never been identified. When Winston Churchill was at Harrow, he got himself into a position where he actually was a fraud; after two years of suffering through Latin class, failing, trying again, failing again, day in and day out, he figured out a way around his troubles with what has long been known to students as a dead language. The way was cheating. He found an upperclassman who couldn't write essays but who was a whiz at Latin, and the two made a deal. The Latinophile would translate young Winston's homework for him every evening and read it to him so that he would get the pronunciation, and the Anglophile would write the occasional essay for the older boy—dictating it to him as he walked around the room, as was his wont. Once the headmaster liked the boy's essay so much, he asked him to come and discuss it and go into greater depth, which, of course, the lad could not do. The two were not openly accused, and Churchill was never put on the griddle, but he fretted regularly that he might be found out.

It continues to surprise me to find that dyslexia affects so wide a variety of people. We all find that there are these affinities that enter our lives. Before I was trained as a learning specialist, I never heard about people who were dyslexic; now I encounter them everywhere, in all situations; at parties a person newly met often confesses his dyslexia to me, friends ask my advice about their children and their nieces and nephews, and I have had many conversations with seatmates on trains or planes who, when they find out what I do, tell me of their struggles, or their children's struggles, or their husbands' struggles. The person who gives me financial advice is dyslexic, as is my accountant, who has several advanced degrees. Recently I was talking to the chairman of a board I am on, another smart dyslexic who received a progressive early education much like Nelson Rockefeller's and who graduated from the University of Chicago at the age of nineteen. His dyslexia entered our conversation when he asked me to call a radio station and enter a complaint "in high dungeon." The same day the brilliant computer expert I hired to help me understand how to get on the Internet, a woman who is sought after by companies to write their manuals and who built her own house with her own hands, misread the instructions to install my software, reading *through* for *though* and confusing the direction. When I suggested it might be the other word, she cringed, very embarrassed, said she was dyslexic and that she had thought she was stupid until she was accepted into a doctoral program at Columbia University, then added, poignantly, "Please don't judge me on my words."

John S. was identified as dyslexic on his own, when he was in his thirties. He wanted a college education and had not been able to get one—he had flunked out of St. John's University on Long Island when he was nineteen—but he was determined that one day he would succeed. So he had himself tested and found out his strengths and weaknesses, and he also got himself a second chance. I met him when he was thirty-five and a student at Marymount Manhattan College. Before we started working together, John had been described to me as "crazy but not dangerous." As it turns out, he was neither, but he was certainly among the most valiant people I have ever met. John had a strange life, it's true. He was a college student indeed, but, unbeknownst to the faculty or his fellow students, he had been supporting himself for years as a fortune-teller, and he had a whole other life where people consulted him regularly, almost like a therapist. I don't know about John socially—his life was too murky for me to want to find out—but I observed him at school. He was, of course, older than most of the other students at Marymount, but he had friendly relations with many. He was quick-tempered, though, and would get angry at teachers and fellow students at the drop of a hat.

John was tall and handsome in a very Irish way—black hair, blue eyes, mischievous smile, and glib charm; he seemed to have great potential as a con artist. He was a real Mr. Malaprop, though, always using a word similar to the one he wanted to use but just different enough to subvert his meaning completely. He had trouble speaking, he had trouble reading, he had serious trouble writing, and his study skills were nonexistent. He hadn't a single clue about how to get around a library—he didn't even know how to use a card catalog, much less any of the more technological resources—and he had great trouble trying to organize the information he did find. But no one was more willing to work than John, and work he did. He wanted his education, and he wanted it badly. John had never felt part of the mainstream world; he always felt different, strange, incompetent. A bachelor's degree was going to be his passport to respectability. We met a minimum of two times a week, often more, sometimes more than once a day. Whatever I could give him, John wanted. I taught him how to decode words by syllables; I taught him how to write a coherent English sentence and, more important, how to know when it wasn't coherent. He learned ministep by ministep how to write a research paper, and he finally—

after weeks and weeks of work and six or seven rewrites—turned in a fine history paper.

As hard as English and history were for John, math was even more of a challenge. He had to use graph paper when trying to figure out any sort of math problem because otherwise the numbers just jumped all over the page. When we worked together, he was taking a required course called Developmental Math, with basically sixth-grade-level material—the math that we use in our daily lives. It was very difficult for him. Math facts did not stay in his head, and multiplication tables made no sense to him whatever. I used manipulatives—particularly coins—with him as I would with a young child until he finally understood things like what a quarter of something was. John never minded or felt condescended to; anything that would help him learn was fine by him. He never gave up, and that seems to be the one thread that runs through all the stories of dyslexics who have "made it," whatever "making it" means to them. Whether a head of state, an Oscar winner, a successful businessman, or a thirty-five-year-old undergraduate, dogged determination is what links them together, and what made John a member of a distinguished fraternity.

What makes me describe him as valiant is as follows: John was permitted to take his tests with me, untimed. One day he had a very important math test, *the* test that would make the difference between his doing okay in the course or not. In the classroom, the students would have been given an hour to finish, and most students would have been done long before the time was up. I put John in a room with a one-way mirror and watched as he worked on this test. He had a fistful of pencils, a pile of scratch paper, and a very anxious look on his face. He spent three hours in that little room, and he never stopped working on the problems that whole time. When he was finished, the wastepaper basket was filled, and he was empty, utterly exhausted, used up. The next day, his professor came to tell me that John had received 97 points out of 100 on the test. That was the day John broke the back of mathematics, the day he realized that he could understand it after all. All I could think of was what I would have done in his place, and I thought that it was quite possible that I would have given up, that I didn't have it, that if something were that difficult for me, I would simply avoid it. John S. is another of the many faces of dyslexia; he will always be a hero to me.

CHAPTER TWO

Dyslexia Defined

Pinning Down the Elusive Elements

EVERYONE THINKS he knows something about dyslexia, even if what he "knows" is incorrect. Everyone also knows someone who is dyslexic, or who might be dyslexic, or who is just wondering if indeed dyslexia might be the reason reading is so fatiguing or writing so tedious. Dyslexia knows no age, gender, or class boundaries; it afflicts upwards of 15 percent of *all* Americans. The brilliant are as likely to be affected as those of average intelligence, the rich as likely as the poor, the adult as likely as the child. There is no cure for dyslexia, either; it doesn't go away. Dyslexics have to learn to work with and around the condition, not dream about getting over it. But just what is this thing called dyslexia? That is a question that I am asked regularly. More than a hundred years after the disorder was first identified, confusion and misinformation continue to surround its definition. So, before we get into just what dyslexia actually *is* (and what to do about it), here is a list of things that it definitely is *not*:

- It is *not* stupidity;
- It is *not* laziness;
- It is *not* willfulness;

- It is *not* lack of interest;
- It is *not* difficulty seeing or hearing;
- It is *not* simply the reversal of letters, numbers, and words;
- It is *not* anything to be ashamed of;
- It is *not* the end of the world;
- It is *not* necessarily permanently disabling; and
- It is also *not* "curable."

Even though this list of "nots" is also a list of facts, not opinions, most dyslexic children and adults have at one time or another been called stupid, or been accused of being lazy, or been told they were just being stubborn, and that is why they were having such trouble learning to read, or that they would be able to learn much more easily if they just wanted to . . . if they were just more interested . . . if they would just pay attention . . . if they would just work a little harder. Most have also been ashamed of being dyslexic, have tried to pretend they weren't, have thought it made them less smart than and inferior to others. Most have also felt at one time or another that being dyslexic was the end of the world and that they would never be able to get out from under the weight of it.

I met Valerie McCarthy when she was a junior in high school; I asked her to be a member of a panel of students with learning problems who would explain what school was really like for them to a group of their teachers at a workshop I was conducting. She became the star of the event. Attractive, intelligent, and extremely articulate, Valerie told her story, and throughout the room there were gasps and tears from faculty members who all thought they knew her well, but who had no idea what she had gone through before meeting them.

When she was just a little girl—and a privileged, loved, adorable little girl who went to a well-regarded private school in Manhattan—Valerie had felt ashamed, had felt inferior to her classmates, had felt it was all her fault, and had been terrified of the future. Toward the end of first grade, Valerie had not yet learned to read. Her school did not approve, and, as is often the case, her teachers blamed her. They thought she just wasn't trying hard enough. As her difficulty continued, they became less and less patient. One day during an arithmetic test, she became confused by the directions given and was unable to follow them properly—a typical experience for a dyslexic. When everyone else was finished with the test, Valerie was still at the beginning. And she knew the material, too, but no one bothered to find that out. Instead, her teachers made the seven-year-old stand up in front of the class and explain to the other students just how stupid she was. They told her parents she was stupid as well. Valerie believed them, but, luckily, her parents did not. In second grade, her teacher even occasionally whacked her on the back with a meter stick to cure her of what he thought was her stubbornness, her refusal to learn, and her lack of attention and effort. This did not take place in Victorian England, either; this was the 1980s, in New York City.

Often Valerie's papers looked like the jumble that was inside her head when she tried to read and write. Once during a test, the teacher dealt with her difficulty by walking by the child's desk and sweeping books, papers, and pencils onto her lap and the floor. Then he told the humiliated eight-year-old to pick everything up. As soon as she started tidying up, however, he told her not to do that, to concentrate on her work. When she went back to try to finish up what she had been doing, he scolded her for her messiness and told her to clean everything up. The little girl could not win no matter what she did, and she received small comfort from her classmates, who were all so shocked and afraid they would be treated the same way that they shunned her. Soon Valerie constructed a protective shell around herself that was all but impenetrable. She tried to appear "normal," but she was in agony, and her parents were at their wits' end. They didn't know what was wrong, what to do, or how to help. Finally, a friend suggested they have her evaluated, which they did. The diagnosis: dyslexia.

I met and worked with Rebecca Tomasini the summer after what should have been her senior year in college. Rebecca had had no trouble learning to read as a child. In fact, all through her grammar school days in western Massachusetts, she was an honor student, and on the gifted-and-talented track. Then, in ninth grade, she hit the wall. She couldn't do the work. She could think, and think well, but she couldn't read what she needed to read, and she couldn't express herself in writing. Her teachers blamed her as well; they said she was lazy and needed to work harder, that was all. As she says now, "Even in grammar school my papers looked as though an orangutan had written them. Anybody with proper training would have known something was wrong." But no one did. Rebecca was scared. She was confused. She was humiliated. And she was furious. Her grades plummeted; she was taken out of the classes for the gifted and talented and put in with less and less able students. Her behavior bottomed out as well. In very little time, Rebecca changed from a spirited, curious, smart kid into a rebellious and insolent teenager. She was miserable. She wanted so much, and she was able to get so little. Hungry for intellectual stimulation, she ended up at a mediocre college where most of the all-female student body was preparing for a Mrs. degree, while Rebecca dreamed of becoming a scholar, an expert on the Renaissance. She knew she was smart; she didn't know why she couldn't achieve what she wanted so desperately, but she knew something was drastically wrong. She had to find out, and she had to fight for what she wanted. She found an educational psychologist, and she was tested. The diagnosis: dyslexia.

For most of the century-plus that people have been interested in dyslexia, discourse about the disability has been marked by disagreement and dispute. Even now there is more than one "official" definition, and terminology is still in flux. For years the condition was referred to as *specific reading disability;* another term often used is *developmental dyslexia,* or even *specific developmental dyslexia.* All are meant to distinguish it from the word problems caused by brain injuries or disease—called acquired dyslexia, or alexia. The World Federation of Neurology offers a definition for specific developmental dyslexia as follows: ". . . a disorder manifested by difficulty in learning to read despite conventional instruction, adequate intelligence and sociocultural opportunity. It is dependent upon fundamental cognitive disabilities which are frequently of constitutional origin."

The International Dyslexia Association, which used to be the Orton Dyslexia Society, named for Samuel T. Orton, the American doctor who, with his wife, did pioneering work in the field in the early decades of the twentieth century, adopted a newer, more precise, more inclusionary definition of the reading disorder in 1994 to replace the many vague, exclusionary definitions that had been floating around. "Dyslexia is a neurologically based, often familial disorder which interferes with the acquisition and processing of language. Varying in degrees of severity, it is manifested by difficulties in receptive and expressive language, including phonological processing, in reading, writing, spelling, handwriting, and sometimes in arithmetic. Dyslexia is not a result of lack of motivation, sensory impairment, inadequate instruction or environmental opportunities, or other limiting conditions, but may occur together with these conditions. Although dyslexia is lifelong, individuals with dyslexia frequently respond successfully to timely and appropriate intervention."

At about the same time, the Orton Research Committee proposed its own working definition for research purposes, as follows: "Dyslexia is one of several distinct learning disabilities. It is a specific language-based disorder of constitutional origin characterized by difficulties in single word decoding, usually reflecting insufficient phonological processing. These difficulties in single word decoding are often unexpected in relation to age and other cognitive and academic abilities; they are not the result of generalized developmental disability or sensory impairment. Dyslexia is manifested by variable difficulty with different forms of language, often including, in addition to problems with reading, a conspicuous problem with acquiring proficiency in writing and spelling."

So, even now, and even within the organization that has done the most to spread the word about dyslexia, there continues to be a measure of debate about definition. For our purposes, the official Dyslexia Association definition makes the most sense; it is clear and quite broad-ranging, and it also includes the notion that something can be done about all of this, that dyslexics often "respond successfully to timely and appropriate intervention." Margaret Rawson, a pioneer in the field and a founder of the Dyslexia Association, described dyslexia a bit more succinctly and poetically when she said, "The differences are personal; the diagnosis is clinical; the treatment is educational; and the understanding is scientific."

Valerie is one who certainly responded successfully to her just-in-time appropriate intervention. When her parents told her school about her diagnosis, officials there said, "Nonsense. There is no such thing." The McCarthys flew first into rage, then into action. They changed their daughter's school to one that understood what was wrong, that appreciated her, and that knew how to teach the little girl. Then they got a properly trained learning specialist to work one-on-one with her after school, to teach her to read in the ways that she could learn. When she first started at her new school, Valerie couldn't believe how friendly the other students were or how nice the teachers were. She soon came to feel safe and enjoy it, though, and she had an unexpected plea- sure as well. "Because my first school was somewhat accelerated," says Valerie now, "I was ahead for the first time in my life. It was great, but it lasted one month at most. Then I wasn't exactly sure what was going on or how to feel about it." Most surprising to Valerie was the fact that she wasn't the only student having difficulties; there were several others in the same situation as she, and they talked about their problems, shared their fears. "That was comforting in a way," recollects Valerie, adding, "but some of them seemed to have surrendered. It was scary, too, and it made me realize I had to push myself to do more."

One enforced activity in the highly structured school turned out to be a very felicitous event for Valerie. Each of the eighth-graders at her all-girls academy was required to try out for the spring musical; the year Valerie was in eighth grade, the play was *The Wiz*. Valerie had no interest in being in the production, but she had no choice. A day after the auditions, the teacher in charge called Valerie's mother. The child had exhibited such a powerful natural singing voice that they wanted her to play Dorothy, but they were afraid she would be unable to mem- orize all her lines because of her dyslexia. Would her mother be willing to help? Would she! She had been so worried about her daughter that she would do anything. Now, finally, there was some hope. Here was an area where Valerie was not being left behind; in fact, she was leading the pack. Mrs. McCarthy seized the opportunity. She helped her daughter learn her lines and lyrics for *The Wiz*; she helped with Valerie's homework, and she enrolled her daughter in Saturday singing lessons, which had unexpected benefits. Valerie was a smash hit in *The Wiz*; she went on to star in every other musical during her years in high school, and she went from voice lessons to theory to ear training, from an hour or so a week to all day Saturday, 8:30 A.M. to 5:00 P.M. She had found something she truly liked and something she excelled in. She has since graduated from college, and she is currently in Italy, training for an opera and concert career.

As for Rebecca, she would have been a great deal better off if her intervention had come much earlier in her life. After struggling so in high school and then finding herself in what she felt was an utterly inappropriate college, she really hit bottom. She knew she could do and have more, but she was locked into an inability to show others what she could really accomplish. Things got so bad she found herself on Prozac. Then somehow she discovered pools of energy and strength. With the help of a professor who recognized her superior intellectual ability and was willing to speak up for her, she was accepted into Smith. At last she was reaching her own level; she was thrilled and terrified. She started Smith that January; the following summer we worked intensely together, laughed uproariously together, and cried together.

Over those few short months, Rebecca learned how to monitor her reading, how to form a thesis statement, how to tame dense text. It was a fabulous start, but she needed more, and the college was committed to giving it to her. The school was new at this, though, and unsure of how to proceed. Rebecca's years at Smith were not easy; she had constant battles to fight, and many times she thought about chucking it all, but she didn't. She is now a graduate of a Seven Sisters college, where her mind was permitted to grow and be challenged as she had always dreamed, and she has also received an M.A.—in Renaissance studies— from the University of London.

Educators were not the first to be aware of dyslexia; ophthalmologists were. The first description of "word blindness," by Dr. W. Pringle Morgan, appeared in the British medical journal *The Lancet* in 1896. Not long after, in 1902, another ophthalmologist, James Hinshelwood, described a patient of his who was thought to be bright in many ways but who couldn't seem to learn to read. Hinshelwood thought the difficulty was somehow with the boy's visual memory, with his ability to remember what the letters and words looked like, and that the cause was either an injury to his brain or some sort of congenital problem. Dr. Samuel T. Orton, a neuropathologist and psychiatrist, in 1925 used the term *strephosymbolia,* or "twisted symbols," to label the "difficulty with words" that he saw in patients in his psychiatric practice, and he also described the reversals and mirror writing that many dyslexics experience but that is not limited to dyslexics. Even while Dr. Orton was doing his work at Columbia University's College of Physicians and Surgeons, though, Ph.D.'s at Columbia University's Teachers College were saying what Valerie's teachers much later said, "Nonsense. That can't be right. No such condition exists."

As it turns out, even though Dr. Orton was one of the first to link dyslexia with language, a concept agreed upon by all today, his early work concentrating on visual processes and deficits was what he was long known for; those reversals became *the* symbol of dyslexia, and people became convinced that the only thing a dyslexic had difficulty with was keeping letters and symbols in the right sequence. Many people today still think that that is all there is to dyslexia. Jokes on the subject even continue to make the rounds, such as, "If MADD stands for Mothers Against Drunk Driving, then what does DAM stand for?" Answer: "Mothers Against Dyslexia."

Once people began to believe that reading problems were centered in the eyes and the ability of the eyes to translate what they saw, treatment plans started revolving around training a person's visual perceptual abilities, and optometrists and others offered visual training as the key to remediating reading problems. For years this training was sought by many, including the parents of Walker Harman, Jr., a young man currently in law school with whom I worked when he was a student at Marymount Manhattan College.

Walker is from Texas; his mother is on the obsessive side, particularly about him, her eldest son. So, when it was recommended that Walker not move on to second and then not to third grade because he had not yet learned to read, Mrs. Harman rallied her troops and contacted every known expert in the field. At a very tender age, Walker was consulting a series of doctors and specialists. He saw several around Dallas, and he came to New York every six weeks to receive treatment that was meant to retrain his eyes, body, and brain to see symbols as they actually were. Walker did eye exercises; he walked on balance beams; he batted at balls dangling on strings from the ceiling; he even carried a pegboard around with him so that whenever he had some free time, he could practice inserting different colored pegs in it in an assortment of ways. Did any of it do any good? "Well, it did help me to learn to love New York," says Walker today with a sly smile. And that is about all it did; it certainly didn't teach him to read.

Yet, despite the lack of documented success in remediating reading difficulties, vision therapy for learning problems continues to be offered today by many, many optometrists. It is a therapy that appeals to parents to whom a connection between reading difficulties and eyes makes sense—after all, what is the major pathway of written words to the brain? The eyes. It is hard to resist thinking that if only what went into the eyes were somehow dealt with differently by them, then things would improve, and reading would be a much easier task.

There is widespread agreement now that dyslexia is a language disorder, meaning that the difficulty is not in the eyes, or even in the ears, but in the language acquisition and processing centers of the brain. So, training the eyes or training the ears won't make any real difference. It's the brain that needs to be trained. For a long time, it was thought that those language acquisition and processing areas were centered exclusively in the left side of the brain, while logic and artistry and spatial awareness were the specific purview of the right. We know now that it is not as simple as that. There is much more interchange between the brain hemispheres than we had once believed, and although the left side is the primary locus, language processing involves, to varying degrees, both right and left sections. Therefore, dyslexics are not *just* "right-brainers," as they were long described, although many often show great strength in conceptual thinking—seeing the "big picture"— as well as in visual and spatial skills, all of which are more associated with the right hemisphere of the brain than the left. Many graphic designers, architects, computer animators, filmmakers, athletes, and dancers are dyslexic, but then, so are many lawyers, doctors, teachers, and writers, even writers who create some of the most complex and eloquent language. Yeats was dyslexic and so was James Joyce (which might not come as a complete surprise to many who have struggled through *Ulysses*).

At the moment, the most intense concentration in reading research is on phonology, most particularly phonemic awareness as the "most potent" indicator of the ability to learn to read, and on deficits in this awareness as a prime underpinning of dyslexia. Phonemes are the smallest sounds we hear in words, most often the sounds of one letter; every word in the English language is a combination or recombination

of just forty-four phonemes. Phonemic awareness is the ability to identify these sounds, to isolate them within a word or syllable, to move
them around, and to count how many there are. A very simple example
is the ability to determine that there are three sounds in the word *cat*
(c-a-t), that they are *kuh-aa-tuh,* that if you were to say them backward,
you would say *tuh-aa-kuh,* and if you were to leave out the *aa,* you
would have *kuh* and *tuh.* Without this ability, it is much more difficult
to learn to decode words, to translate print into sounds.

The late Isabelle Liberman did landmark studies on phonological
awareness in the 1970s at the Haskins Laboratory in New Haven. She
showed that children develop these higher-order skills as they mature,
and that by school age, they should be proficient at them. Her experi-
ments, which asked children to tap out the number of sounds they
heard in words, showed that none of the four-year-olds in the study
could identify the correct number of sounds (they were too young),
that 17 percent of the five-year-olds could, and that 70 percent of the
six-year-olds were able to do so. That meant that 30 percent of those
who were old enough to be able to tap out the sounds couldn't do so.

To look at whether this ability to isolate sounds was a real indicator
of their future reading capability, Liberman gave reading achievement
tests to that six-year-old group when they started second grade. Of the
30 percent who could not earlier identify the sounds correctly, half
were in the lowest reading group; not one was in the highest. So 15 percent of the children in her studies were having a very difficult time
learning to read. Current statistics from the National Institutes of
Health estimate that at least 15 percent of school-age children are
dyslexic; Isabelle Liberman's studies of almost three decades ago would
tend to support those numbers.

In order to read, write, and spell English, an alphabetic language, one
must be able to decode, that is, be able to relate the symbols, the letters, to the sounds, or phonemes, and the sounds to the symbols. And it
has to be done quickly. Fluent readers sail through a passage with few to
no glitches; they can process with ease all the different phonemes that
make up the words. Dyslexics have difficulty doing this; they have to work
much harder to recognize or sound out each each word, so their processing is much slower and less smooth. Also, their capacity for holding

the individual sounds of a word in short-term memory can be weakened, so they might forget the first before they have figured out the third or fourth, and have to go back and try a few more times before they have the whole word. In addition, their ability to call up a word stored in memory can be much slower and less reliable than that of nondyslexics. That is why dyslexics often grope for words and have difficulty answering direct questions, why they talk around and describe the answer while the exact word or "label" remains slippery, why they frequently end up saying, "Forget it." On the other hand, skilled readers, who can find stored words more easily anyhow, also increase their ease with word recall by reading more and using words over and over, which helps to fix them firmly in their memories.

Phonemic awareness, the underlying foundation of reading, is also enhanced, enlarged, and reinforced by reading. Therefore, skilled readers can read more because they have this ability to manage the parts of words, and the reading they do makes them more and more adept at manipulating the language. A study at Jerusalem's Hebrew University confirmed this theory. It showed that training at-risk kindergartners in phonemic skills helped them learn to read more readily and that kindergartners and first-graders improved their skill in chunking words into phonemes drastically once they learned how to read. Nothing builds muscles like weight lifting, and the stronger you are, the more weight you can lift. The same goes for reading.

Keith Stanovich of the University of Toronto takes this thought one step farther. He posits that there is a core of phonological deficits that interferes with the ability to learn to decode words, and he goes on to describe an unfortunate reciprocal relationship that he has termed the Matthew Effect. It starts with the dyslexic having difficulty learning to read words because of this core, this lack of phonological-processing abilities, including a lack of phonemic awareness. Then, because reading is so difficult, the dyslexic reads fewer books, magazines, and newspapers than the stronger reader, and also reads easier books, less complicated and sophisticated prose. So, while the more fluent reader's basic phonological skills are growing and developing because of his ability to read and his greater exposure to the written word, the dyslexic's basic skills do not get nourished and strengthened and instead remain a hindrance. And on it goes, in a downward circular movement. Where does Matthew come in? Well, as in the Bible, if you apply the concept of reading to Matthew 13:12, you find that poor readers get poorer while rich readers get richer. Nothing succeeds like success, and nothing begets failure like failure. There is a great deal of research to support Stanovich's theory. Studies recently conducted in California found the not-so-surprising information that the fifth-grader whose reading scores are very high, in the 90th percentile, reads approximately two hundred times more text per year than the fifth-grader whose scores are very low, in the 10th percentile. Many of us in the field can also corroborate it anecdotally; we have taught students who were not diagnosed until late and were caught up (or actually down) in the Matthew Effect whirlwind.

It doesn't have to be that way. Dyslexics don't have to be left out of that particular success loop. They don't have to become victims of the Matthew Effect. They *can* join the upward spiral, they *can* learn to read and understand sophisticated material, but they *must* be taught to do so in ways that work for them. And believe me, there is nothing in the universe more satisfying than working with such a student and reversing that spiral.

According to the Dyslexia Association definition, dyslexia is "neuro-logically based"; it's right there in the neurons, the building blocks of the brain, in the arrangements of them, in the sizes of them, and in the quantities of them. Getting to the point where the Association could make such a statement wasn't easy. Though most involved with the field felt from the earliest days that there had to be a neurological basis for dyslexia, for a long time the only possible way to draw any con-clusions was by studying the behaviors of dyslexics and relating them to behaviors of people with known neurological conditions. It was hard to get a look at the brain. So, much of the early research was based on observing people who had lost various language functions because of accidents, strokes, or diseases.

Dyslexia is still a disorder that is identified by behavior—reading is a behavior, and so is being unable to learn to read—but modern tech-nology now makes it possible to create various computer models of the neural networks of human brains and to see how they behave, and to watch real brains in action during the reading process and to see what is going on where. That doesn't mean that vital information was not gathered before fast and powerful computers and assorted scans and MRIs came into existence, but it does mean that more information is being gathered by more people faster and more accurately. Early, non-invasive machinery like EKGs didn't yield much valuable information about what goes on in the brain to make reading easy or hard, and animal models are no good for most studies because reading is a distinctly human activity. Now, though, neuroscientists are marching rapidly across that bridge to the twenty-first century, and they have a wide array of expensive toys to help speed them along. PET scans and functional MRIs have made it possible to look at and compare brains of living beings and quite noninvasively to study the brain during the act of reading. Brain imaging with functional MRIs has been an intense focus at several spots, with Sally and Bennett Shaywitz and their colleagues at the Yale Center for the Study of Learning and Attention publishing the most in mainstream journals and receiving the most mainstream attention for their efforts. What the studies have been trying to show is which areas of the brain are at work when its owner is reading or trying to read. With two groups of adults, one dyslexic, the other not, the Shaywitzes have been able to track the reading process through the brain and vividly demonstrate what happens where and what the differences are between the good and poor readers. This is the first time that it has been possible actually to see that there is, in G. Reid Lyon's words, "a neurological system that undergirds all the components of reading and that a neurobiological signature underlines poor performance on reading."

Their research really began with a French brain surgeon and anthropologist named Paul Broca. He discovered that language functions were localized in the left frontal region of the brain, the inferior frontal gyrus, now known as Broca's area, in 1861. Over the years since then, many others have contributed greatly as well. One hundred years after Broca came the "father" of modern behavioral neurology, Norman Geschwind, a graduate of and professor at Harvard Medical School. Geschwind was one of the very first to study structural differences in the brains of dyslexics and nondyslexics, and he was the first to look at the possibility that the language areas of nondyslexics' brains might differ in size from each other, while those in the dyslexic were the same size. Study continues actively on these brain "asymmetries," as well as on the connections between areas, the nerve fibers that carry information.

Geschwind was also interested in the relationship of gender and dyslexia, left-handedness and dyslexia, and immune and allergic disorders and dyslexia. He connected all three; he thought it might be possible that the male hormone testosterone acted on the fetus to weaken the immune system and the left hemisphere of the brain. Norman Geshwind died prematurely in 1984, at the age of fifty-eight. His research has been carried on by Albert Galaburda and others, who are still looking at what is called the testosterone hypothesis. They have found enough in their studies, particularly as related to handedness, to keep on looking, but they have not yet come up with conclusive evidence linking either left-handedness or immune disorders to dyslexia. Geschwind was certainly not the only person interested in reading disorders and handedness, the main reason being, of course, that the opposite side of the brain controls handedness—that is, if you are left-handed, it is quite possible that your right-brain hemisphere is more developed than your left-, where so many of the language areas are located. Those of us who work with dyslexics would tell you that many are left-handed, that left-handedness stands out as one of those red flags, and that it is more difficult for someone who is left-handed to adapt to the left-to-right sequencing required of readers of English.

Geschwind wasn't the only one interested in gender and dyslexia, either. Until quite recently, it was thought that male dyslexics outnumbered female by at least four to one. Now it is clear that is not so. Anecdotal evidence would indicate that two societal biases were at work in these numbers. The first is the fact that the education of boys has always been much more highly valued than that of girls, so there was traditionally much more concern when they did not do well. Dyslexia research and treatment pioneer Margaret Rawson, in her 1968 book addressing the adult accomplishments of the dyslexic boys she studied at a coeducational private school in Pennsylvania, commented, "With girls, schooling and employment outside the home take a role secondary to homemaking, and homemaking, however important, obviously cannot be graded for comparative purposes." The second societal

bias in favor of identifying more boys with dyslexia than girls is that traditionally girls who struggle in school tend to become shy and with-
drawn, while boys with difficulties tend to "act out" and call attention to
themselves. More recent studies, such as the Connecticut Longitudinal
Study (1983–1996) at Yale and others, have indicated that females
seem just about as likely to be dyslexic as males. In fact, according to G.
Reid Lyon of the National Institutes of Health, even though schools
continue to identify as dyslexic 3 or 4 boys for every 1 girl, studies the
NIH has funded around the country (including the Yale study) show
that the real numbers are 1.2 boys for every girl.

According to the Dyslexia Association definition, dyslexia is also
"familial"; brothers, sisters, cousins, and others of the same families are often dyslexic, and it is "heritable," passed down from one gen-
eration to another. Familial and heritable do not necessarily mean that
having a dyslexic parent or sibling guarantees you will be dyslexic, but
they do mean that there is about a 50 percent greater chance of having
the disorder if a relative has it. Walker Harman's father is dyslexic; academic success was so nonexistent for him when he was a teenager that
school officials tried to take him out of high school and put him in a vocational school where he would get some practical training, but his
mother intervened ("threw a fit," says her grandson), and he stayed in a
college preparatory program. He went on to Baylor, where he graduated
with fairly respectable C's, then to the University of Oklahoma Business
School. He is now a very successful businessman/hotelier, who, according to his son, still can't spell or read, who didn't read a book for pleasure
until he was forty years old, and who didn't discuss his difficulties with
his son until Walker junior was grown, so ashamed was he of his early
memories of failure. Neither one of Rebecca Tomasini's parents is
dyslexic, nor is her brother, but she has an uncle who is.

Cyprian is a dyslexic boy I have worked with longer than any other
student in my practice. He is now in high school; we met when he was
in the second grade. Cyp was having a terrible time learning to read,
and his parents and teachers were as confused and frightened about it
as he was. After a few months of working with him, I arranged for a
conference with his parents to discuss their son. They were very nervous, afraid of what they were going to hear, but after I described the

real progress he was making, as well as the difficulties he was facing and learning to deal with, his father blurted out, "Well, you know, I've never really been able to read."

Studies are ongoing constantly on the genetic aspects of dyslexia. Researchers at the Boystown Institute, and on the Twin Project at the University of Colorado, Boulder, among others, continue to yield important information. Scientists have been searching for the "dyslexia gene," and they appear to be closing in on a candidate or two. Genes located on both chromosome 6 and chromosome 15 appear to be the most likely—with phonemic awareness deficits linked to 6 and single-word-identification deficit linked to 15—but they think others are involved as well, and much more detective work needs to be done before any conclusions can be drawn. Bruce Pennington, professor of psychology and head of the Developmental, Cognitive and Neuro-science Program at the University of Denver, says, "There is a great deal of genetic involvement in building a brain. Thirty to forty percent of the one hundred thousand genes in the body are uniquely expressed in the brain."

Okay, so dyslexia is genetic. What isn't? One beautiful, charming mother of a seventh-grade boy I worked with felt very guilty that her son had inherited her learning weaknesses. She could hardly forgive herself. Yes, he had, I explained to her, but he had also inherited her good looks, excellent sense of humor, and natural charm; he was hand-some and the most well-liked boy I have ever known. Plus, she was get-ting him the help that he needed, help that no one knew to get her. Many geneticists talk about the fact that hereditary predispositions that seem negative often also have a very positive side: that is, sometimes a seeming genetic weakness offers protection against something much more dangerous. Perhaps that was at work with this young man and his mother.

Anyhow, is the fact that dyslexia is genetic all there is? No, not at all. Dyslexia may be genetic, but it is not *just* genetic; there is more to it. If you have the gene or genes, are you guaranteed to be dyslexic? No, no, no. First, interestingly enough, it appears that some people are born with the gene but unaffected by it. Second, our brains are not "hard-wired" at birth; they are not completely formed, set, unchanging and unchangeable. Quite the contrary. They are incredibly plastic, malleable, capable of change, growth, development. We can alter and improve ourselves in all ways. Bruce Pennington says the brain is an "open system," and he adds, "The developing brain must use its environment to shape its patterns and connections, and as the brain learns, its structure changes, so does the size, and even how many synapses there are. Not all the structures of the brain even show genetic influence, and some, like the cortex, develop late and are much more susceptible to environmental than genetic influences."

Studies of the human brain not devoted to unearthing the etiology of dyslexia and other learning disabilities have yielded similar information that could and should have a huge impact on how we take care of children, particularly very young children. These studies show that the electrical activity of neurons that takes place even in the prenatal brain, which used to be thought of as a by-product of the building of the brain, actually has an active role in the shaping and wiring of that brain. The firing of neurons is spontaneous before birth and is controlled by sensory experiences once the child is in the world. Nature and nurture. According to these studies, it appears that the sensory experiences are the overseers of the lopping off of superfluous neurons that takes place in every brain as the child develops and grows. In other words, what goes in through the senses exerts a great deal of control over which neurons and neural networks will be permitted to stay and labor in the brain and which will be eliminated. Humans are born with all the neurons they'll ever have. Those that receive stimulation grow and develop; those that are not used are discarded. Therefore, obviously, the better the sensory input, the better the development. And the most important time for this development? Ages one through three are all vital, but the first year of a baby's life is the most powerful one. This doesn't mean that parents should be reading *War and Peace* to their six-month-old babies to get them ready for reading, but it does mean that all that talking and cooing and singing and touching and snuggling that parents tend to lavish on babies helps their offspring develop properly in all areas, including language. Evidently, nature and nurture are not separate, discrete entities. Nature certainly affects nurture; there is that genetic component to dyslexia, but nurture has its strong impact, too. Remember, part of the Dyslexia Association definition says that "individuals with dyslexia frequently respond successfully to timely and appropriate intervention." Every indication is, though, that the earlier the intervention, the more successful. That intervention can change how a dyslexic reads, writes, and learns, and it seems that it is possible that it can even change the makeup of the brain itself.

Says Bruce Pennington, "We are in the middle of a scientific revolution in understanding how the brain works." Leaders of this revolution, like most others before it, have found a great deal of government money available to buy their weapons. The 1990s were designated the Decade of the Brain, and during that time, the NIH doled out funds to nineteen universities and centers from coast to coast to establish a Learning Disabilities Research Network. Some of these studies began quite a bit before the decade designation—in fact, Haskins Lab, where Isabelle Liberman did her studies, was the first to receive NIH funding, as far back as 1965—but the extra attention certainly didn't hurt. Harvard has received money; so has Yale, Johns Hopkins, Florida State, Denver, Boystown, and the University of California at Irvine, among others. G. Reid Lyon, blessed with brains, energy, and a fabulous sense of humor, is the research director who oversees this work. Lyon is also iconoclastic and passionate about what he does, and he is a born showman, holding audiences rapt and then startling them with statements like "Whole language sucks for dyslexics" before darting behind a podium, and "That's Al D'Amato's brain thinking as hard as it can," when describing a slide of a brain showing absolutely no activity.

Above all, though, Lyon is dedicated to scientific rigor, to establishing a science of education. What is discovered in one lab must be solid enough to be created anew in another setting. Says he, "If you don't have generalization and replication, you have belief, not science." Lyon also describes the NIH's job as "knocking down theories, not supporting them." The research initiative of the National Institute for Child Health and Development, part of the NIH, says Lyon, is to uncover which methodologies or combinations of methodologies, which developmental level, which stages of reading, and which combinations of setting have the greatest impact, and for how long and for what reasons. He goes on to say that NIH-funded studies have shown that early language disorders in children are highly predictive of reading and writing difficulties, and that early intervention is extremely important. So important, says Lyon, that "if you're not given informed help before the third grade, you're in trouble."

• • •

Nature and nurture combine their effect before a child is born, as well. Sometimes reading and learning problems are the result of environmental damage the fetus has sustained; cigarettes, lead, alcohol, drugs, disease can all create problems that are much more difficult to deal with than dyslexia. The first student I ever worked with, at the clinic at Teachers College while I was doing my graduate work, was a victim of fetal alcohol syndrome. He was severely impaired, and the kind of intervention that is appropriate for dyslexics did not help him much.

Paul was nine years old; he could read very little and write less, and he had very little stamina or attentional capability. He also had the distinctive flatness in his face that distinguishes those who have been damaged by their mother's drinking. He was sweet and sensitive; he was painfully aware of his lacks, and in the two years I knew him, he talked more than once about being so tired of disappointing people all the time that he wanted to die. Learning anything was exceedingly difficult for him, retaining it was even harder, and he was emotionally very fragile as well. He wrote his name, first and last, completely backward, and if we were walking down the hall and I asked him to turn left, he invariably turned right. Once I took him to a New York Knicks basketball game, and he got sick in the cab; he couldn't stand the motion. He was an adopted child; I found out that the much older woman who was his mother had been his baby-sitter. When he was three months old, the woman who had given birth to him dropped him at the sitter's one day and never picked him up.

A couple of years after I taught him, I supervised another graduate student who had become his tutor. She was, as I had been, beside herself most of the time because she felt she could do so little to help Paul. Once she called me in tears because when she asked him what he wanted to do when he grew up, he replied that he really didn't know and that he thought he would probably be out on the street, selling drugs. At the end of that school year, Paul's time at the Teachers College clinic was up; he had to leave to make space for a student who had been on the waiting list for some time. Where he is now I don't know.

Acquired dyslexia, or alexia, is another kind of damage, generally from accidents or strokes or illness; it usually responds quite well to appropriate intervention. Actually, a great deal of what works for dyslexia works also for alexia—carefully thought-out, very direct, multisensory teaching. It feels like a mantra, I say it so often, but there it is. The late A. H. Raskin was the national labor correspondent of *The New York Times* for more than forty years, and the deputy editor of the editorial page of the *Times* for another fourteen, until he retired in 1976. In September of 1992, Mr. Raskin described eloquently on the Op-Ed page of the *Times* his struggles with processing language caused by a stroke he had suffered two years before.

> . . . I was forced to remain silent and could not follow either verbal or written commands. Words sounded to me like jargon, as though the people around me spoke a foreign tongue. I could neither comprehend nor use language. It is difficult to convey the depth of my emotional solitude. . . . I now had a new self, a person who no longer could use words with mastery. Privately I could do nothing but cry. With the tears came feelings of anxiety and depression. . . . Reading was just as difficult. The printed word at first resembled hieroglyphics. Later, individual words became recognizable and took on meaning, but I could not decipher a printed statement. Looking at a group of words was overwhelming. It was as though the words were catapulting off the page, and I could not make sense of their significance. . . . I felt mournful and frightened, then tense, anxious and full of rage. . . . Initially, when I tried to write my name, I just scribbled. . . . Spelling was no longer automatic. . . . Gradually I combined words in order to form sentences, although I tended to omit the articles and prepositions. Verb tense was yet another chore.

The octogenarian Mr. Raskin learned to read and write again the same way young developmental dyslexics do. He was taught the basic structure of the English language; then he graduated to learning about syllables—until, step by step, he regained the ability to communicate his thoughts vividly in speech and, as the above so clearly shows, in writing.

According to Kate Moody of the University of Texas Medical Branch in Galveston, there is another kind of acquired dyslexia. What she describes, with a bit of poetic license, is not the result of stroke or degenerative diseases; it just looks the same. Difficulty with words is at its heart, though. Moody (and others) posit that the same brain plasticity and ability to change that offer so much promise are also very much endangered by not receiving the right kind of stimulation, particularly in the language areas of the brain, which, as Bruce Pennington pointed out, develop later and are therefore very susceptible to nurture. The cause of this paucity of correct stimulation for the brain is definitely environmental, too, but it has nothing to do with chemicals of any sort. The culprit Moody points to is television. Studies she quotes have found that heavy television viewers are less adept at reading than those who watched moderately or not at all—and dyslexics were not included in these studies. Comments Moody, "Larger and larger numbers of children who were born with the equipment to read are becoming less and less able to read." She continues, "Since the 1970s children have spent more time watching television than doing anything else. The eyes and hands and brain all play a big role in learning. TV uses none of the above."

It's scary, but it makes great sense. If a child is born with all the neurons he needs and if that child spends the first decade of his life sculpting a brain by shedding neurons the way an artist sheds the extra marble to create a statue, it seems only logical that all those neurons that are waiting for the kind of stimulation that will make them build networks to be used for reading and writing are being sloughed off in favor of the neurons that have nothing to do with creating or translating language. Certainly print and TV ask very different things of us, and we use very different skills in dealing with each. Moody describes the differences as follows:

NATURE OF PRINT	NATURE OF TELEVISION
Linear	Nonlinear
Sequence is important	Sequence is unimportant
Stable—stays on page	Unstable
Phonological awareness is necessary	Phonological awareness is unnecessary
Mind creates pictures	Pictures are ready-made

NATURE OF PRINT	NATURE OF TELEVISION
Saccadic eye movement (from left to right) is required	Saccadic eye movement is not used
Pace is reader's own	Pace is rapid
Left-brain activity is amplified	Right-brain activity is amplified

It used to be that fussy children were read to, or sung to, or cooed at and coaxed with loving words from whoever was caring for them. Now, more often than not, restless, cranky, attention-demanding young ones are often in the care of parents and others who are overworked, overstressed, overbusy, and so are plunked in front of that great attention diverter and pacifier, television—which might just be lying in wait to destroy the neurons those children need to become good communicators, patient observers, voracious readers. And in our own living rooms. Think about it.

There is another kind of poor reader who has all the building materials he needs but who seems unable to learn to deal with text. These students often start off well, then soon they are not reading on grade level: they are unable to express themselves in writing. No one can figure it out. Typically the children receive the blame for their decline: they are not working hard enough, they are fooling around instead of paying attention, etc., etc.—the usual litany. In fact, it is the education system that is to blame. These are the children who are at the heart of the debate over whether the structure of the language should be directly, explicitly taught, or whether the children should be expected to figure it out for themselves. These children are victims of another sort of environmental hazard: They have received inadequate instruction. They have not been taught what they need to know to learn to read; they are described as "curriculum disabled" by those who see them applying to schools for the learning disabled. I taught just such a student back in the Teachers College clinic.

Carlos was fourteen, from Texas. He was so bright and had shown such promise when he started school that he was included in an experimental reading program that bathed the children in language, surrounded them with books, and believed wholeheartedly that osmosis would do the rest. Lucky Carlos. Osmosis proved to be a poor teacher. P. S.: English was not Carlos's first language; Spanish was, which complicated the situation even more. Carlos seemed to enjoy all of that bathing in English and all of that exposure. At least, he enjoyed it until the day he was supposed to magically read. He couldn't. He tried, but it just wasn't working. What Carlos needed was proper, organized instruction in the rules of the English language, in phonics, in sight words, in grammar, in syntax. But such instruction was not the style in his program. Soon this cheerful, achieving boy became less and less able to do his work.

First he was taken out of the experimental program that was for the higher-performing students and put back in the "regular" class. Then he fell to the bottom of that class. By fourth grade, Carlos was in special education and considered not very bright. His slide was quick and disastrous. He lost all interest in schoolwork; he thought he couldn't do it, and everyone agreed. Elementary school took away all his expectations of success and all his confidence in himself, as well as all his family's pride in his abilities. He didn't learn to read, he didn't learn to write, and his teachers blamed him. It was all his fault. Sound familiar? Sound like Valerie and Rebecca and probably several people you know? It sure does. It sounds just like what has happened to so many dyslexic, misunderstood students. Only Carlos was not dyslexic, even though he was certainly misunderstood. Still, his academic life continued to get worse and worse as he slid farther and farther away from his hopeful beginnings. From gifted and talented to special ed. in only a few years, and plummeting. His teachers wondered how they could have been so wrong about him in the beginning; his mother was dismayed; Carlos was a wreck. His parents divorced, and he and his mother moved east. By the time I met him, he was in junior high school in New York, depressed, overweight, so used to failure in school and in life that he was utterly convinced that the only thing he would ever be good at was skateboarding.

Over the course of just a few months, I tested him and I tutored him. It was clear he was bright; it was also clear that he wanted desperately to be able to show how well he could think, but he didn't have the tools to do so. At our first session, I asked him if he knew the short vowel sounds. He said, "The what?" And we were off. I taught Carlos how the English language works; I taught him about vowels and consonants; I taught him about syllables; I taught him about sentences and about syntax, and how to go back and check whether he was right about what he was reading. Carlos was a sponge; he was so thirsty from his years of drought that he drank up everything I could give him, lesson after lesson; the only thing that would quench his thirst was learning the skills that would free him from his prison of ineptitude and what he and everyone else thought was stupidity. Each session was more exciting than the one before it, for Carlos and for me. He made progress faster even than he had bottomed out.

The most fun was that all the phonic rules and elements that I taught him made immediate sense to him. He didn't have to struggle to learn them and remember them and find the right place for them, as dyslexics must; all he needed was to be taught, and osmosis is a poor substitute for teaching. Our time together was limited because Carlos was moving back to Texas, but he made incredible improvement over the weeks we worked together; he became energized and enthusiastic about learning and about his growth. He even sat up straighter, which is really no surprise. He was getting his pride back. I did not stay in touch with him after he left, but his mother had vowed to ensure he continued the work we had started until he no longer needed it. I'm sure she did, too. As a going-away present, I gave Carlos a copy of the book he most wanted to read and now could: *Brave New World*.

There is one more thing dyslexia is: big business. There has been an enormous growth in the number of identified dyslexics over the past decade or two, and an industry has sprung up to deal with them. I am often asked why there are so many now. People are skeptical. They seem to wonder whether there isn't some sort of scam that lets people think or claim they're dyslexic when really what they are is . . . who knows. I can't support the following statement with numbers, but I truly believe that no one would be interested in faking dyslexia; too much pain comes with the designation. There certainly could be over-diagnosis, or incorrect diagnosis, but I doubt that there is much. I think the reasons for the substantial growth in numbers are twofold: First, we know more now; we know what dyslexia is, how to diagnose it, and what to do about it. So we can spot it more readily. Second, there have been laws in effect for somewhat over two decades that insist that children be sought out, diagnosed, and treated. So of course the numbers have skyrocketed. Many of those students who were thought to be just a little stupid now can be given the chance to learn that they deserve. We humans have not been reading for all that long, but as long as we have, there have been dyslexics. Now they can find help.

CHAPTER THREE

Dyslexia Across the Age Range

Leaving or Staying in the LD Closet

W HEN JOHN Charles Waterfall, known as Bruce, was in his thirties and courting the woman who was to become his wife, he almost lost her by being forthright and acknowledging his reading problems. It was in the spring, and the Unitarian-raised Waterfall joined his girlfriend's family for a Passover seder. He was having a wonderful time; he thought the whole experience was terrific. He got a kick out of her relatives; he loved the ritual, enjoyed the food, drank down the sweet wine, and waited eagerly for Elijah to come and sip from his own special cup. Then the prayer book, the Haggadah, was passed from person to person, and soon it was Waterfall's turn to read the holy words. Tensely he received the book. Nervously he looked over the passage that he was supposed to read. It was in English, but it might as well have been written in Hebrew for all the sense it made to him. Calmly, he looked his girlfriend's parents straight in the eye, said he couldn't read it, and passed the book to the person sitting on his right. His host and hostess gasped with surprise; no guest of theirs had ever refused to read at Passover.

After a few moments, they seemed to recover from their shock and carried on with the seder graciously. Deep down, though, they were frantic. The minute he left, they took their daughter aside and told her that he was clearly an anti-Semite and that she must get rid of him immediately. It never occurred to them that in fact this man really couldn't read the words, actually was unable to read them. He was a successful businessman with an MBA from Harvard. They thought he meant he *wouldn't* read, wouldn't take any real part in the service. Their daughter wasn't so sure, and besides, she was crazy about him. Lucky for him. Eventually, when she realized he had trouble even reading street signs, Susan Solomon was able to convince her parents that it was okay to become Susan Waterfall, that her groom was not anti-anything, that he really couldn't read the unfamiliar words of the Haggadah, and that he really couldn't read much of anything at all. "You know," he says, bemusedly, "that's the second time a religious service got me in trouble. The other was when I was a teenager and on a bicycle trip with three other boys and an adult. One Sunday we all went to church, and I was given the honor of being asked to read to the congregation. I couldn't do it. I had to hand back the book. Give me words out of context, and you will hear silence." That, gentle reader, is the classic definition of a dyslexic, right from his own mouth.

Visiting Waterfall in his midtown Manhattan office, you'd be convinced he'd never had a problem in the world. He is sophisticated, elegant, funny, graceful, slight and fit, welcoming and relaxed. His firm, Morgens, Waterfall, Vintiadis and Company, of which he is a founding partner, buys the debt of distressed companies, then restructures them. "It's about a billion-dollar business," he says quietly. Like Waterfall, the offices are streamlined, calm, and quiet, the colors muted and earthy, the art modern and interesting. There is light everywhere; walls filled with windows bring sun, trees, swimming pools, gardens, the Hudson River, and points west into this twenty-sixth-floor aerie, and one can just about make out down there—way down there on the street—regular folk rushing to and from Rockefeller Center and the shops of Fifth Avenue. This space and this man symbolize success, ease, and confidence. And I'm here to talk about Bruce Waterfall's learning problems, his dyslexia. Like Nelson Rockefeller, like Winston Churchill, like Charles Schwab, Waterfall is another one who has succeeded in spite of, and perhaps even because of, a difficulty whose name he didn't even know.

Bruce Waterfall was in his forties when he was diagnosed as dyslexic. It wasn't that he suddenly discovered or admitted his difficulties; he'd never been able to read or write properly, and he had always been the first to say so, as we have already learned. He didn't decide to submit himself to the testing necessary to give a name to his reading difficulty because clinicians were looking into his children's reading problems, either, as is often the case. It wasn't even that he wanted to further his education or his career; after all, he'd already graduated from Cornell University *and* the Harvard Business School, and he was financially successful. What led him to the evaluation that declared him dyslexic was a desire to come to terms with many parts of his life, most particularly with his mother's death. It was the psychiatrist he was working with who first brought up the subject. He said, simply, "You know you're dyslexic, don't you?" Waterfall didn't know what that meant, or what dyslexia was. The doctor told him that a language-based learning disorder was one of the things keeping him from broadening his horizons, and that he needed to deal with it. He told him that he too often spoke in monosyllabic words, that his sentence structure was simplistic, that he needed more flow, more sophisticated language, that he needed the access to language that only reading permits in order to be able to express himself in a way that would reveal his true self and his enormous intelligence.

Waterfall hadn't felt very intelligent for most of his life, in spite of his accomplishments. He had certainly felt driven; he had certainly felt he needed to have areas of distinction to make up for his weaknesses; and he had also felt that he needed to use his considerable personality to be a part of the "smart crowd" and not be deemed a "less-than": less-than-able, less-than-smart, less-than-popular. He didn't know why he couldn't read, and that lack of understanding was as confusing as could be. His father, an engineer, was an avid reader who kept "the thickest damned dictionary" by his side most of the time. He read daily to his only son and only child, and he read only serious literature. "*Peter Pan* didn't make it in our house," says Waterfall. "No animal fables, either, and no fairy tales were permitted. I can't believe all the wonderful stories my children have."

It wasn't just literature that was taken seriously in the Waterfall household; everything else was somber, too. His parents, Waterfall feels, had the entrenched mind-sets of many who made it through the Great

Depression. Work was valued above all. Nothing was ever wasted; nothing was ever squandered; there were no frivolities, no music or dance. Waterfall's mother loved the theater, but it never occurred to her to foster such a love in her son. His father, he says, had but one interest: "Me." Waterfall *père* wrote his son a letter once a week, every week, though they lived in the same house. He kept a book, *Things for Children,* listing his son's accomplishments and updating them every year: in it he recorded how many steps the boy could take with a normal-sized book on his head, or how many X's he could make on a page in one minute. All the things the young Waterfall was able to do; no mention of what he couldn't. Something was wrong with this beautiful, bright boy, but his father didn't have any idea what. "My father couldn't believe that a son of his couldn't read. He never expressed anger about it, but he just couldn't believe it." Assorted therapies were tried, the standard approaches of the day. "At first they thought I had a hearing problem— 'Maybe that's why the kid is so stupid.' But there was no hearing problem. Then they thought I had an eye problem. So I got glasses and moved to the front of the class. That didn't do it. So then they decided the eye problem must have been worse than they had thought. I did all kinds of exercises: I watched things move around; I watched parrots; I did it all, and still I couldn't read."

The Waterfall family moved north from Maryland after Bruce had finished fourth grade, and the boy was horrified and dismayed to find himself at the bottom of his class at P.S. 104 in the Bronx. Then he figured a way to survive the humiliation. "I decided that the reason was that the southern school I had attended wasn't as tough as the new one. That's how I avoided feeling really stupid." Waterfall muddled along for a year or so, with his family still flummoxed by his difficulties. Then his problems became secondary to the tragedy that befell his mother. At the age of forty-two, she had a stroke that was to leave her unable to move one side of her body for the rest of her life. The family was immediately torn apart. Bruce was sent to boarding school, and his mother spent a full year in the hospital. "It was so awful," he recalls. "I didn't know where I was." From day one at the Hackley School, Waterfall was assigned a tutor, several times a week during the school year and all summer as well. Still he couldn't read. "I was always embarrassed," he recalls. "I was embarrassed about spelling and about reading. Even if I knew what I was going to be given to read, if I had to read it aloud in front of the other boys, I couldn't do it. I was okay in math and science, but I felt proud if I could ever get a C in English." What he determined then, and what he continues to determine today, was that he needed to compensate. "Because I was dyslexic, I needed something to distinguish myself. So I became a championship swimmer and a respectable runner in track and in football. Back then one-hundred-and-fifty-pound football players were possible," he says with a smile. "Compensation is *it*," he continues. "I didn't know it at the time, but using strategies and compensation is the intelligent way to go when you're dyslexic. In everything I do, I compensate for my lack of reading skills."

Bruce Waterfall finished Hackley, but he didn't graduate. "I got a general diploma because I couldn't fulfill their foreign language requirement. I was the only one in my class who didn't graduate." "For a lot of good reasons," he spent the following year in England on a foreign exchange program. He was miserable; his family was still stunned by his mother's illness; his father was coping with taking care of her as well as working full-time. But when he came back, he got a break. Cornell University had been interested in him because of his athletic prowess. "I had set all kinds of swimming records," he recalls, "and I was the second-fastest runner in Westchester County. I was strong, and I was competitive. I had the attitude that athletes must have; I needed to win. Life was such a goddamn struggle that I had to be tougher than anyone else around. So I was able to tell myself I was going to hurt less than the other guy, and I learned to take whatever pain came my way." At the time—the mid-1950s—Cornell had a special program designed for returning Korean War vets who'd gone into the armed forces before graduating from high school. For a short time, it was possible to be accepted to Cornell with only a general diploma. Says Waterfall, "I never even applied anyplace else." So off to Ithaca went Bruce Waterfall, Mr. Ivy League without a high school diploma. There was one other thing he did have, though—money, money of his own, and the knowledge that he knew how to make money. During his second year at Hackley, his grandmother had died and left him some money, which he invested and reinvested until by the end of high school he was quite well off on his own. So, it would seem natural that he would become a business major, wouldn't it? Well, he didn't, although that was obviously where his heart and talents lay.

Just what did he study? Why, engineering, of course. Because he liked it or had any affinity for it? Not on your life. "At the time, I didn't have many choices—or at least I didn't perceive I had any choices. If I'd had to take English courses, or history courses where there was text after text, it would have been the March of Death. Engineering took a lot of time, but there was not much reading." So engineering it was. Did he like college life? "I hated it! I had no pleasures. I had no free time." He studied; he swam; he was among the most popular of students. He coped, and he compensated. "It was very important to me to do whatever it took to get the job done," he recalls. "I am the most organized person in the world—I have to be because I get confused, dazed, if I'm flooded with too much information or too much stimulus. Cornell is where I learned that organization. I had to learn it. I had to get rid of everything except what I wanted to do. There were just not enough hours in any day. I also had shortcuts. I had all the smartest kids in the class lined up; they were my fraternity brothers and friends. I knew the results of most of the labs before I even started. I got tests from years gone by. If the professor was dumb enough or lazy enough to give the same test year after year, that wasn't my fault. On every exam I knew at least one question before I went in—knew it, had done it, whatever it was. Today somebody might say that was cheating, but back then it was survival. I had to do it to save time." Nowadays, of course, students of Waterfall's caliber would be given language waivers, extended time for tests, people to help them with note taking, etc. Back then he was on his own and had to figure out his own accommodations. And he swam, from the first of September until spring vacation. Says he, "The demands were incredible. The Harvard Business School was easy next to Cornell." He made it through, this time with a full, bona fide diploma. He graduated above the middle of the class, he was president of his fraternity, and he proudly held a number of swimming records.

By the time Bruce Waterfall got to Harvard, he was rid of engineering for the rest of his life, and he was as focused as a microsurgeon. Every night he and the other students were expected to prepare three cases for the next day's classes. "That was so much more than I could possibly read in an evening, it was ridiculous," says Waterfall. So, as usual, he did what he had always done: he coped; he compensated. He figured the odds, focused in on what he needed to do, and then did it. Every night Waterfall prepared one case thoroughly and well, and the next day volunteered like mad to discuss that one case. He hadn't any idea about the other two. Every single day of his time at Harvard he was prepared—and prepared beautifully—for but one of the three demanding graduate school professors he faced. He lived in terror of being found out, but, he says, "I was never caught unprepared, even though I was unprepared in sixty-six percent of my classes. That's because I was always very well informed—when I was informed—and always very verbal." When he discussed a case, he had a great deal to say about it, and, as we have already learned, he is not short on opinions. He impressed his professors, as he continues to impress anyone who talks with him. "There were plenty of guys who never volunteered in any classes, making it clear all the time that they weren't sure of what was going on. They were the ones who got caught."

Exams at Harvard were never the strain or struggle they were at Cornell—or even at Hackley—because Waterfall was not locked up in a room and made to perform for several hours, trying to call on an anxiety-addled memory, trying to write essays in minutes that would take him hours at best. He was not put on the spot, having to deal with questions he couldn't answer. Harvard Business School exams tested what he needed to know. For each exam, he was given a new case and told to prepare it and deliver it back within a specified number of days. He was provided plenty of time to do his usual splendid job on one and only one case, and he also had time enough to have a typist prepare his answer and someone else correct his grammar and spelling. He had a chance at Harvard to show what he really knew, what he could do, and how he could think. He did very well there, and he's done very well ever since.

Out into the real world he took his focused, adventure-in-the-stock-market-seeking self. It wasn't long before he'd earned a well-deserved reputation as a very aggressive, confident money manager who knew exactly what he wanted, who made fast, fearless decisions, and who made lots of money for himself and for others. After working for those others for several years, Waterfall and a friend from his Cornell days started their own company, where he continues his daring and dazzling dyslexic ways. "My partner describes me as often wrong but never in doubt," he reports with a grin. "In fact, the strategies I learned to deal with my dyslexia have given me a great advantage in what I have chosen to do. A dyslexic can't know all there is to know about a company before deciding whether to buy or sell its stock. There are four or five essential things, and those are the things I know. I refuse to get confused by the bullshit."

Unconfused, seemingly dauntless, happily married, wealthy, powerful, and in his forties, Bruce Waterfall found himself submitting to a psychoeducational evaluation. "I was the only person in the waiting room over the age of about eleven," he says with a wry laugh. Not only did he go through all the testing to discover his dyslexia, but he also faithfully attended about a school year's worth of thrice-weekly remediation. He learned the phonetic rules of the English language; he learned what sounds two vowels make when they are paired together, what adding a silent *e* does to a word, what syllables are and how to break words into them. "I had no ability to decode," he says. "I'd never even heard of it. But I had what I thought were strategies. I'd look at the whole word, the shape of it, and try and figure it out. When I read, I read every single word, so naturally I was a slooow reader." Bruce Waterfall is a much faster, more skilled reader now, and he even pursues books for pleasure, claiming he does so best in the peace and quiet of airplanes. A particular favorite is *A River Runs Through It.* "I love fly-fishing," he says, "and that book has the best first line in history. 'In our family fly-fishing was a religion.' That tells you just about all you need to know, doesn't it?" Still, Waterfall has no illusions about himself; those would come under the heading of "confusing texture," something he avoids. Even after his remediation, he remains convinced that "compensation is still the name of the game. Look around my office. I don't have a single paper cluttering up my desk: everything is dealt with immediately and put where it should be; otherwise I'll get confused. I have a secretary who is an Oxford graduate. Most of the people who work here are lawyers. I never read a document; that's what they do. They tell me what's there and I pick out the three or four things that are very important to me. Sometimes I'll know something is wrong in a deal, sometimes even before the lawyers know, but never because I've read all the papers. The same goes for writing. If I need to write a letter or a note, even something like a sympathy note, it is composed for me, and I copy it over in my own handwriting."

Waterfall is so at ease with who he is now that he doesn't shy away from telling his daughter that not even his great love for her can make it possible for him to read the book that she wants to hear, that she'd better ask someone else to read it to her or learn to read it herself. Being able to read newspapers is a different issue, however. It is of vital importance to him, personally and professionally. "I have a neurotic need to know," he says, amending that self-deprecating statement with the comment that to be really effective in life and business he needs the "cumulative knowledge" that only comes with regular attention to serious papers. He reads two a day, *The New York Times* and *The Wall Street Journal.* "The tutor I had got me to reverse my strategies for reading a newspaper. Instead of reading every single word, as I was doing, she taught me to read the first sentence of each paragraph, to look for key words, things like that. She really changed my confidence. I realized I could get eighty percent of any article without reading all the words. Every day, though, I spend an hour, minimum, on the papers. I need the time, and I need it early, when it is quiet, before everyone is up," he says. "I can't read on the subway." So Bruce Waterfall gets up at five-thirty every morning to have quiet time to read the newspapers. Coping again; compensating again.

Compensation, like virtue, might just be its own reward. Waterfall happily describes a list of quite recent, pleasure-giving compensations. "It didn't occur to me until later in life that culture was important," he says. "I never saw art with my father, never went to a concert. I never even saw a ballet until I was forty. Now I love it all. I love going to the Philharmonic and to dance performances, and I would go to any and all art shows if I could." How to deal with all the reading he needs to do to understand what he sees? The self-acknowledged master of the game wins the prize for Creative Compensation in the World of Culture. He and his wife find and hire experts to be their guides through the art world. They have a former dealer who accompanies them to galleries, and a docent at the Metropolitan Museum who accompanies them through shows there. "I can't read all the information about each piece of art quickly enough to understand it, enjoy it, and get something out of it. This way I can look at the painting and have someone read about it to me, adding information he or she knows that will tell me even more than the printed materials. It makes the experience such a delight." He pauses, thinks for a moment. "I'm always compensating for my dyslexia. Now I substitute money for reading skills."

F ew can achieve what Bruce Waterfall has even without being dyslexic, and adding the reading disorder to many people's list of struggles can tip the balance too far. There are some scary and shocking statistics compiled by the National Institute for Literacy. Before Public Law 94-142—the federal legislation that mandates the identification of learning disabled students as well as their appropriate instruction—was enacted in 1975, 25 percent of those with what they term specific reading learning disability completed eight years of schooling or less, while only 4 percent of the non–learning disabled population had such a meager education. In 1993 the results of the U.S. Congress–authorized National Adult Literacy Survey, which included 26,000 adults, ages sixteen-plus to sixty-five, were released. Unfortunately, these showed that even after the federal legislation that made it possible for so many to stay in school and (theoretically) receive the kind of education they needed, the dropout rate for the reading disabled in high school or earlier was 52 percent, versus 16 percent for nondisabled, and a very small percentage—8.7—of those surveyed who had stayed in high school went on to graduate from either a two- or four-year college. Of course, lacking substantive education drastically affected the job prospects and earning potential of those who made up those numbers, and an astounding 42 percent ended up near or below the poverty level. And we all know that jails around the country are filled with learning disabled convicts.

Lack of knowledge about reading disabilities was rampant until very recently. Even Bruce Waterfall, with all his advantages—educated, caring parents who could afford therapies, regular tutoring, and private secondary school—fell through the cracks as a child and didn't find out and address what was preventing him from reading until he had been a full-fledged adult for some time. Most teachers and most schools didn't have Idea One about what to do for people who couldn't learn to read the way everyone else did (some still don't), and most everybody blamed the student. And then there is Keith Stanovich's Matthew Effect. It doesn't stop at fourth grade; it gets worse the longer the person continues to be unable to read. So adults who are reading-impaired can seem far less cognitively able than they really are. Their access to the sophisticated thoughts and language found in books that require advanced reading skills has often been blocked, so their ways of expressing themselves can be more concrete and simple than those of adults who have developed more complex language skills. Reading sophisticated material also develops the ability to make inferences, draw conclusions, and think critically, which are keys to problem solving; often these higher-order thought processes have not been able to grow in these adults as well as they would have if the adults had been able to read better. The reading-disabled have also been beaten down and discouraged by so many years of continuing to be unable to measure up, of failing. These problems can combine and compound until an adult who has never been diagnosed and never been taught to read seems on IQ tests to be much less intelligent than he really is, because he does not have the experience and information expected from all adults. Waterfall is right when he says it is the cumulative body of information that counts and brings real knowledge, not each little bit. And it's the inability to read that prevents that body of knowledge from accumulating and growing in people of normal intelligence. For so many years, so many people of normal or better intelligence either dropped out of or limped through school without ever gaining a real education that adult illiteracy in the United States became a problem of gigantic proportions.

But the literacy and dyslexia folks have not been able to agree on much over the years, so the problems of reading-disabled adults have been misunderstood in literacy programs for decades. The philosophy underlying early (and often continuing) efforts at eliminating adult illiteracy was that it was a social issue, a learning issue only in that those who were unable to read enough to function well as adults had not been given a chance to learn, had not had enough schooling, and that goodwill, attention, and instruction would properly address the issue. Great amounts of money were hurled at addressing this very important social issue; literacy centers were established; hopeful clients lined up. Volunteers were gathered around the country—still are—and hordes of well-meaning people put in time and effort trying to help countless adults learn the reading and writing skills they need to get them more into the mainstream of American life. The success rate has been far from stupendous. There have been some triumphs, of course, because there has been a segment of the nonreading population who did indeed need just the opportunity to learn. That segment has decreased in number considerably, though, and the group who needs specialized instruction has grown.

These people are of at least average intelligence; they have been in school and have received instruction, but they have not learned to read in spite of that instruction; they have not been educated. That is part of the definition of a dyslexic, that he has not learned to read in spite of having the intelligence that would make it possible and in spite of having been taught in school. Adults seeking help often have had twelve years or more of schooling, and those who dropped out had at least the early years, the years when reading is taught. So it is not deprivation— or at least deprivation of general instruction—that has caused their difficulties. According to the National Institute for Literacy, 40 to 60 percent of clients in literacy settings have learning disabilities. That is an astounding number, and they are indeed deprived, deprived of the kind of teaching that would enable them to learn. Many are so eager to improve their skills that they try one program after another without finding what they need; they fail at one, try another, fail there, and so on and so on, feeling more and more as though it's their fault and adding more and more failure to their experience—after years of failing in school.

Still, there has been little or no communication between the worlds of literacy and learning disabilities. That is starting to change now, but the pace is glacial. It's almost like the struggles between the whole language and skills-oriented approaches in primary schools. Like the whole language advocates, the literacy folks talk about motivation, inspiration, respect for the students' experience—all social and emotional issues that are valid and valued aspects of adult education. Also like the whole language group, though, they leave out well-thought-out, explicit instruction, and they leave out fully training the volunteer tutors. Niceness has never taught anybody to read, especially somebody who has been through the educational mill; the committed volunteers who want to help need the kind of intense, specialized training that equips them to recognize and remediate reading disabilities. They all have goodwill and good intentions, but they need more; they need guidance themselves so that they have the tools to understand the difficulties that are faced by their clients and what they can do about them. Then their goodwill will be invaluable in helping them put into action what they know. They also need mentors, people with whom they can discuss their cases who are experts and who can give them the advice and supervision they need.

Clearly there is no dearth of people who are interested in helping others to read, and many of the volunteer tutors would be happy to be properly trained and could do a fine job if they were. Indeed, many of those who go into the field, get training, get advanced degrees, and become prominent began their work simply because they wanted to help. Often they knew just who they wanted to help, too: their children, their other relatives, themselves. Look at Diana Hanbury King, founder of the Kildonan School. If she hadn't had a dyslexic child, she would never have gone into the profession, many children and teenagers would never have learned to read, and those of us who are teaching now would be much the poorer because she would never have developed the methods and materials that are so vital to our work.

Another woman I know, an award-winning teacher in Connecticut, was a young mother in rural Vermont when she realized her child was not learning to read in spite of good "normal" instruction. Her son was in second grade, and his teacher said she didn't know if he would ever be a reader. She was distraught, and so was her neighbor who had a child in the same situation. Then one day my friend saw an ad in the local paper announcing that an educator from Maryland who had a summer house in the area was going to give a talk on the Orton-Gillingham method of teaching reading. My friend went, and after the talk, she sought out the lecturer and told her about her son. The woman put her in touch with a trainer at Massachusetts General Hospital, and my friend began accumulating the necessary skills for what was to become her vocation. At the time, she thought she was just learning how to deal with her own child, and at the time, that is exactly what she was doing. But she learned so well that she also started teaching many other people's sons and daughters, and has done so now for a quarter of a century. Way back then, she and her neighbor studied the Orton-Gillingham method together, and they convinced the principal of their children's school to let them come in and teach each other's offspring. It worked, and my friend found her calling. Her son also learned to read. He became a successful lawyer, and her second child, a daughter who was also dyslexic, graduated from college and has begun her own career working with learning disabled children.

Another colleague of mine got into this profession for exactly the same reasons, but it took her until her children were almost grown to do so. She, her husband, and their sons all had some measure of dyslexia; how it affected their lives depended as much on when they were born and when their reading or writing difficulties were discovered as on their coping and compensating skills—and it is clear how important those particular skills are. Ron and Elaine West (now Elaine Mitchell) raised three children with reading disorders, and both parents actually learned about their own dyslexia through their sons. Each of their boys had completely different experiences, in and out of school, even though there are only five years between the eldest and the youngest. I met Elaine when we were in graduate school together. We had an enormous amount in common: we were the same age, which was a good deal older than most of our fellow students, and we shared many interests. We even looked a bit alike. We had two real dissimilarities as well. She, like so many others who diagnose and teach children and adults with reading disorders, had gone into the field because of the experiences she had had with her own children, and she knew so much more than I about the subject that she was a constant source of aid and comfort when I was getting started. On the other hand, I was used to writing and therefore had no trouble with the zillions of reports we were learning to compile, while Elaine's dyslexia was centered in difficulty putting words on paper. We were a great team, and we have remained good friends personally as well as professionally.

Ron and Elaine met in the late fifties, when they were in high school in Indiana. She was a year or so younger than he, a very good student and very popular. Ron wasn't quite so fully established. He was a bit on the fringe socially, and academically he had what he calls a "ragged production ability"; he always did very well in math, pretty well in science, and poorly in English. "Displaying or presenting the knowledge I had was always the hard part," he explains. "I was never able to communicate really well, and if I wasn't in my element, I was lost." After a pause, he adds, "But there was one thing in English I was always very good at, could do better than anyone else," he says, "and that's diagramming sentences. To me that was easy because it was just like math. I couldn't write sentences very well, but I could diagram someone else's."

Ron had had trouble learning to read "from day one," and his troubles didn't end just because he got older. He remembers elementary school well, and he particularly remembers being The Only Person in the whatever-early-grade class who couldn't finish some reading exercises. I'm sure there were others who were not able to finish and who were suffering just as much as he was, but I have never met one single dyslexic soul who didn't feel that he was The Only Person in the room, class, grade, school, or world who couldn't do *it*, whatever *it* was, when everyone else could. Ron was yet another dyslexic who also stumped his teachers and his family. He says his mother was an "education-aggressive" farm girl who had not had more than a sixth-grade education herself, but who was going to do the very best for her beloved, adopted, only child. She knew he was smart, and she insisted on taking an active role in his early education, constantly asking the school if he was all right and describing to them the things she saw in his work—his reading inaccuracies, his enormous difficulty writing, his impossible spelling—that she felt should be addressed somehow. Those in charge at the school wanted to help, but they didn't know how. They did try some of those charming old-fashioned remedies, though. His third-grade teacher had a lovely little paddle that she used to spank the children to make them read faster. Talk about motivation! Ron tells with glee about the day she lurched after him with the paddle, gave a big windup, missed, and broke the instrument of torture on her desk. "It was a triumph," he says, re-relishing the brief moment of escape.

Socially Ron did fairly well as he stumbled his way through primary and secondary school. He was never really a part of the "in" crowd, but he was also never so "out of it" that it caused him pain, and he had some enlightened mentors who emphasized his strengths, such as math, and tried to reduce the focus on his weaknesses. So he was able to get through school with a group of friends, some extracurricular sports at the Y (he was too uncoordinated to make the high school teams), a "catch" of a girlfriend, Elaine, and a reasonably intact sense of himself.

And what did he study in college? Engineering, the dyslexic's best friend. He went to Purdue (with Elaine following the next year), and tried to avoid all courses that included large quantities of reading material. He was mostly able to do so, and he had the bonus of having to take a developmental English course for engineers. There he met a teacher whose attitude was not "Oh, let's see if we can do anything at all with you," but was instead "Let's find your talent and develop it." Ron was sure he didn't have any talent for writing, but he and this gifted woman discovered that he did; together they found things he could write about more readily than others, and they found ways to get him to write more and better than he had ever done in his life, or even thought he could do.

Ron got out of college in 1961 and went to work at IBM, where he stayed until 1992. He had all kinds of jobs at Big Blue over those thirty-one years, but, he says, "They all had something to do with teaching." Nowadays he teaches computer courses full-time, at a community college near where he lives in Roseburg, Oregon, with his second wife, Lynn, and where he enjoys life and even has developed a taste for literature. "For many years, I never read anything that I absolutely didn't have to," comments West. "Then, when I was in my mid-thirties, someone gave me the collected works of Arthur Conan Doyle, *Sherlock Holmes*. The structure was simple and easy to read; the stories were short enough that I didn't have to labor and labor, and the mental pictures they painted were so marvelous that I was almost instantly hooked. I started reading; I discovered what joys can be had from reading, and now not a day goes by that I'm not involved in one or two books—usually fiction. Fiction is easier to read for me; it's more fun and more liberal in presentation. Histories or biographies are not for me; they're too hard, but I love sci-fi and mysteries." He goes on. "Writing continues to be the most difficult thing I do. One morning I'll sit down and write four or five pages that all make sense, and there is not one misspelled word. Another day I'll write one paragraph and not be able to spell one word properly. It's particularly bad late in the day. My work teaching takes so much energy and 'mind effort' that by the end of the day, I'm just too fatigued."

It wasn't until after the Wests became parents that their education about dyslexia began, and it was a difficult journey, filled with the dead ends and confusion that accompanied the search for understanding in those years. Their eldest son, Mike, was never diagnosed or given any assistance until he was in college, but he says today that he hasn't a single doubt that he was and is dyslexic. "I saw so many of my own problems in Mike," says his father, "but when he was in school, we still didn't know what to do about it." Mike is the one who had the hardest time in school and who has been the most deeply affected by his dyslexia—even though he may not be the most disabled of the boys. Mike, too, is an engineer in Texas, working for Texas Instruments. Mike also has a devil of a time writing. It took him eight years and four schools to get his B.S.—"It took me five years to figure out how to study," he says, but he graduated from Rensselaer Polytechnic Institute in Troy, New York, a very distinguished school of engineering. Even after Mike learned to read well enough to get by, writing was always an issue; it was forever in his way. Then, finally, at RPI he found people who understood, who knew he was smart and talented, and who valued what he could do and supported what he had difficulty doing. They helped him. "The people in charge at RPI were diverse and interested in diversity," he says. "They were accepting." What the school did was what many schools would do nowadays: it made "reasonable accommodations." The writing requirements that were so impossible for him were waived; his professors let him use his energies to learn what he needed to learn, and he was able to demonstrate his knowledge in a variety of ways. They also gave him extended time on tests and his own, private room. The combination worked, and it brought out the knowledge and talents of Michael West. When he graduated from RPI, he did so with a 3.0 GPA.

Mike was so glad to get out of school, he could hardly believe his good fortune. He went to work; he married and built a life; he was free. And now, of all things and of all people, he is back in graduate school, studying at the University of Texas at Dallas for a master's degree in International Business. He told the dean that he was a most unlikely student, that he had really hated school; but this time he has found a way to study and matriculate that seems absolutely designed just for him and other dyslexics. He goes to the campus about once a month for a few hours, and the rest of the time Mike takes his courses at home over the Internet. Extended time is a given; privacy is a given; a chance to go over the material again and again is a given. "Even at that I have to be very organized," he says. I have a weak memory, so I have to have all the reference materials right in front of me all the time. I need to know where everything is and where I am in regard to it. But it's great. I'm in charge of how I study and when I study. Recently I took a midterm exam, and I spent nine hours on it." (He got a very good grade on it, too.)

Weak memory or no, like his father, Mike remembers well his early days in the education system. No wonder he has always hated school. He and his family lived in Texas when he was little, and in the early grades, he says, "The teachers treated me like a retard. They also blamed me every time I couldn't finish something. They would throw material up on the blackboard and tell us to copy it down. I have to write slowly, word by word, so I could never finish it. They were always impatient. And then we had to use script. When I write in script, the letters never come out the same way twice." As a youngster, Mike found a way to compensate, the same way Bruce Waterfall found: he developed something he could be proud of—he became a champion swimmer. It wasn't easy, though; it required six hours of pool time a day, a demanding regimen that grows old very, very fast. Swimmers burn out faster than any other athletes, and it's no wonder. Think about being wet and cold and disoriented from having your face submerged in chlorine-filled water for hours on end, while a coach urges you, pushes you, yells at you.

When Mike was older, and the family was living in Poughkeepsie, New York, an IBM stronghold, he found other ways to compensate besides swimming. He got a job in a ski shop and worked there for ten years, which was great. At the same time, his academic life was a mess. "I just couldn't do well in school," he says. "The only way I can really learn is hands-on, and they didn't teach us anything that way, not even science. I'm great at things mechanical, though, and the ski shop was a terrific outlet." He also fell in with an older, more sophisticated crowd, and he got involved "more deeply than anyone knows" in drugs for a while. "It really was all part of the dyslexia," he says now. "Life was so painful, and the drugs eased the pain. Then, when it was time to stop, I stopped. I couldn't ever blame anyone who did what I did; it's hard to blame someone for getting into drugs. What you have to blame them for is not getting out."

Mike is married to a woman thirteen years his senior, and he has a stepson who is now of college age. Mike and his wife have become avid scuba divers; they travel as often as possible to the Caribbean to see what they can see under those beautiful blue waters, and he says that the thing he would like most in the world is to run a diving shop on some island somewhere. Sounds to me like yearning for those happy, carefree days in the ski shop. In a way it is. He is doing exceptionally well at his work and in life, but though Mike can be lonely, he is never alone; he is always accompanied by his dyslexia and its attendant aggravations. Recently he has had to do a great deal of traveling for his job . . . all over Europe and several times to Japan. Traveling is not easy for dyslexics; it can be very confusing. Dealing with different customs and several languages in a brief time is taxing for anyone—and much more so for those who have difficulty with words. Traveling for business is even more complicated, with local customs and protocols taking on much greater weight and proving much more important than they are for tourists. After all, in some cultures, a wrong gesture can break a deal. Then, after all that effort and pressure and all those dilemmas, when Mike gets back from a trip, he has the dreaded report to write.

Mike could do with ease most of the kinds of writing he faced before his job included this international travel; they consisted generally of filling in technical information on templates. These reports, though, are much more complicated and detailed, and they require much more sophisticated writing skills and vocabulary. "I don't have a secretary," he says, "so I write and rewrite and then write them again. I don't trust anyone else to do it. I can't tell that person exactly what it is I want; I just have to do it myself. I accept that fact. I know what it should say, and I just have to work on it until it says it." Mike has done so well with his travels that there is some possibility he will be sent abroad to live for a time. "Can you imagine it?" he queries with a sigh. "Learning another language? Beyond conversation, that would be just like pulling teeth for me." The thought of writing or reading in another language makes Michael West just shake his head in dismay.

Mike doesn't even read in his own language for pleasure because reading is no pleasure for him. "*National Geographic* is the only magazine I read; beyond that I find it difficult to keep in my head what I need to remember about the person the story is about," he says. He doesn't have much of a social life either. "I don't have many friends; having friends takes a lot of effort, and I don't want to exert that effort right now. Also, I had plenty of friends in high school, and that didn't turn out to be so positive. I always had friends who were older. Now I'm afraid of having close friends. I mistrust many of the people I've known. They've let me down in so many ways. I should probably work for the CIA; I'd be a perfect spook."

Tom West is the youngest of the three brothers, half a decade younger than Mike and three years younger than Patrick. Tom is also, according to his father, probably the one who is "the most afflicted" by dyslexia. By the time he came around, though, the Wests knew more of what to do about it; they had been through this before. Tom got his first diagnosis and his first extra help when he was in the second grade. Says he, "I was not only diagnosed, I had the most aggressive education for dealing with dyslexia." And still it wasn't easy. Still they all suffered. Says his mother, "You get so down when you've done what you can, and then you have a kid in the fourth grade, and at the yearly conference, his teachers just look at you and say, 'Oh, dear.' " Elaine West had had it by the time Tom was in fourth grade, and she decided to do some-thing about her feelings of helplessness. She decided to learn about this thing called dyslexia and to figure out ways to help her son. She studied up on how his learning was being affected by his difficulties and what techniques would help him compensate; she kept after his school and fought hard to get him what he needed. It didn't work.

In November of his eighth-grade year, after some IQ testing, Tom and his parents were told by his school that he didn't have what it took to be a student, and that Elaine and Ron should forget about any col-lege prep track and look around to find a vocational program for him. Elaine could hardly believe her ears. She knew they were wrong; she knew that Tom could develop academically if he were just taught in the right ways, and she vowed that somehow she would find a way to unlock the keen intelligence she knew was in him. "*Someone* has to believe in these kids," she says now with determination. Then, after intense searching, she found the key—the Kildonan School in Amenia, New York.

Kildonan was still run then by its founder, Diana King, and Tom feels blessed by having the opportunity to go there and to know her. He boarded at Kildonan for the rest of eighth grade and for all of ninth. "I don't know what the school is like today," says Tom, "but when Diana was around, there were no politics. You knew that the students came first, before anyone else, even the faculty." He goes on to tell about one spring when he was there. British-born Diana always felt it was good to get the students out into the air and working with their hands, so she had them plant gardens all around the school. They dug, they weeded, they composted, and they planted, and when they were done, they had planted two lovely gardens in the shapes of the words f— and sh—. "Diana burst out laughing," says Tom, who goes on, "She had them replant it all, of course, but she enjoyed their prank and got a kick out of their courage."

The two best things about Kildonan, according to Tom, were, one, that "the first thing they did was tell you about all the advantages of being dyslexic," and, two, that "then they said, 'Now there's this written language, and you have to learn some coping mechanisms to deal with it.' " Tom learned to cope well enough with "this written language" that he graduated from a prep school in Vermont, with a "pretty good academic record." He then decided to get himself accepted into college without any special programs or elaborate accommodations. "At some point, your value in the world has to be without extra help," he says, echoing the sentiments of most dyslexic students I have ever known who had the advantage of early intervention, so he took his SATs untimed and got a 1300. Maybe not good enough for Harvard, but not so bad for someone who was thought to be such poor college material. Tom chose the family profession and went to the Rose-Hulman Institute of Technology in Terre Haute, Indiana, where, he says, all the classes were taught by full professors, which you won't find to be true at Harvard. Tom also did his academic work at Hulman without any assistance, except for writing papers for his humanities classes. Says he, "I've been a mechanical engineer all my life. I've been designing and building things since I was in the fourth grade. I started with go-carts and graduated to race cars. But I am still dyslexic. Writing is torture."

His time at Kildonan had given Tom back what the "regular" school system had stolen from him because of its own inabilities, not his. The "special" school returned his sense of accomplishment to him, his sense of intelligence, of worth. It did one other very important thing for Tom West; teachers there taught him to read. Before he went to Kildonan, he knew only one way. "I read ninety-five percent by word recognition, and I often had to read the same line four times to get it," he says. At Kildonan he learned how to decode the English language; he learned the word attack skills that are so necessary for figuring out otherwise unrecognizable configurations of letters and syllables, and that dyslexics must be taught and taught in ways they can learn. "Now I'm an avid reader," he says. "I don't have to go over everything a million times anymore, so I can really enjoy it. I started off reading articles about my passion, race cars; then I graduated to reading the manuals, then went on to fiction. Kildonan gave me the skills, and then all the work I did in college made a huge difference. My short-term memory quadrupled in college. Now I can read anything, and I make sure I read a lot all the time, enough to ensure I don't regress."

Whether Diana King convinced him or not, Tom West is sure that there really *are* many advantages to being dyslexic. Says he, "There are things I do much better than the average other person because I am dyslexic, things like visualizing and conceptualizing on a magnitude of problems. If I look at a toaster and I see the front, it's apparent to me immediately what the back looks like without my being able to see it. It's tough to see what the whole thing looks like without looking close, but I don't have to look close. I can also put together complex mechanical engineering models in my head; I can think in three dimensions." Tom has put that ability to work for himself and has designed and created several contraptions with combustion engines. Before, during, and after college, race cars have always been a passion, both building them and racing them; in college he won an award in a competition with 100 other engineering schools when he designed a formula car based on a 600 cc motorcycle engine. "I worked on that more than my regular schoolwork," he says, "to the detriment of my grades perhaps, but not my education." Tom now works for a company called Dynatorque, which manufactures gear boxes that open and close valves on the Alaska pipeline, among other places, and he holds a couple of patents himself.

"One of the biggest reasons my brothers and I are as successful as we are is because our parents stood up for us one hundred percent of the time," says Tom West. "When my school said I was not academic material, my parents said, 'Don't be ridiculous.' They always knew we could achieve what we wanted to achieve. I see two future possibilities for myself . . . either I'll start my own manufacturing company and build, market, and sell something to make a lot of money, or I'll go back to school, get a Ph.D. in mechanical engineering, and teach. Look at my dad; he can't spell, and he's a college professor now. I hope that one day I can get a job like he has."

Patrick is the middle West son. At the moment, Patrick actually has the job he has always wanted. He is not an engineer, though. He is the vice president in charge of marketing and sales for the biotechnology division of a huge corporation. That means that he is responsible for the introduction of a new health care industry company founded around a key product—a genetically engineered protein that causes bone to grow—and for making the company successful around the world. It's a high-stakes game, with travel, deadlines, pressure, and uncertainty. He loves it. In terms of finding out about his learning problems, Patrick is also in the middle of the family—his were discovered earlier than Mike's and later than Tom's. Patrick had an evaluation when he was in junior high school. His diagnosis was stronger on attention deficit disorder than it was on dyslexia; the tester wasn't completely sure he was dyslexic, but his experiences have certainly been those of someone who is.

Patrick had the standard dyslexic's introduction to school. Attempt . . . failure . . . inch forward . . . setback . . . inch forward again. "Reading was painful," he says, "and writing a nightmare. Then there was spelling! I had all the classic reversals. It's still a nightmare. To this day, I don't write letters or notes because I'm afraid of the words I'll misspell. At work I have to write a fair amount, but I've developed systems and found coping mechanisms. I use bullet points and write many short memos. But I still fret about it, and I still have trouble with things like *to* and *too;* and as much scientific writing as I have done, I always have to think about whether it is *vial* or *vile.*" He thinks he uses the ADD to his benefit, though, particularly in his work. "I try to use it as a tool, an advantage," he says, "to harness that energy. I think it works. I know that I am most confident when I have eight or ten balls in the air at once," he goes on. "That pressure allows me to achieve some sort of equilibrium, and to really focus in." Comments his father, "Patrick is the master of compensating mechanisms."

When Patrick was only eight years old, he started playing the cello. His teacher spotted a genuine talent almost immediately, and by the time he was nine, Patrick was commuting from Poughkeepsie to the Juilliard School in New York City every Saturday to be trained in their elite preparatory division. He stayed there for seven years. Every year the stakes at Juilliard rose and rose; the music became more complicated, and the difference between playing chamber and orchestral music became wider and wider. By the time he was in high school, Patrick lived constantly in fear because he knew it was just a matter of time before someone found out that he could not read music. "It was a real cat-and-mouse game," he says, "trying not to get caught. And what an ego buster. Playing the cello had always made me special. In fact, in the beginning, I think I liked the attention even better than I liked playing the cello. Then I found myself in the back of the orchestra and seen as a goof-off, a bad kid."

Basically Patrick, who has a strong musicality, had learned to play by ear. "And by instinct," he says. He tried to learn to sight-read as well, but he still needed to hear the music. Every day when he practiced, his mother played on the piano whatever he was practicing so he could listen to it. He learned that putting his finger on the right place on the right string would get him the note she played, and eventually he internalized the knowledge that a particular dot meant an E-flat, and that if he put his finger on the right spot, he achieved an E-flat. "It's not as accurate as sight-reading," says Patrick, "and it's very slow, but I could do fine when I was young. Basically I achieved a fourth-grade level of sight-reading."

Juilliard is the number-one music school in the country—for performers. Teachers there do not train teachers; they train performers. Performers have to sight-read all the time, and Juilliard expects its students to be sophisticated and fluent sight readers. It's just part of the deal. The school will probably never officially alter its methods of teaching to accommodate gifted but dyslexic musicians like Patrick, but one of his teachers did, unofficially, and with fabulous instinct and insight. She did for him what Valerie wishes people had done for her. It was a class in music theory; they were doing solfeggio, the attaching of the sol-fa syllables to the tones of the scale. Patrick was having extreme difficulty. His teacher had an inspiration and said to him, "I'm going to color-code your notes, make them visual." This is the kind of instruction designed for dyslexics, and Patrick flourished and mastered the material.

Unfortunately, another requirement of Juilliard's was proficiency in piano playing, no matter what your instrument. That meant learning to read two lines of notes at the same time and having the coordination to play them accurately at the same time. "That added an even bigger hurdle," says Patrick. "It was just like sports to me. I am very good at the sports that require constant, regular movement, like kayaking and skiing. I am no good at the stop-and-start types of games, like baseball and basketball. Learning to play the piano is akin to hitting a baseball to me. I can't do it."

A team sport Patrick could play and play very well was soccer. Of course, it's also a sport with constant, regular movement; soccer players run an average of four and a half miles a game. The team he played on was very successful, so he was a standout player on a standout team. This and the fact that he had a girlfriend made him a "semicool guy" by the time he was a sophomore in high school and eased his way socially through his final years in Poughkeepsie. After graduation Patrick went to DePauw University and graduated with a major in music performance. To do this, he showed great creativity—he convinced the officials at the school to call music his foreign language and therefore fulfilled that requirement. He also told them that he wasn't able to play the piano, and they said that was acceptable, too. In addition, he explained, he was a serious soccer player, which helped because although school officials may or may not care much about musicians, they all seem to love jocks. In fact, Patrick was the only string player in the school who earned a varsity letter each of the four years he was there. "It was weird," he says. "I was semialienated from almost everyone else, and it was a self-induced alienation. I was a musician who played sports, and I joined a fraternity where there were no musicians and no soccer players. I was all over the place."

Now in his early thirties, Patrick is all over the place literally, but he is very centered personally. Like his father, he says he copes by being hyperorganized, in the office and at home, which is also a happy place for him. He has a significant other with whom he lives in Boston—she is an assistant district attorney—and they are making many plans for the future. Those plans don't include staying on this very fast track for the rest of their lives; they do include looking into other ways of spending their time together. "All I wanted was to prove that I could perform at this level," says Patrick. "If it goes well, I will be among a very small number of people who have taken something like this all the way and been successful. I've always been unique and different, and I wanted something unique and different."

Genetically speaking, Elaine West Mitchell says that her kids didn't stand a chance; they got their dyslexia from both their parents. Their father never met the people who gave birth to him, never had any interest in doing so. "My parents were the wonderful people who adopted me and raised me," says Ron West. So he doesn't know about his genetic history, but Elaine knows about hers. It would never have occurred to her to call herself dyslexic in any way until she learned what she learned from her three sons. She never had any trouble reading, she never had any memory weaknesses; memorizing came easily to her, and it wasn't until the demands got intense that she had any serious trouble with writing. But she worked very hard for her good grades in school. Ron recalls that "I used to give her a bad time for working so hard for an A in college. Now I realize that she had some difficulty assimilating information. I remember how hard physics was for her."

Elaine does remember that neither one of her parents could give directions to their home, and that her mother had great difficulty pronouncing long words—little clues to subtle difficulties with language processing. She says that she herself has always had difficulty with organization in addition to struggling with writing. "And I still have trouble with overloading," she says, "the same way Patrick does. If I have too much visual or auditory stimuli, I short-circuit. For instance, I can't drive into a city and have the car radio on at the same time." She pauses, thoughtfully, and adds, "And sticking to the point of a story is a problem for me, too."

The West boys are all grown-up men now, each with his own way of coping with and compensating for his dyslexia, and each with his own set of scars as well. Elaine sometimes wonders what their lives would have been like if she had known earlier what she knows today about learning difficulties, differences, and disorders. Maybe her sons would have had it easier. But she knows for sure that she could never have been prouder.

CHAPTER FOUR

Living the Life
of the Dyslexic

Complications Outside the Classroom

ALTHOUGH SCHOOL is the most difficult place for dyslexics
because of the constant reading-and-writing requirements,
life after school can be hell, too. One young woman I know
who was taking tennis lessons couldn't keep the sequence of steps in her
head, and her coach just kept shouting them at her again and again, which
only served to confuse and scare her. Finally, he smartened up and gave
her two steps at a time, and then two more, and then two after that, and
she actually became a very proficient player. For almost a whole summer,
though, she felt as clumsy, stupid, and inadequate as she ever felt when
a teacher asked her to read aloud in front of the class.

Team sports are booby traps waiting to bewilder the uncoordinated
dyslexic; music lessons can be as enigmatic as calculus; and even
reading in church can present an occasion for shame, as we learned
from Bruce Waterfall. Basic social situations can also be complicated,
because dyslexics often have difficulty with subtle cues and can be as
awkward in the drawing room as they are on the playing field. It seems
that life offers constant opportunities for even the most brilliant
dyslexic to feel like a dunce; there are daily challenges to be met and
conquered.

By the time she graduated from high school, Valerie McCarthy was finally convinced that she was not actually the stupidest person in the world. She didn't exactly think she was the brightest, either, but she had begun to give herself a little hard-earned credit. Valerie had starred in every one of her school's annual musical productions since she first wowed 'em in *The Wiz* in eighth grade. Her musical abilities had grown and her commitment to lessons had expanded until she was a highly active and very valued Saturday student at the well-respected Mannes College of Music. And her academics were on solid footing. As she started eleventh grade, she vowed to give up all outside help with her studies—no tutoring, no major editing of her papers, not even assistance with the reading from her mother. She was determined to become independent, to struggle through herself. "Even if I wasn't going to make it," she says, "I wanted to try. And it was really good for me. I felt much better about my work, and I got B-minuses as my lowest grades." In her senior year, she applied to fourteen colleges "just to apply." She says with a chuckle, "I even included some Ivies just to be able to say I'd applied to them. It felt good." Getting accepted at some of her "reaches" felt even better. Then she had to make the big decision. Should she attend Johns Hopkins and study psychology, one of her major interests, and think of singing as just a hobby? Or should she go for it, and become a music major at Northwestern? Never one to shy away from a challenge, Valerie decided to give her voice a real chance. Northwestern it was.

Valerie planned to spend the summer between high school and her first year of college in Italy, as one of about twenty-five students attending six-hour daily master classes in Florence, being critiqued in front of all the others by renowned voice teachers. The air would be thick with competition, anxiety, envy. Valerie thought it would probably be more like the real world than any situation she had had to deal with so far, and she felt the experience would be invaluable in terms of learning about her voice, of learning how to deal with the pressure and all those emotions, and of gaining greater stage presence. A friend of her family's, a French opera singer, concurred and added that it would be even better if Valerie were to stop off in France on her way to Florence and study with her own, aged, revered coach. Valerie was thrilled. "What a glorious opportunity!" she thought.

Brimming over with youthful enthusiasm, self-confidence, and optimism, Valerie boarded her Air France flight to Paris. The minute she got to her hotel on the Left Bank, she called Madame. "Come right on over," she said, and off Valerie went, not even stopping to think that she hadn't had any sleep and might just be suffering from a bit of jet lag. She arrived at Madame's studio; it was a scene from an old sepia-colored photograph, and Madame herself seemed to step from another century. She was about eighty years old, small, frail, serious, dressed in black. Valerie thought they would just visit for a while, but Madame instantly asked her to sing. Valerie began an aria, but had a little difficulty because of the eight hours she had just spent breathing recycled airplane air. She paused for a moment and cleared her throat. "She just yelled at me," Valerie recalls in horror. " 'What are you doing?' she demanded. 'You can't sing!' " Suddenly Valerie was nothing more than that little girl who couldn't do it—who couldn't read, who couldn't spell, who couldn't sing. She was right back in her elementary school days, with the teacher throwing her books on the floor and telling her she was stupid, stupid, stupid! "Right away I had a vision of grammar school, and there I was." At her hotel that night, after a good cry, Valerie had nightmares about her early school experiences; she had nightmares about a ruined future; she had nightmares about losing her voice completely. When she woke up, there was no relief; it was a new day all right, but in just a few hours she would be expected to subject herself to the tortures of Madame again. And there would be twelve more of these new days until her two weeks were up. Could she possibly live through it?

The second day was worse than the first. If Valerie breathed wrong in one phrase, Madame punched her in the stomach. If she thought something was wrong with the way she held her neck, Madame twisted it. The mental, verbal, and physical abuse continued and intensified. Up went Valerie's protective shell, the shell she hadn't needed since she left her first school. She hated how it felt; she hated needing it; she determined to shed it. It was then that Valerie grew up and became truly wise. She could survive almost anything now. "I said to myself," Valerie recalls, " 'This cruelty is not what she really means. She just wants to get to me, so that I can do and will do exactly what she wants. Well, she's supposed to be so great . . .' " she mused. Right then and there she decided to surrender herself to Madame. And surrender herself she did. She discarded her protective shell, an act of supreme courage; she followed every single instruction Madame gave her, no matter how tiny, no matter how outrageous, no matter whether she thought it made sense or not. She lived, breathed, ate, drank, and slept Madame's teachings. Her sessions improved daily; Madame's attitude softened. At the end of the two weeks, Madame kissed Valerie on both cheeks, bid her *"Adieu; à bientôt,"* and said, "See? That's my girl."

Valerie spent the next three weeks in Florence, having her work picked apart and picked apart by more than one teacher, in front of all the other students, students from all over the world. Most found the pressure very difficult, but not the intrepid Valerie. What she had learned in Paris was hers forever. "The Koreans could handle it," she says, "and so could I. The others couldn't. There was this one teacher. She taught once a week. She was hard, but she was great; she knew exactly what she wanted and how she wanted it, and you had to do it her way." Other students regularly burst into tears and stomped out of the room, sobbing, saying, "She's horrible! She's insane!" Valerie just laughed, then gave the teacher what she wanted. The next summer, she worked with that same teacher four times a week for a full month. "She took me in as her daughter; she wants me to succeed." Valerie is living with this teacher now, and studying with her full-time to prepare for her career onstage.

Valerie turned her nightmare into a dream by using what she had learned about coping with her dyslexia and what she had learned about people and teachers through the years, but France wasn't the last time her dyslexia caught up with her and made her miserable outside of classic academics. As a voice major at Northwestern University, she had to do some acting, and she had to join a group of drama majors, who were used to reading scenes cold and memorizing them quickly and regularly, at least one a week. Valerie was terrified. "Reading in public is still a problem for me," she says, wincing at the thought. "I just can't do it. If I absolutely have to, I feel like an idiot. I had to do something, so I got them to let me look at scenes in advance before reading them in front of everybody. I just told them I was dyslexic and couldn't do it any other way." Valerie also needed time to memorize, and she didn't know how to rush the process; she had to do it small section by small section to do it effectively, and she didn't have time to do it her way. "I was trapped," she says. "I had no choice. I knew I had to figure out a method that would let me memorize faster; I had to jump in and do it, or they would say, 'Get out! You can't do this.'" She developed a system, and it worked; she learned to memorize much faster. She doesn't read a line the normal way, the way she says it or sings it. She starts off setting a beat, and she says a syllable for each beat. She keeps it up and keeps it up, slowly, tapping out the beat . . . on the wall, while bouncing a ball, doing sit-ups, something physical, something that activates her kinesthetic memory as well. "It works as long as I keep going. I can't lose the beat; that's the most important part."

Like so many other dyslexics, Valerie regularly faces social complications invisible to others. Sometimes she has problems listening; she overloads when bombarded with too much visual or auditory input. So she can lose the thread of the conversation she is having with a group. Lovely to look at, with a vibrant smile, sparkling eyes, and an effervescent personality, she is also a klutz, uncoordinated and accident-prone, another common characteristic of dyslexics. She spent her entire childhood with skinned knees and elbows, and was always bruised. Her lack of ease physically also made P.E. classes a nightmare for her throughout high school, where she was subjected to rather relentless teasing from her classmates. Now, though, she is free of enforced athletics, free of feeling like a fool because she can't hit or kick a ball. Now she only has to worry about stumbling in the street, and, "Finally," she says, "I have decided that it's amusing."

What she doesn't find amusing is the difficulty she continues to have reading music and the fact that she can't learn to play the piano. She is not alone; playing an instrument is something most dyslexics must forgo, although the cello seems to be more conquerable than most. Some of Winston Churchill's letters home from school are filled with pleas to his family to let him take cello lessons; Nelson Rockefeller entertained his family with cello recitals; and Patrick West, whom you have met, was quite a prodigy on the instrument. For Valerie, "Learning to read the music to sing was hard enough, and I still simply can't read scores. I have to be able to hear it; there has to be a recording, or someone has to play it for me." As for piano, she agrees with Patrick West. "It's just too complicated. You have to do two different things with your hands at one time and read two lines of music at once. I can't do that. What would make it easier for me would be colors and shapes. That would make a real difference. If each octave were color-coded and each note had a different shape, I could read the music and learn to play the piano. Maybe someday I'll devise a method of teaching music that way." Patrick's former solfeggio teacher might help.

Valerie never had the problem "reading" people that many dyslexics do who find body language and social cues hard to interpret. She is actually very good at figuring out even the subtexts of what people are saying; she is very intuitive, part of the reason she was considering psychology for a career. She also enjoyed, from an early age, the attention and devotion her voice brought her. Her singing made her special; it went a long way in helping compensate for the troubles she experienced as a dyslexic. Her particular combination of strengths and talents made her social life much, much easier than it might have been. She never had trouble making friends, once she was in a safe place where there were people she could trust and was able to drop her invisible shield. If only some of that had been true for Walker Harman. He struggled for many years and suffered mightily before he found a place safe enough to begin to make real friends.

Walker had trouble in school from the first day of first grade, both academically and socially. Kindergarten had been great; he had been left to his own devices, never forced into any kind of traditional group play, allowed to grow plants and play with the animals that were around, and never forced to get over what he calls his early antisocial behavior. Then his family moved, and Walker changed schools. Suddenly there were rules, rules, and more rules. He was told not to do things—not to talk, not to go outside, not to cross the street—and he was expected *to do* other things, like read. He was furious, he was scared witless, he was disappointed, and he was dismayed. He also remembers feeling great embarrassment all the time, and he remembers being—or at least feeling—very isolated from the other kids. He couldn't do what he wanted to do, he couldn't read at all, and his eyehand coordination was so poor, he couldn't even play any of the games. He just didn't fit in. In a panic, his mother took charge, and he started going to his many rounds of doctors and "shrinks" and educational psychologists; she was determined to find out what was going on with her son and to help him get over whatever it was. She dragged him all over Texas trying to find the answers she sought; she flew him east to New York, and to many places in between. He was studied and questioned and tested and examined. He felt like a "weirdo." He had no friends anywhere near his own age, but he did enjoy all the attention that he was getting from the adults. Walker had always preferred grown-ups to children, and now he was with them most of the time. By third grade, he was in a third school, one where he finally received the kind of instruction he needed, and he began to read. He also began to feel more like a member of the human race. "At last," he says. "There seemed to be much less pressure at that school—less social pressure and less teacher pressure—and I became less overcome by fear and isolation." Still, he gravitated toward adults, and the friends he did make were mostly teachers.

In sixth grade, Walker changed schools again, back to a "regular" public school and to what he viewed as another chance to prove himself in the "real world." That year was fine, but seventh grade was the worst of all . . . so far. Walker had managed to get his academic life somewhat together, with the aid of daily sixty- to ninety-minute tutoring sessions and remedial reading classes, but he was still no good at sports and no good at being with people his own age. "I was just a geek," he says, "and I got beaten up all the time. In shop class, the teacher even sided with the bully." Walker skipped lots of school that year, and he forged his mother's signature on many notes claiming doctor's appointments. Eighth grade was better because he had a teacher who understood him and what he needed, but there was little improvement in his social life.

Although he began to make friends in high school, those years were pretty dramatic for Walker. He went to four different schools before he graduated, including the Christian Reform School in Missouri, where, he says, he learned more about drugs than he could ever have imagined at home, and where he went to AA meetings, not because he was an alcoholic, but because that was the only place he could smoke. "It was a horrific experience," he says. "My parents and I had not been getting along. They could not stand what the people I hung out with looked like—purple hair, nose rings, that sort of thing. They had become very, very strict, and I disobeyed regularly, but much of it was really pretty adolescent and benign. At least, I thought so, but my parents obviously felt otherwise. At one point, I went to visit my grandmother for a couple of days. When it was time to go home, my father picked me up in his plane—he is an amateur pilot—but instead of taking me back to Dallas, he whisked me off to Missouri. I never saw it coming. They had completely shut the door, and I wasn't even allowed to communicate with them for ninety days. When I got there, I stayed in bed for three days, until they threatened to send me to a dirty old hole called the Johnson Brothers Boys' Ranch. Suddenly I knew that I had to toe the line, or I would never get back to a real school or ever see my parents again." Walker stayed at that grim place for nine months and, amazingly, kept on schedule academically, so he did not have to repeat any schooling.

He spent the next year in a Jesuit-run school where he was intellectually stimulated, where he found close friends, and where he started experimenting with drugs in earnest. ("I wanted to have some fun," he says. "I thought I had earned it. I had just finished a terrible year in Missouri, my mother was battling cancer, and I felt as though I was grabbing hold of life.") He wasn't able to fulfill the foreign language requirement the priests insisted on, though, and had to change schools. By this time, drugs were a regular part of his life. He fooled around with and sampled a fairly wide variety of substances, but speed was the most appealing and what he used most often. "I would never have admitted it then," he says now, "but what really appealed to me about speed was the fact that it focused me and helped me get done what I needed to do." Interesting observation, since speed is chemically much the same as Ritalin, which is used to focus students with attention disorders. I have heard many stories of people with dyslexia self-medicating to ease the pain their disorders bring to them; Walker seems at least partially to have been self-medicating for some therapeutic purposes; perhaps others do the same. At any rate, his relationship with drugs ended after about nine months, when he decided that the lack of sleep associated with speed wasn't worth the enhanced focus it gave. Things hadn't improved much at home, though; they had in fact declined so, that Walker ran away and lived with various friends' families for an entire semester. "You may call it rebellion," he says. "I call it survival." For his last two years of high school, Walker had one-on-one instruction at a tutorial school. Then came college rejections. "You know," he says now, ruefully, "school was never about learning for me; it was about finding the right place where I could learn."

Walker's friends were all going either to Bennington or Sarah Lawrence, but he didn't get into either one. He did get into Fordham, but his parents would not hear of his going to school in New York City. Once again he was off to the professionals; they sent him to an educational evaluator to take a whole new battery of tests. Once again his keen intelligence was overlooked in favor of his difficulties. The evaluator determined that Walker would never survive in a regular college setting. She convinced his parents that he should go to Landmark, a college for learning disabled students in Putney, Vermont. "It was tiny," says Walker; "it was freezing; there was nothing but academics; it got dark at four o'clock. I was miserable." He spent every weekend visiting his friends at Sarah Lawrence, and returning to Vermont on Sundays just made him feel wretched. He went home for Christmas vacation and said he would not go back. His parents told him that officials at Landmark said he would not be able to make it at a mainstream college, to which he replied, "Fine. Then I won't go to college, but I'm not going back there!" He had a friend who was going to go to Marymount Manhattan College, so Walker applied. He was accepted, he enrolled, and that is where we met and worked together.

I was instantly impressed with Walker's verbal skills, his organization, his courage, and his pain. He took part in a great deal of theater at Marymount, and he was really quite good. He acted, he directed, and he studied. He made friends, too, and not only did he survive at this mainstream college, but he flourished, graduating with a 3.7 GPA. "I grew up at Marymount," he says now. "I wish I had done it a little differently, and I still resent my parents for not saying, 'That evaluator doesn't know what she's talking about. We're going to find you a good school, and you're going to go there.' I don't know how they could have done anything other than what they did, but I always believed they didn't have any faith in me."

Walker took some time off after he finished Marymount to figure out what to do next. He sampled the world of acting, full of auditions and rejections and waiting on tables. He tried a few other potential careers as well, and when he decided he wanted to go to law school, he got a job as a legal assistant in the litigation department of a big law firm. He stayed there for a year and a half. He became a star among the assistants: he was always ready for work on time or before; he worked long hours; he traveled for the firm; and because he looked for opportunities to learn and grow, he got them. "It was really good work experience," he says, "and decent exposure to the court system. I learned what is involved in filing a lawsuit." Walker studied for the law school exams diligently for about six months. For two of those, he devoted himself entirely to LSAT preparation; he took a Princeton Review course; he did fifteen practice tests. When it came time to take the exam, he took almost twice as long as the others to finish. And he scored in the 93rd percentile.

Older, wiser, calmer, reassured of his own abilities to think and to deal with his difficulties, Walker entered Fordham Law School in September 1996, convinced that this would be the one exception to his experiences to date, that this time he would really belong. He would slide right in, have an easy time of it, and would quickly make a good solid group of like-minded friends. However, it didn't quite work out that way. Law school posed the greatest challenge to Walker of his whole life, and it sent him right back to his early unable-to-do days just as thoroughly as Madame had sent Valerie back. Suddenly he had to read far greater quantities of far denser material than ever before, which was difficult enough, but Walker could read quite fast by now, and his comprehension was excellent, so all that took was time and effort. That was okay. He was prepared for that, but he wasn't prepared for the toughest part—class. Aggressive, fast-on-their-feet students grab the discussion in law school classes; they set the pace and the agenda. Less aggressive students pick up the crumbs. Said Walker after a few months, "I'm going through some of the same things I went through before. I get so nervous, I shake, so overwhelmed by the experience, I freeze, and I can't say what I do know. Then it gets worse. I get so paralyzed, I can't even look down and read my notes. When things aren't going as well as they might, I start behaving like a typical dyslexic. I misspell words; my thoughts are jumbled; I misspeak. When I'm comfortable, my notes are beautiful; when I'm frustrated, they're a mess. When I'm relaxed, I excel. Why can't I do that all the time?"

Walker didn't slide right in. It wasn't easy, and there wasn't that instant group of good friends. That seemed to make him saddest. "Well," he commented, "as the work of school weighs heavily, you want to balance it out. I look around and I see bonding, I see study groups forming, and I'm not a part of it."

Rebecca Tomasini never joined any study groups at her first college—she thought she was far too brainy and independent for most of the other students. "No one wanted to be a lawyer there," she moans. "They all wanted to be legal assistants!" And all Rebecca did was want . . . and want . . . and want. She wanted to be part of a group that wanted more and got more, that thrived on intellectual stimulation and challenge, that was daring and brave, that would encourage and somehow unlock what she knew was her superior brain power. So, four days before she was supposed to return to the campus to begin her senior year, she decided not to go back. Instead she fought for herself for the first time in her life; that is when she got herself admitted to Smith College, her dream school . . . at least it was before she got there.

Rebecca didn't want to join any study groups when she was first at Smith, either. She found intellectual stimulation in that community, all right, and pressure enough that she wasn't sure she could cope. She knew she was smart, but she was having a terrible time keeping up with the work—with the volume, with the complexity, and mostly with the pace. Every other week, she was convinced that she was going to drop out anyhow, so why bother getting involved with a study group? She was also sure that she would be so much slower than the others that she would not be able to hold her own and would in fact bring down the general level of the whole group.

Rebecca was just getting used to the idea that she was dyslexic; she was diagnosed after she started at Smith, and she wasn't yet fully in touch with what it all meant. Her first reaction to finding out about her dyslexia at almost twenty-two years of age was outrage. "It was a real blow," she says. "I thought it undermined everything I had done. I had slipped through so many cracks, through so many people, so many times. . . . I had wasted so much time. All I could think of was 'Smith is hard; Smith found out.' I must have gone to all second-rate schools because none of them found out. I cried and cried and cried. I felt so cheated, and I was so mad, I wanted to hurt someone." The psychologist who diagnosed Rebecca finally said to her, "Oh, stop it. Now you know what's wrong. So go do something about it!" "Then," says Rebecca, "I rethought the whole thing and decided that I actually might be pretty brilliant to have made it so far on my own. I thought again. Wouldn't the dyslexia explain why I was so depressed? Finally, I decided that I could wallow in it or use it, learn and grow from it, and then I felt fortunate to have found out. Once I came to terms with my dyslexia, I changed my way of thinking completely, from confused and angry and humble to 'Look out, world, get out of my way!' " Rebecca joined a study group and found that she had a great deal to contribute, also that she didn't slow anyone down. It was an amazing comfort; her friends helped her understand a great deal of whatever she couldn't get from trying to read about it, and they also gave her huge quantities of emotional support. She says that being at Smith really was the key and the answer for her; she feels strongly that she couldn't have found such solidarity at a coed school.

Rebecca never had a problem having friends. Warm, outgoing, wickedly funny, she stayed a part of the elite "artsy" group all through high school, even after she was not in the same advanced classes as they. Once an astonishingly cruel comment from a French teacher—"I'm so surprised you hang out with Doris and those kids. Are they really your friends?"—sent her to the bathroom in tears. Those friends were the only validation of her own intelligence she had left; they were her only defense against the creeping feelings of inferiority that were contaminating her sense of herself. They still appreciated her; she could always keep up with their conversations, with their interests in theater and art, and she could always make them laugh. It was a very cohesive group; they were not competitive with each other; they were all successful. They helped buoy her spirits, they helped her with her papers, and they tried to help her with math, too.

Mathematics completely eluded Rebecca, as it does many dyslexics, and she was having great difficulty trying to pass Algebra I. She tried doing her homework with her father, having him explain the abstract concepts to her. He was a very adept mathematician, but he had no idea how to teach her and have her actually learn what he was teaching; their sessions together always ended up with his saying in frustration to his brilliant but seemingly obtuse daughter, "Why don't you get it? It's right there! You must see it!" (A few years later, she had to enlist parental help once again, this time her mother's. She had decided to make a quilt by hand; carefully she stitched all the squares and then found herself totally unable to arrange them so that they would form the design she sought. Mom was able to rescue her this time.) Even Doris and all Rebecca's other successful friends were unable to succeed in keeping her from failing Algebra I, though, and not just once—twice.

They were also unsuccessful in keeping her from sinking into the morass of unidentified dyslexia. "I gave up," she says. "I'd work twenty hours on a paper and still get a C. Then there were all those low-level classes. How I hated them! There was a Shakespeare class my junior year that I wanted to take, but they wouldn't let me. I went to it anyhow, and the guidance counselor came and took me out. Can you imagine anything more humiliating? That's when I really got mad." Rebecca, who had been a great student, a superior athlete, and such a darling of teachers that they asked her to baby-sit for them, turned into an angry, disrespectful adolescent, particularly when confronted with anyone in authority. During the classes she knew were so beneath her, she would deliberately read something other than the book being discussed, usually something harder and more sophisticated, just to show that she really didn't belong there. She became bitter, and her conversations with adults deteriorated from interested, enthusiastic, and cooperative to surly, churlish, and sour. She was not getting along with her parents, either, another common experience for teenaged undiagnosed dyslexics who feel that no one understands them. "My mother or father would say hello to me," she recalls, "and I would whirl around and spit at them, 'What do you want?!' " It got so bad that Mr. and Mrs. Tomasini were at the guidance office at school all the time, and reports about their daughter were sent home to them every two weeks. Basically the reports said that what she really needed was a swift kick in the behind; it's a remedy that has never actually proven very successful in treating dyslexia, although many have tried it.

Rebecca never got involved with alcohol or drugs; food became her comfort and her vice. Eventually it became her enemy, too. She gained weight, which, of course, only made her feel worse, so she had to eat more; she fought with her parents constantly, convinced that they didn't trust or value her; and finally, when she started drawing swastikas on walls around the house, her situation hit rock bottom. Mrs. Tomasini was deeply worried about the daughter with whom she had shared so much joy, and she felt that something had to give, something had to be done for her; the whole family needed relief. Maybe Rebecca would be better off living someplace else for a while. So she packed a suitcase for her, rushed her into the car, locked the door, and started to back out of the garage, on her way to an agency to seek help and guidance. As her mother put the car in reverse, Rebecca leaned out the window and cried to her father, "Okay, go ahead, just stand there and let her do this! You don't care!" She might as well have walloped him; her words were fists that struck him and hurt him deeply. He was devastated, so completely devastated that he stood behind the car and made it impossible for Mrs. Tomasini to continue down the driveway. It seemed briefly that Rebecca had even been able to divide her parents, but in the end, they were all relieved and very glad. They had always been a close family and they knew they could be again. Eventually they got through it, and things went back to normal. Rebecca says, "My parents are fabulous. I don't know how they stood those years, or how I stood them, either. They felt so guilty when they found out that I was dyslexic; they had spent many hours with the guidance counselor when I was in high school, but there was no real help, and they felt as though they should have been smarter about it."

By spring of his first year of law school, Walker Harman had found his place, his sea legs, and the friends he had hoped would appear in this first truly grown-up phase of his life. The pain he had in the early months was so intense and so much like the pain he had had so many times for so many years, he decided he was simply not going to suffer it anymore. He knew himself now, and he was going to take more control of his life. Like Valerie when she was in Paris, he determined he would not let this new challenge defeat him the way others had. So, like Valerie, Walker truly grew up, and he became wise. "Just before winter vacation," he says, "I decided I had to sit down and really think about what it means for me to be in law school. It means an enormous amount, and I don't intend for it not to happen. I've worked too hard to get here; I intend for it to be a success, and I'm going to make it a success. I realized I had to set goals, one of the most important being not to drive myself crazy. Then I went home and had a really great vacation with my family. It had taken a while for us to be completely reconciled, but we have a fine relationship now. Being with them was very nurturing."

Rested, refreshed, revitalized, Walker returned from vacation and was immediately invited to join three different study groups; he joined them all. The other students in the groups ranged widely, from astonishingly talented and quick to struggling to "get it." Some found it easier than Walker did; some found it more difficult than he. He fit in beautifully. At last he had a group of like-minded, like-suffering souls to share ideas and frustrations with, a support system. He was no longer alone and isolated; he was no longer the geek. His workload didn't slow down any, but Walker did. He began to rekindle his faith in himself and in his abilities, and he realized he didn't have to do 100 percent of the reading every single night to understand what was going on. He even found romance on a blind date and recaptured a social life. Balance is all, it seems; there is that old *Liebe* and *Arbeit* again. With his newfound place in his society, Walker even began to look different. Medium-tall, slender, fair-skinned, and sandy-haired, he is quite handsome. He is also graceful and elegant, with excellent taste in clothes and the easy good manners of a born gentleman. During the fall and winter, though, the tension and anxiety that dogged his first months of graduate school were etched on his face. By May they were gone. He looked older and less harried at the same time; he spoke more easily, smiled more readily and more warmly. His peace of mind shone through his eyes.

"Finally," he said over dinner one soft, rainy evening, "I'm really enjoying law school. I had some humiliating experiences last fall; I remember people laughing at me as I misspoke while answering. Now no one is interested in how anyone else performs, and now I also feel more composed. It's so nice not to live in fear every day as I did in the fall. The freedom has given me the opportunity to learn so much more and absorb so much more—and I've made tons of friends." To top it all off, Walker was chosen for a plum summer judicial internship, one coveted by many, and he was selected based on a letter he wrote himself and hand-delivered. When he got to the office where he wanted his letter read, he saw a huge box of applications waiting to be opened. Instead of adding his to the mix, he slid it under a locked door and hoped. His enterprising effort paid off; his letter was opened quickly, and the reader was impressed enough to seek him out. Not bad for a young dyslexic who worries about sending thank-you and get-well-soon notes.

Walker Harman now feels that he received too much attention because of his dyslexia, that all the poking and prodding of him inside and out got in his way, even though it also got him (eventually) the kind of instruction he needed to go ahead. "All the special attention I got for being diagnosed hindered me," he says. "It made me feel as though I had a disease." Rebecca Tomasini, on the other hand, had no diagnosis, no testing, no special help. She spent her high school years floundering, wondering, worrying. Still, her ideas about what might have happened to her are frightening, far worse in her eyes than what actually did happen to her. "In the long run," she says now, "I'm glad I was not diagnosed, because I would have lost that vision of myself as smart because my friends were smart. I would have been put in a self-contained special ed. classroom with Down syndrome kids and kids who threw chairs. At my school, it was called the Zoo Room." What about if she could have stayed in the classroom and been pulled out for extra instruction? "That would have been ideal," she says. "I wish I had been pulled out. If I could have been given the hour I needed to finish the five-minute essay, my entire high school life would have been different."

Cyprian was tested and began remediation just in the nick of time, just before his feelings about himself really plummeted. He did not get off scot-free, of course—no dyslexic does—but his pain was minimal compared with that of so many others. Cyp started his days in a tiny private school in a rural community not too far from where Rebecca lived; he was evaluated about halfway through second grade. It was not a grueling process; the testing was done by someone he knew well and could see without having to travel far. At just about the same time, we started working together during his school day and on weekends. His school seemed like a sweet and gentle place, but it wasn't. It was run by parents, whether they knew anything about education or not, and there was a very competitive atmosphere. The classes were tiny, the children well fed and intelligent, but the faculty members were not properly trained, and they had grand ambitions for their pupils, sometimes bordering on delusion. Cyp's first-grade teacher bragged about having her students read *The Secret Garden,* an utterly inappropriate selection, from which they couldn't possibly glean the reading lessons they should have been learning. A few could, of course, struggle through the book in some fashion, which only encouraged the lunacy. This is a book she should have been reading *to* them; if she had, then everyone would have been happy and free to enjoy the beautiful story. Imagine how Cyp must have felt; he couldn't read *The Cat in the Hat,* much less the dialects of some of the characters in the Burnett book. He must have been utterly bewildered. He knew something was very different about him, but he didn't know what. I don't know if he felt stupid, but I would be willing to bet he did. I would also be willing to bet he felt afraid; in fact, he was so nervous when we began to work together, I think it might be guaranteed that his school days were filled with fear. The innocence of youth is a real myth; children know everything. They may not be able to understand—the adults in Cyp's life didn't even under- stand then what was going on with him—but they know. All of them know. Cyp knew he was not like his classmates, and his classmates also knew it. And, as is typical of children, they were not always so kind about it, either. One youngster who was blessed with high intelligence but not much generosity regularly made fun of Cyp and laughed over his struggles and stammers as he read aloud or tried to answer a ques- tion. I spoke to this boy more than once, to try to get him to understand how hurtful his chuckles were and how crushed he would feel if the sit- uation were reversed, but he was young and unable to hear me or put himself in another's shoes—or at least unable to stop what he was doing.

How did Cyp cope with all of this? We humans are very resource- ful and clever in our survival techniques. Cyp was then and still is a very appealing child; when he was small, he looked as though he had stepped out of an old English painting. He is intelligent, and he has a very gentle nature and an easy smile. Aggressive behavior is not and probably never will be a part of his personality, so he chose a good- natured, heartbreaking way of handling the situation. He employed a time-tested method for dealing with being made fun of, one that many of our favorite comedians have employed to help them manage the pain of being the odd man out. He became the class clown, a silly cutup. Cyp's coordination was somewhat like Valerie's—not so hot. So, if he were to trip or stumble, he made it a slapstick trip and did a flop. He fell off his chair on purpose; he dropped things again and again until the other boys were in stitches. When he made mistakes reading aloud, he giggled more than anyone else; he tried to make it seem that he had done so on purpose and that making mistakes was the coolest thing to do. He also had a wide repertoire of faces and noises with which to distract and amuse his classmates. They thought he was a hoot, and they enjoyed his antics. They didn't try to join him, though; they didn't need to. So they had fun with him, but it was really at his own expense. His teachers were not nearly so amused; they often commented on his fooling around in their reports. None of them understood why he was doing it and what they might have done to help him give up his defenses. Instead, as is so often the case, they blamed him. Eventually his parents made the difficult but life-saving decision to take Cyp out of that hothouse environment and send him to the local public school. There they found true professionals, there he was fully tested, and there he received the assistance he needed. In addition, there his classmates were much more varied than the insular, narrow group at his private school. He wasn't the only child with difficulty; he didn't have to feel like The Only One who struggled. Soon he was able to give up his antics and win the affection and respect of his fellow students. He did so very quickly; at the end of fourth grade he was voted the "coolest kid" by his classmates, not for clowning around, but for being a good friend and an important member of the class.

Cyp has lots of friends. One in particular, another dyslexic boy he met at a camp that included daily tutoring and sports, will likely be his soul mate forever. They are really Mike and Ike; they even finish each other's sentences, and they plan to become professional fishermen together. Cyp is also popular with the girls and an utterly fearless athlete. The lack of coordination that bogged him down when he was small certainly doesn't stop him from snowboarding tricks or mastering the moves of a bicycle that spins and turns. Musical instruments have eluded him, though; he has tried three times and become very discouraged. He is convinced that one day he will be able to play something, though, and have fun doing it. Perhaps Valerie will have developed a dyslexic-friendly method of multisensory music instruction by then.

Once Cyp's mother and father broke through that guilt-and-denial barrier that confronts the parents of children with learning problems and understood what was going on with their son, they became as informed and supportive as parents could be. They have given their son the correct educational opportunities, and they have also given him many chances to develop other strengths and to feel terrific about the fact that he is an ace fisherman, that he can design computer games, and that he can also cook. If all children had the benefit of such a committed family, they might have a chance to be as successful as he is, and Cyp is now a very successful dyslexic.

For many, remediation is not enough to become successful; dyslexics and other learning disabled children and adolescents often need some counseling or therapy in addition to remedial aid to help them deal with the issues around their disability and the lack of self-worth that so often accompanies it. Studies have shown that learning disabled youngsters have a tendency toward "learned helplessness" and can have serious difficulties with motivation. After all, if it's so hard and takes so long, and the results are not going to be so great anyhow, why put in all that effort? Most of us would at least be discouraged by, if not depressed about, the prospects. Depression is a serious issue among the dyslexic and otherwise learning disabled population; more than one student I have worked with has attempted suicide at about the age of sixteen, and low-level depression is rampant among both children and adolescents. A sense of being damaged also often accompanies learning disabilities, and with that sense of damage and inadequacy can come a rigidity that further gets in the way of learning and developing. I have several children I work with who need constant effort devoted to helping them learn to look at things in more than one way and develop more flexible approaches to problem solving, both academically and personally.

Dr. Emily Ostrow (to protect the privacy of her patients, I have changed her name) has been practicing psychiatry for twenty-one years. She sees mostly adults, and an occasional teenager, and while she is not quite the Psychiatrist to the Stars, her patients are usually as high-powered and high-achieving as she is. Among those in treatment with her have been rich businessmen and -women, Oscar-winning actors, a Pulitzer prize–winning playwright, a famous lyricist, high-level book and magazine editors, and singers and conductors who regularly receive standing ovations amid blizzards of tossed roses. Many have sought her assistance at least partially because of their dyslexia; she hears tales of pain in school and feelings of worthlessness from the most surprising sources, from people whose lives we might often envy, they seem so glittery and triumphant. Dr. Ostrow sees that sense of damage and sense of inadequacy all the time as well. "There is often an intense sense of woundedness, with dyslexic patients sometimes thinking of themselves as defective or 'spoiled goods,' " she says. "It's a function of the reverberation of the low self-esteem that comes into play when they are very young and cannot learn to read. Dyslexia surfaces so early that it becomes a part of their clear self-image." She also finds that "feeling like a fraud is a theme that runs through all their stories, no matter how much public acclaim they have. They are always thinking that they'll be found out, that they are not really as smart or as successful or as talented as they seem. Many of my patients were or at least felt as though they were early academic underachievers," she continues, "and they have compensated enormously. Still, there are real issues."

Dr. Ostrow sees a rich Wall Street trader who is so embarrassed by his reading difficulties that he won't try to read even simple books to his children or listen when they want to read to him. Another patient is an actress who takes so long to learn her lines that every audition looms like a sheer, icy cliff to be scaled. Still another is a famous actor who has an intense yearning to be seen as a good person to compensate for all those years he felt he was a bad person because he couldn't read. "Many come to me who have great talent but who are stuck, who can't go further, because they also have this gigantic expectation of failure," she says. Sometimes they are so filled with shame and so out of touch with their feelings that they can become very intolerant of others who show similar weaknesses. We've all known bullies who pick on the weaker kids just because they feel weak themselves, and it has been proved that the children in a family who are abused are often the ones who most remind the abusing parent of him- or herself. One mother that Dr. Ostrow sees certainly does not abuse her child, but she has great difficulty perceiving that her dyslexic daughter is capable, just as she has great difficulty feeling capable herself; it is an issue they work on constantly in her therapy.

Dr. Ostrow says that many of her patients also have enormous fears about forming relationships and that often when they do, they're very tumultuous. She says that it is very hard for those who have been made to feel so inadequate when they were young to trust being valued by someone else, to believe that they are worthy of being loved. So they often create difficulties and strife just as they are starting to succeed in relationships, just as the other parties are beginning to care more, to come closer; it's a way of avoiding that "being found out" that they are not really what the others think they are.

She also sees pockets of helplessness that are quite unpredictable and that are redolent with the kind of helplessness that is learned: an enormously successful businessman who feels totally incapable of traveling alone, of making his transportation connections, of taking care of his bags, of managing to get to the right hotel room, of being able to read the maps necessary to get to where he needs to go. A great deal of her treatment consists of catching the negative, self-defeating patterns, where the individual reframes situations or acts in situations as though he or she actually is inadequate—such as self-destructing in a relationship, or not attempting a role that is perfect—and dehabituating the behaviors, helping the person to stop creating ways to continue to validate the conviction that he or she is less than everyone else. It's not an instant cure; it takes lots of practice and reinforcement to counteract those early impressions and memories. In fact, there are no instant cures for the kinds of damage dyslexics can endure simply because they are dyslexic. Right now there are no drugs that can be prescribed, either, to ease the symptoms of dyslexia the way prescriptions like Ritalin help attention deficit disorder sufferers. Talk therapy does work, though; it can be very successful in helping dyslexics to dig deep, to learn to understand and to rid themselves of those residual agonies.

Although many studies indicate that women often compensate for their dyslexia more easily and successfully than men do, Dr. Ostrow finds that the women she sees are substantially less achieving than the men, that because of their learning difficulties, they often just stay away from the competition in the business, financial, and medical worlds. The deck is still stacked against them in the fast lanes, she believes. Still, some of the women she has treated because of their emotional difficulties due to their learning disabilities have made highly successful lives for themselves in fields such as computers, or in teaching learning disabled students. One even became a top teacher of speed-reading, of all things. Also, there are those who have more high-powered success stories to tell—like the gorgeous black model who came to Dr. Ostrow because she was frantic about wanting to make a better life for herself, about wanting a different career, about getting older, about being stupid and unable to do anything but pose for pictures, about not being able to read well, and about having had a terrible time in school. She was so damaged and thought so little of herself that she had no idea how articulate and well spoken she was. Finally, after months and months of psychotherapy, she sought and landed a job in public relations, and started a steady rise to the pinnacle, where she now sits happily, as head of the large PR department of a very popular magazine.

Dr. Ostrow also tells proudly the story of another woman patient she helped. When the woman began her treatment, she was entrenched in a marriage that made her feel more and more diminished each day. It was all she thought she was entitled to. Her husband was quite a bit older than she, and a true pedant. Because of her dyslexia, she had always had trouble academically; she had always wanted to have more education and to do better in school, and she was very resentful of her husband's formidable academic credentials. She was incapable of doing anything to dig herself out from under and to alleviate her pain. Therapy gave her the courage and the insight into her own abilities to enable her to decide she was certainly able to do a great deal more than she had been doing. So she went back to school and set about proving to herself and others that she really did have a brain, that she, too, had some impressive strengths. She kept at her schooling until she earned a Ph.D. in applied mathematics, and, since receiving her degree, she has developed a very impressive career. In fact, she now has working under her, doing economic research, several professors with as lofty credentials as her husband has. Perhaps even more important, though, through learning to understand and value herself and her own dyslexia, she has developed a deep understanding and sympathy for the reading disability of her daughter, and she has done all the right things to help her. She has helped her husband understand both her and their daughter better, and she has become her child's advocate at school. She has found the best tutors for her, and she has spent much time and energy helping the child develop her natural talents, which, not surprisingly, happen to be in math. She has been determined that her daughter will not have the same difficulties and wounds that she had, and she has been successful, at least so far. She has a happy, well-adjusted child who is achieving academically at her highest level, and who also has friends and fun. Comments Dr. Ostrow, "Without the therapy, she would have done nothing. It was lucky she started when she did."

Part Two

Diagnosis
and
Treatment

CHAPTER FIVE

Detecting and
Diagnosing Dyslexia

The Key to Breaking the Chains

O NE OF THE clinicians at Teachers College loved to tell the
story about the teenaged boy who gallumphed into her
office one day and hurled himself into a chair with a quick
half-turn. There he collapsed, all six feet three inches of him, replete
with baggy, baggy trousers, a Michael Jordan T-shirt, a Yankees cap on
backward, and zillion-dollar sneakers. His eyes were guarded, his body
language hunched and protective, and his face tender and young under
a slight dusting of adolescent acne. He mumbled his name and said he
was there for his whatever o'clock appointment. "So," said the clinician
to the obviously depressed lad, "what brings you here?" "I dunno," he
replied, adding, "They tell me I'm les-dyxic."

Guess what? He was.

The teenager's story notwithstanding, there are no reliable ways to
self-diagnose dyslexia, no at-home tests that you can clip from a magazine or buy in a drugstore, no ten easy steps to determining whether
you fit the profile or not. However, there are clues, and dyslexia is one
of those conditions that is quite reliably defined by "If you think you—
or your child or your mother, father, aunt, or friend—are dyslexic, then
you probably are." And if you suspect it, the next appropriate step is to

seek a real and proper diagnosis. Once it has been confirmed, you can find out what you should do about the particular situation. The way to get this diagnosis and accompanying recommendations for remediating any difficulties is to have a psychoeducational evaluation. Anyone can have one; the person does not have to be actively enrolled in either therapy or school. It is called psychoeducational because the current criteria for determining learning disabilities, of which dyslexia is but one, are based on a discrepancy between intelligence (the *psycho* part) and achievement (the *educational* part).

When I was doing the educational part of these evaluations at a clinic at Marymount Manhattan College, I diagnosed a twenty-something English woman who had had a terrible time in school—who had in fact been made to sit in the corner of her first-grade class wearing an authentic dunce cap—and who was working as a nanny. She thought it was the best she could do: she liked children, she was blessed with patience, and she thought she was too stupid, of course, for more intellectually demanding work. What she really wanted was to become a nurse, but she was afraid she would not be able to do the coursework required, particularly pharmacology, which required quite intricate math, an area of particular difficulty for her. She was very anxious about what the evaluation would reveal, but she simply had to know if she had any chance to fulfill her ambition. Most of the time, testing is a very positive step; it usually shows that the person is much smarter than everybody thinks. Testing points out strengths as well as weaknesses, and a good evaluator makes reliable recommendations for help. All that proved true in this case; testing indicated that Angela was a fairly classic dyslexic who, with the right help, could indeed become a nurse. She was as happy as if she had won the lottery; she began remediation immediately, was accepted at a nursing school in Florida, and began her education.

It is enormously valuable for adults like Angela or like Bruce Waterfall to be evaluated, so that they can understand and put a name to just what has been getting in their way all these years. It is essential, though, for elementary and high school students who are having difficulties to be evaluated. Without a proper diagnosis, they will linger in the shadows; without a diagnosis, they most likely will not get the help that is due them and that will make it possible for them to survive and thrive in school and beyond.

School districts are required to offer full psychoeducational testing at no cost to school-age members of their community, whether they attend public school or not. There are also clinics that give evaluations, usually with sliding-scale fees. Many of these are at hospitals and offer a team approach, which can be very useful if, in addition to reading difficulties, you think you or your child has a problem such as attention deficit disorder, which must be diagnosed by a neurologist or psychiatrist to be really certain. There are also clinics at universities, such as the one at Teachers College, where I was trained. The costs are quite low, but the staffing is by professionals-in-the-making—supervised but not yet fully accredited. With all of the lower-cost options, also, you will have little or no control over who is to do the testing and interpreting, and the experience might be wonderful and valuable or much less than that, depending on the quality of the testers and administrators involved. There is also the issue of expediency; often at clinics, there is a several-months-long waiting list.

If you have the evaluation done privately, you can choose who you want to do it, and you can interview several people before making your decision. Private evaluations are not inexpensive, however—they can cost anywhere from several hundred dollars to over two thousand. And the cost does not necessarily determine the value; some of the most expensive people may not be the best. You must do your homework and seek out recommendations from doctors, teachers, school administrators, and experienced friends. If your child goes to a private school, officials there will recommend people they have worked with successfully. Still, you must find the person you think will be best for you and/or for your child, someone whom you respect and who also makes you feel comfortable. So you must be diligent about making your selection. At the end of the chapter, I will list questions that should be asked of any potential evaluator, but first let's have a look at what the components of an evaluation are.

Basically the testing is in two parts, spread over one, two, or three days, cognitive (IQ, or intelligence quotient) testing and educational testing. Sometimes various tests of emotional or psychological state are added as well, depending on what the examiner(s) is looking for. The IQ tests used are either the Stanford-Binet or one of the Wechslers, the WISC-III for school-age children, or the WAIS for those who are older. There is also a Wechsler for younger children, the WPPSI, but while it may have predictive value, it does not point the way to actual reading difficulties per se, because the children are too young. The Wechsler tests are what are called "protected" by the American Psychological Association. That means they can be given only by licensed psychologists. All sorts of psychologists are permitted to give them—neuropsychologists, school psychologists, clinical psychologists—but they all must have extensive training in administering and interpreting the tests before they are permitted to do so without supervision. There are two scores, Verbal IQ and Performance IQ, that are derived from the many subtests that make up, say, the WISC-III, and there is a Full-Scale Score as well. That is the number people brag about when they have just been admitted to Mensa. It is also the number that is important in determining whether a student is to be classified as "learning disabled" and eligible for services, because the legal definition of learning disabled requires at least an average IQ. With the WISC-III, average means a Full-Scale Score of 100, with a standard deviation of plus or minus 15 points, so those with learning problems that are classified "learning disabled" have at least an 85 Full-Scale IQ. Lower than that would fall into the below-average range, and below that borderline retarded; lower still is categorized mentally retarded.

The ten required and three supplementary subtests of the WISC-III measure a number of language and logical abilities, some under time pressure and some not. None of the Verbal subtests requires a written response, and only one has a time limit—*arithmetic,* where some word problems are presented orally and others must be read. The other subtests are *information,* which asks questions intended to measure just that, how much information the person has gathered and remembered; *similarities,* which with limited language seeks to measure abstract reasoning; *vocabulary,* in which the person being tested is asked to define orally presented words; *comprehension,* which tries to see how much commonsense reasoning the person has in social situations with conventional American mores; and *digit span,* an optional, supplementary subtest that sees how many numbers at a time the person can hold in short-term memory and recite back to the tester. None of the Performance subtests requires a verbal response; some require a written one, and all of them are timed. These are the ones on which dyslexics often don't do so well. They are *picture completion,* a subtle (some might say sneaky) test where the object is to find the missing detail, an exercise that requires the ability to separate essential from nonessential information and to retrieve the right labels; *coding,* a pencil and paper task that measures processing speed and that, with its added motor component, raises the dyslexia red flag like no other; *picture arrangement,* which asks that images be arranged in a logical order to tell a story; *block design,* another indicator of potential reading weakness, in which one must be able to break down a three-dimensional, whole abstract shape and put it back together again; *object assembly,* which requires the putting together of puzzle pieces to create known objects without any sort of visual model; *symbol search,* a supplementary pencil and paper test that also measures processing speed, memory, and attention to detail; and *mazes,* which tests organizational and planning ability, as well as attentional capacity and impulsivity.

Put them all together, and you have IQ scores.

Margaretha Arienti is a school psychologist in Stockbridge, Massachusetts, who gives the Wechsler all the time. She has great respect for it as a measure; she feels she can glean compelling information with it. Little is learned from the Full-Scale Score of the WISC, though; evaluators find their information in the subtests, in comparisons among them, and also from looking at what is called "scatter," high scores in one area and low in another. Arienti insists that even looking carefully at all the subtests is only part of the puzzle, that educational testing is equally vital to the whole picture. She also insists that when scoring the WISC, the tester must take a great number of other bits of information into consideration besides the numbers, such as behavior and anxiety, and that experience enables one to bring a great deal more to the basic instrument. "You can't just get stuck judging each test by the rule book," she says. "You must look at it in combination with other factors." Instead of merely following the directions in the manual, an experienced psychologist looks at clues with a keener eye, more like Sherlock Holmes than Inspector Clouseau. Arienti does indeed compare her work to that of a detective and says that full testing isn't even enough. She has parents fill out a questionnaire designed by noted pediatric neurologist Mel Levine; she also asks questions and listens very carefully the whole while she is working with someone, trying to find out what he says and how he says it, and she takes copious notes. When she scores the WISC, she always does the basic scoring first; then she does another kind of scoring, a factor analysis, which clumps scores and indicates patterns; and then she adds a third, a personality assessment, which uses the first numbers she obtained, to determine style of learning, problem-solving approach, and social awareness. With all of these, she pulls much more information out of the test than someone would who simply scored it, and she spends hours doing it.

"It's important to look at what the person does with what he or she has," says Arienti. "I always look for that. And if the test results don't give me a clear picture of the person, I must look for more clues," she says. "Sometimes I call the teacher or the parent; other times I go over all the tests again and again. After the second or third time, something might pop out." One time Arienti evaluated a teenaged boy who mumbled almost unintelligibly. She had to ask him to repeat virtually every word he said in order to understand him. She thought he might have some lingering speech and language problems that needed to be addressed. Each time he repeated himself, however, he spoke clearly and correctly. She was puzzled, so she contacted his teachers; they were aware of and concerned about the mumbling. Then she called his mother; she was completely unaware of it. This boy was a middle child; his other sibs were superstars, highly verbal, and he was not. He was overpowered most of the time, and he felt so inferior, was so convinced that what he had to say was worthless, that he tried to hide it by mumbling. He was afraid to speak up, and he was entirely used to not being heard. One of Arienti's important recommendations was that he must be heard; his teachers must make sure that they listened to him and let him know how valuable his contributions were. Says Arienti, "To get a real picture, I have to look at every single factor. I have to construct a hypothesis and try to prove it. If I can't prove it, I have to keep digging. Everything has to make sense, and I spend as much time as it takes for it to make sense."

Intelligence quotient testing is absolutely necessary to determine, under current guidelines, whether there is or is not a learning disability, but do these so-called "intelligence tests" really measure intelligence? That is a subject that inspires much debate. There are those who would argue that they do, because they measure the intelligences required to do well in school—language and logic. Some say they do not, that they are culturally biased no matter how the authors try to arrange the subtests to eliminate such bias, or at least that they don't measure the various kinds of intelligences that are necessary and valued in our society if not our schools. Some would even go so far as to say that they are archaic and not worth the paper they're printed on.

Psychologist, Harvard and Boston University Medical School professor, MacArthur "genius grant" receiver, and all-around intellectual upsetter of the status quo Howard Gardner maintains that there are seven, not two, intelligences that are valued in our society, several of which are more accommodating of dyslexia than the two that are valued in schools. Gardner's seven, which include the two that are measured by the WISC, language (which he calls linguistic) and logical mathematical, also include musical intelligence, which is self-evident; spatial intelligence, which young Tom West describes he has when he says he can create a mental picture of the back of something just by seeing the front; bodily kinesthetic, which dancers and athletes have to a high degree; interpersonal—the ability to understand other people—which is so important for politicians, salesmen, and teachers; and intrapersonal—self-understanding—which is important to us all.

None of these last five kinds of intelligence is measured by any standardized tests in existence, but all have individual worth outside of school. Gardner explains that his theory is not just plucked out of the air, but biologically based—he is talking about how brains have evolved and what they are organized to do. He also asserts that minds are "organized in terms of content," and that each content has its own laws of learning—that the laws for learning language will not be the same as the laws for learning about other people or the laws that govern learning about bodily space. Gardner's plan for getting the educational establishment to recognize and capitalize on this theory and the teaching and testing principles that accompany it is no less lofty than the complete reform of education in America. He says that now, "in traditional schools, educators put language on a pedestal," and he is right. His idea of a better way would be to have assessment specialists in schools who are charged with somehow figuring out the assorted kinds of intelligence each child has, and to have curriculum brokers who help students find the right kind of subject matter and the teaching methods that would enable them to master the material. He then would have school-community brokers who find vocational and avocational opportunities in the larger world outside of school and who direct students to them. Here Gardner is particularly addressing the students who do not excel in language or logic, and his goal is to make sure that they are encouraged to make use of their other intelligences. "These students," says Gardner, "will be well served by an educational system which brings to their attention those opportunities in the wider community which make particular use of their combinations of intelligence." Books could be written about Howard Gardner—thirteen have in fact been written by him—so it is impossible to do any real justice to him here. He is mentioned only to illustrate the notion that not everybody believes the current form of IQ testing is valuable or accurate. What we are focusing on, however, is the series of tests needed to diagnose dyslexia, and at the moment, an IQ test is among them.

Also among them is a battery of educational tests to get an in-depth feeling for particular skills the person has or hasn't developed and learned in school, and for how he is able to use them. These tests take three to four hours or more, spread over one, two, or sometimes three sessions, depending on the age, stamina, and attentional capabilities of the test taker. Susan J. Schwartz, of the Institute of Learning and Academic Achievement of the New York University Child Study Center, taught me diagnosis at Teachers College, and I remain as impressed with her now as I was when I first met her (even though she continues to be a dozen years my junior). She knows her stuff, and her manner with children—I have observed her testing several different children, but never an adult—is calm, warm, and reassuring, but never condescending or saccharine. Her voice is clear, her diction impeccable. She understands kids with learning problems completely, and it shows. She also likes children, and that shows, too. She loves to play with words, and she makes kids laugh. Her sense of caring combines with her sense of humor so smoothly that she can wring at least a smile from even the most anxious child. All of that really helps, because being tested is exceedingly stressful for both children and adults. They don't know what to expect; they feel that they are being judged; and they are, in fact, on the spot, performing and performing. Some of the tests are fun, but others take them to their limits to see what their limits are, so the tasks get harder and harder until they can't do them anymore. Also, all the tests relate to schoolwork in some way and of necessity tap the child's greatest weakness. That is not fun, and it's not great for the old ego, either. So the manner of the person doing the testing makes a huge difference.

A little personal aside here. When I was four years old, my mother took me to be interviewed for a spot in the nursery school, then called junior kindergarten, of the Rye Country Day School, a private school in our town. The then-head of the school conducted the interview, and he was so mean and scary that I would not talk to him. After unsuccessfully trying to intimidate me into responding to his horrible questions, he said, in his coldest, most officious manner, to my extra-shy mother, "I don't even know if this child *can* talk." He humiliated her completely and insisted that she bring me back to be tested to see whether in fact I could talk and think and do all those things necessary to get along in junior kindergarten. In fact, then as now, I talked constantly, and I had already started reading. When I went back, a nice, unthreatening lady gave me the required tests. She, of course, put me right at ease and made me want to please her, so I did well enough on the tests that they had to put me in *senior* kindergarten, not junior. As you can see, I know firsthand the importance of being kind to those under testing pressure.

Something that Susan Schwartz likes to do while she is testing a child is talk about what she is doing and what it might mean; it's as though she is entering into a partnership with the person. Schwartz also likes to take her time when she is testing a child; she refuses to be rushed. "I like to go slowly and think about what's going on as it's going on," she says, "so I tell the kids, 'I'm really thinking about you as we're working.' They like that. Then, as we get into the testing, I give them feedback regularly, and I let them see my thinking. I say things like 'I see you can recognize whole words.' Or, 'You like to look at words in pieces, don't you?' Sometimes I go so far as to say, 'I will help you, or I will tell your parents what you need, and they will help you.' " After a pause, Schwartz adds, "You know, we don't really understand how dark children's lives can be and how it makes no sense to them that they can't read." Then, a moment or two later, "And the smarter the child is, the less sense it makes." In her private testing practice, Schwartz often greets parents who need a second look at their sons or daughters, who need more information to understand and help them. "Lots of people who do this testing lack the ability to do a real, qualitative assessment," she comments. "Often they're just looking for the numbers, and when you look for the numbers, you lose the child underneath."

Finding the child—or the adult—underneath is really what testing is all about. And to find whether there is a dyslexic underneath, the clinician must look at certain aspects of the person's learning ability and achievement. Tests offer unemotional, "clean" information; opinion or the child's charm or lack of it cannot influence their results. Tests tell only part of the story, however; humans tell the other part. Parents, teachers, tutors, therapists, and baby-sitters can all provide information about the behaviors that have led to the desire to be tested. Most important, of course, is talking to the person directly; so much can be learned in so many ways by doing so.

One of the great aspects of young people is their honesty; I have always believed that if you want to find out about a child, just ask. At Marymount I evaluated a thirteen-year-old eighth-grade boy who had been brought in by his frantic parents. He was among the handsomest kids I have ever seen, but short and very self-conscious about it. He was also the middle child, and smart. His grade point average, however, was in the cellar, and he had just punched out the guidance counselor at his school. No wonder his parents were frantic. They did not know what to do with him or why he was such a mess. He tested in the above-average range of intelligence, and he read well and wrote well and could do the math. He showed no signs of dyslexia or other learning disabilities. Basically he scored very well on all the tests he was taking for me, and he also seemed to be enjoying it—alone in a room with my undivided attention. As I talked with him, I asked him if he planned to go to college. "Oh, yes," he said. His father had told him that college was imperative. "Well," said I, "it may be imperative, but you're not even going to get into a good prep school, much less college, if you don't do something about these grades." He looked crestfallen; he hadn't thought much about the future in relation to his school perfor-mance—or indeed in relation to much else except getting taller. "Why," I asked, "since you are able to do so well here, do you do so poorly in school? What's going on?" He waited a bit, then looked me straight in the eye and said, "Well, you see, if I bring home a report card with a good grade on it, they [his parents] just say, 'Oh, that's nice.' But if I bring home a report card with a terrible grade on it, I get lots and lots of attention." Remember, I said he was a middle child; he had been somewhat lost in the shuffle. Negative attention was all he knew how to get, and he was going to get attention one way or another. When I recounted this conversation to his mother, she practically fell off her chair. She had had no idea. She immediately set about creating a plan of behavior modification that rewarded his good school performance instead of his bad, his exemplary behavior instead of his sensational, and her son began to change his ways.

To find the child (or adult) underneath the numbers, to find if there is dyslexia lurking, requires probing assorted educational tasks and abilities that are associated with reading, writing, spelling, and math to see what the person knows and how she learned it. It also requires analysis of abilities at the single-word level, which really separates the dyslexics from the non-, and of phonemic awareness, the underlying ability to manipulate sounds and parts of words. Basically the questions that the evaluator is looking to answer are:

What does he do with words? Does she sound them out, or read them only if she can recognize the whole word? Does he just guess at them or skip over them? Does she understand the rules of the language, and if she does, how much does she understand? Can he sequence sounds and blend them together? Can he read any lists of words? Can he take words apart and put them back together again? Can she name chunks of words and not need to say the whole word? Can she retrieve words, come up with labels for things? If you show him pictures, can he accurately name what is in them? If you ask him to name as many animals beginning with the letter K as he can, how many can he name, and what does he have to go through to name any at all? Can she name things fast? If not, how much time does she need? Can he repeat sentences back to the examiner, and if he can, how complicated can the sentences get before they become impossible? Can she discriminate among similar-sounding words; can she essentially "hear" the difference? How well does she read? How much does she understand of what she reads? What strategies does he use? How does he express himself, verbally and in writing? Can she tell a story with a proper beginning, middle, and end? Can he find the main idea of a passage? Can she add detail? Does she get lost in the detail? Can the child put together pieces of information and draw a logical conclusion or make an inference?

Finding the answers to these and other queries enables the evaluator to paint a portrait of the learning style of the person and to make general and specific recommendations about how to remediate any difficulties. To paint this portrait, each examiner chooses among many instruments of evaluation. A mixture of formal, standardized testing and informal investigation seems to create the best picture, one worthy of the word portrait. Susan Schwartz likes to start off with a standardized measure of academic achievement. Often she uses the Kaufman Test of Educational Achievement, because the many assorted parts of this one umbrella test give her a look at the test-taker's decoding abilities, reading comprehension, spelling, math computation, and math problem solving. With older students, she gets an idea of where their appropriate levels are with the Kaufman and then switches to other reading tests like the Nelson Denny or the Gates-MacGinitie, both of which are silent measures of vocabulary and reading comprehension, for a more in-depth examination. After the person has completed one of the reading tests, Schwartz interviews him to find out how he's thinking, why he chose the answers he did choose. She also likes to ask students in grades five and up to read a short passage and give her an oral summary of what they have just read; that gives her a chance to see what they can do with what they read, whether they can pick out the key parts, and how efficiently they can read and remember. She uses a source such as Jane Erwin's *Reading Comprehension in Varied Subject Matter* to supply the passages. Sometimes she gives more than one measure of the same skill to have a second look at how the person functions and to make some comparative observations. "With ninth-graders and up," she says, "and especially with college-aged students, I do the Woodcock-Johnson Battery, because that's what colleges and LD committees want to see to determine eligibility for services." If she is evaluating a student for whom she is thinking about recommending books on tape, she might read aloud to that student while he follows along in the book to validate that indeed mechanics—his poor ability to decode words—are getting in the way of his comprehension, and that hearing the words read smoothly improves his performance.

After she has gathered information about the student's academic accomplishments and strategies, Schwartz does some more process-oriented testing. In order to understand how someone hears sound sequences, how the person blends and manipulates sounds and discriminates among them—basically how phonemically aware that person is—she does the Lindamood Test of Auditory Conceptualization. This is a terrific measure because there is no room for slide; the person either passes or doesn't, which gives clear, firm information. Next she might give the Rapid Automatic Naming Test to get a look at how fast the person processes language and the Boston Naming Test to see how well he can find and retrieve words. Says Schwartz, "I believe the true roots of dyslexia can be found in the person's ability to blend, process, and retrieve words."

A measure of sentence memory—perhaps from the Clinical Evaluation of Language Function or the Detroit Tests of Learning Aptitude—follows. Schwartz then examines and compares the person's receptive vocabulary—possibly using the Peabody Picture Vocabulary Test—and expressive vocabulary, with the One-Word Expressive Vocabulary Test. "Looking at someone's memory for sentences tells about that person's short-term-memory or storage problems," says Schwartz. "Also, is the person getting details to the exclusion of the whole, or is she getting the big picture and no details? I listen to each one, and I take abundant notes." She also looks at visual memory to see if there is a difference between that and auditory capabilities, usually with an instrument called the Wide Range Assessment of Memory and Learning, depending on the age of the child.

Schwartz gets a handwriting sample from young students and gives most everybody the Test of Written Spelling to see how well they can spell both phonetically regular and irregular words. She doesn't do drawing tests like the Beery or the Bender, which many educational evaluators do to see how someone is able to organize spatially, because she feels that they are more valuable to the psychologist who is giving the WISC, but she does have young children do a few subtests of the

Slingerland Tests of Specific Language Disability to see what their visual perception, discrimination, and memory are like. The Near Point Copying subtest of the Slingerland gives her a look at the child's spatial organization as well as his handwriting and copying strengths. She administers the Reversals Frequency Test to assess the individual's visual discrimination and memory for letters and numbers that are often reversed or confused.

To appraise older students' motor patterns and fine-motor control, she usually asks them to read a passage and write one fully formed paragraph about it, while she observes carefully. With this one act, she can get a look at their thinking and their ability to find the main idea and important details and to express what they want to say, as well as their penmanship, grammar, spelling, punctuation, and capitalization skills. If she wants a more formal measure, one that is normed, she uses the Written Expression Cluster of the Woodcock-Johnson Psychoeducational Battery-Revised, which has two parts, one of which measures writing speed and automaticity, and the other descriptive writing.

Schwartz adds some trial teaching to her testing repertoire as well, giving a small lesson in a selected area, say, reading decoding or comprehension, using the kind of instruction LD students need, and noting how they respond. This gives her excellent insight into a student's ability to learn when being taught in an appropriate manner. Also, if there is to be another session, she has a chance then to see how well the student was able to retain what was learned over the intervening time, also valuable information.

Few choices of test are written in stone; the tester must be flexible, must pay attention to how the person is responding at all times, and must be willing and able to switch gears if necessary. Nothing ever brought that fact home to me more than an experience I had at the clinic at Marymount. I was testing a woman in her thirties. I don't remember her name; I remember vividly what she was like, however. Attractive, chic, and well spoken, she had an aura of sophistication that all but hid her tentativeness and fear. She was widely read and widely traveled. As a child, she had had some difficulty learning to read, but she came under the tutelage of caring, well-meaning nuns at her Catholic school, one of whom turned her on to literature for life. Her smarts and zeal helped her overcome her difficulties, and she became a good, if slow, reader who loved books. She was of superior intelligence; she had graduated from a good college, married very young, and then decided to concentrate on her artistic talents. She designed jewelry, and did so well enough that for a dozen years she had a shop in Greenwich Village where she sold only her own work. Life was sweet. Then her husband left her for another woman. She was devastated, and her sweet life was shattered. She stopped designing jewelry, closed her shop, and began therapy to try to figure out what to do from there. She wanted nothing from her ex, so she took a job as a secretary. She thought it would be easy, emotion free, structured, and healing. It turned out to be just the opposite. All the weaknesses she had been compensating for came rushing to the surface just at the time in her life when she felt weakest. She couldn't spell; she couldn't think fast; she couldn't compose appropriate letters; she couldn't even take telephone messages and be sure of writing down the correct name, company, and number. She was fired, and she was convinced she was a complete failure when I met her.

Feeling like a failure and actually being a failure are, of course, two utterly different things. On all the tests for adults, this woman did very well. She had mastered enough skills and had read enough books to score high on the vocabulary and reading comprehension tests. She was able to summarize well, to pick out those main ideas and relevant details, and, without time pressure, to write an interesting, well-sequenced paragraph. It was very perplexing. The only clue to her difficulties was her erratic spelling, and that just wasn't enough. So, on a hunch, I decided to give her two measures designed for young children. One was the Roswell-Chall Auditory Blending Test, and the other the Rosner Test of Auditory Analysis Skills. She was asked to put sounds together, to take them apart, to leave out middle sounds and determine what was left, and to add sounds and figure out the changes they made. There was no context; intelligence was of no value; none of her coping strategies would help here. She was completely stymied. She couldn't do any of it. We were both astonished. There was the basic root of her dyslexia. I made suggestions as to what she might do—one was never to consider secretarial work again for any reason—and gave her some materials to try working with on her own. As said before, most testing looks for strengths to build on first and weaknesses to remedy next. Understanding just how smart and able she was really helped this woman shed her feelings of inferiority. Discovering where her weaknesses lay also gave her strength and helped define for her more clearly how she should pursue her next career, what she should emphasize and what she should avoid.

Though flexibility is a *must* in testing, as in life, every examiner has a couple of favorite yardsticks that are permanent parts of her testing repertoire. Susan Schwartz always gives the vocabulary part of the Gates-MacGinitie, and often includes the comprehension section as well. So do I; the Gates is an amazing test. It wasn't even designed for diagnostic use, and still it's exceptionally valuable. It is meant for classrooms—to establish the levels, abilities, and instructional needs of groups of children—and it's used in classrooms. Many thousands of American schoolchildren take one level and form of the Gates-MacGinitie Reading Tests or another every single year. It's often the first "bubble test" (where the test-taker fills in the circles or "bubbles" to choose an answer) that anyone takes, whether in public or private school. One of the reasons the Gates-MacGinitie is used so widely is the meticulous, thorough work that went into designing it and that has gone into revising each of its soon-to-be-four editions.

It all began at Teachers College, where Arthur I. Gates was a distinguished professor, pioneer, testing authority, coauthor of reading materials, and author of the first two widely used reading tests (in the 1920s). He was also, according to Walter H. MacGinitie, "a gentleman and a scholar." MacGinitie was Gates's doctoral student; he stayed on at Teachers College after he got his degree and became an assistant professor. Gates was just ready to revise his earlier tests, and he asked MacGinitie to work with him. Revising a test is as complicated as designing it in the first place, because you have to start from scratch each time, and designing a reading test is no mean feat. Designing or revising a really good reading test is an amazing achievement that takes four to five years from start to finish. The Gates-MacGinitie is a really good reading test. In fact, it is a series of tests.

The scale is enormous. The first three editions of the G-M were designed for children from the earliest grades, where the tests examine reading readiness skills, through twelfth grade. The fourth edition, which will be available in September 1999, will have two new levels: one at the very top for adult education purposes, designed with materials appropriate for adults and with adult norms, and one each for Levels (grades) 5 and 6, instead of one for both. From Levels 3 and up, the fourth-edition tests will be the same in concept as the third-, but will have all newly written material. The dramatic changes will be at the lowest levels, for two reasons: one, to more accurately reflect the current trends of reading research, and, two, in response to comments and requests the MacGinities and their publisher have received from teachers who use the tests.

The tests for the children who are not necessarily reading yet, who are in kindergarten and the first part of first grade, will add to the letter/sound and sentence-context components that have always been there, subtests to tap the children's sensitivity to rhyme and to measure their ability to understand what they hear. Another addition will assess their familiarity with beginning orthographic concepts, posing questions such as "If you were going to write the word *people,* what letter would go first?" One more will look at their awareness of the conventions of the language, such as the fact that names begin with capital letters, and yet another, called Basic Story Words, will see how many common words—such as *is, a,* and *he*—the children have learned without being able to read.

Level 2 used to consist of the same two parts as all those of later grades—vocabulary and comprehension—but the MacGinities and their publisher received comments from teachers saying that they felt the vocabulary section tapped students' ability to decode even more than it did their actual word knowledge. So Level 2 in the fourth edition will have one section to test word knowledge, one to measure decoding, and a third to assess comprehension.

Levels 3 and up will be divided into the same two sections for the fourth edition that they always have been: vocabulary and comprehension. Material chosen for either section, or written exclusively for the tests, must pass a huge variety of rigorous examinations before it can even be tried out as a possibility. Up to Level 3, everything is written for the tests; starting at Level 3, the passages used in the comprehension section are taken from already-published materials. They used to be written for the tests, but no longer. Finding and selecting appropriate passages that contain the elements needed is more difficult than actually writing them, but Dr. MacGinitie and his wife, Ruth, his coauthor on the third edition, found that mastering the complications of fitting already-published writings to the demands of the tests was worth the effort, because they ended up with passages that were more vital and interesting than those written only for the tests. "What's difficult," says Dr. MacGinitie, "is that you must find material that will test what you want to test. Most tests don't use much previously published material just because of that."

Students have to read extremely varied material throughout their elementary and high school years, so writing on a wide selection of subjects has to be represented on each level of the test to accurately represent their range of reading. Before selecting any material, Dr. MacGinitie makes up what he likes to call a "blueprint" of what the test will be like; this blueprint comprises works of fiction and writings about the social and natural sciences and the arts, and includes both narrative and expository prose, as well as poetry. Making sure the passages to be read are at the correct level to accommodate a range of students is, as you can well imagine, enormously complicated. Several "readability formulas" are used to determine that the content, style, and vocabulary actually are on the correct level. In selecting materials, the MacGinities have tried to keep abreast of new trends and interests of the students being tested, so that the students will be involved in what they are reading and more apt to pay the close attention that is necessary. Creating the questions that follow each passage is very tricky: each has to tap what is really important; when combined they have to have examined a number of skills; and they have to be both literal and inferential. Also, they must adequately evaluate the whole range of students, from strongest to weakest, so the questions in the beginning of each test must be easy enough for most everyone to answer correctly, then build slowly in difficulty until the last questions present a full challenge for even the most accomplished students.

Selecting the *wrong* answers for the multiple choice questions that follow each passage is an art (and almost a career) unto itself, for it is in the choice of answer, whether right or wrong, that pertinent information about the student's understanding of what has been read surfaces. Incorrect answers are often even more informative than correct—especially when using the test for diagnostic purposes. The MacGinities include three types of wrong answers: *prior-knowledge,* an answer that may sound as though it is correct, but one that is selected because of something the test-taker learned before, and is not based on what is actually in the passage; *text-phrase,* an answer that includes words from the passage and that makes sense in relation to the question, but shows that the person has not thought through the question properly and has just grabbed words from the text for his answer; and *construction,* an answer that is based on some interesting detail taken from the text and given a meaning and importance that is not related to the text.

Cultural diversity and political correctness must also be addressed when designing these reading tests. Selections are made so that males and females of various ethnic groups are represented in the passages, both as authors and in the artwork that accompanies the text. In addition, a panel of Asians, blacks, Hispanics, and Native Americans reviews all the text to make sure that nothing is biased or offensive. Asked whether these concerns have multiplied as our society has become more and more obsessed with political correctness, Dr. MacGinitie replies, "Oh my, yes. There are so many different concerns today. But we want to make sure that, say, a sixth-grader who has been taught at home that evolution is abominable doesn't have to deal with a passage about it on the test. We don't want any of the material *of* the test taking away any student's concentration *on* the test, so we don't want any kinds of passages that would engender a class discussion."

Preparing the vocabulary sections of the Gates-MacGinitie tests is a daunting prospect all by itself. The words selected have to be properly representative of the words students at each level have encountered, and, of course, the range of students at each level is extensive. They also have to be useful words, not obscure ones, and they must accurately reflect real usage. There are analyses of how often we use nouns, verbs, and other parts of speech that the MacGinities employ to make sure their usage on the tests corresponds correctly. Words have to be mostly or completely new for each new edition as well, and the MacGinities have devised several rules governing choices of test words and right- and wrong-answer words throughout the tests, to avoid over-recycling. From Levels 3 and up, the words are presented with brief identifying phrases. The authors are extremely careful to give enough but not too much information in this phrase, or the query will turn into a comprehension question and veer from its specific task of testing word knowledge. What they decided to do was have the phrase suggest only the part of speech of the word being tested, so they make sure that each of the four answer choices is the same part of speech as the test word and that they all fit the context semantically and grammatically. Just as with the comprehension questions, the difficulty of vocabulary questions builds from easy to hard gradually throughout the test.

Discovering how and why students choose right and wrong vocabulary answers gives teachers and testers excellent information about what kind of word-attack and word-knowledge skills the students have. But it is impossible to understand their reasoning just scoring the tests. So it is very important to discuss their answers with the students, to find out how they chose what they chose and whether they can correct their wrong choices by using assorted strategies. On the G-M, wrong vocabulary answers fall into three different types:

Visually similar words: These are words that begin or end with the same couple of letters, such as *timid* as a wrong answer for *solid,* or *carton* for *carpet.* Sometimes correct answers are also chosen to look like the test words, too. Students with poorly developed decoding skills will choose wrong on these questions frequently; if they can't really sound out the word they're trying to identify, they often just pick a word that looks something like it. Incorrect visually similar answers are often selected by the MacGinities to be less familiar to the student than the test word is. That way it is clearer that the choice is made on the look of the word; if the student knows the meaning of the incorrect answer, that can push him away from it, and that important bit of diagnostic information is lost.

Miscue errors: Students who read only portions of words, or who read words incorrectly but don't stop and try to correct themselves, make miscue errors. An example of this kind of wrong choice is the student who sees the *ear* in *earth* but doesn't read the whole word and then selects *sound* as the word most related to *earth.*

Association wrong answers: These trip up students who have some sort of half-knowledge of the word, can read it and have some idea of what it is about, but don't really know it. So association choices have a relationship to the word being tested, but not necessarily the correct relationship. The student might select *grab* as the best answer for the test word *want,* for instance. For both miscue and association wrong answers to get at the information sought, the answer choices have to be as familiar to the test-taker as the word being tested is.

All the vocabulary questions are also reviewed by a multiethnic panel looking for possible bias or offensiveness; in addition, after the field tests, responses of groups of students to both parts of the test are analyzed separately, and if it is thought that certain words or passages are more difficult for any cultural reason, they are dropped.

The Gates-MacGinitie Reading Tests are extensively field-tested. Twenty-seven thousand students were tested for the third edition; they are targeting almost 35,000 for the fourth. Twice the number of vocabulary and comprehension questions that end up in the final tests are prepared and field-tested, so that there is plenty of room for elimination of items thought to be not as good as others. Every state in the United States is represented in the field-testing, large and small school districts are represented, and public and nonpublic schools are represented. The MacGinities, as you can see, are serious about having these tests be as thorough and valid as possible. The field tests are untimed, and the teachers conducting the tests are told to keep going until almost all the students finish. The actual Gates-MacGinitie Reading Tests are timed, but the timing is meant to be generous enough to allow most of the students to complete them. This is a point that the MacGinities are emphatic about: their tests are not what are called power tests; they are not interested in how fast students can read, but how thoroughly and accurately. These are tests of understanding, of competence.

Results of the field tests are analyzed and reanalyzed, charted and recharted, graphed and regraphed. The field tests for the third edition were conducted in both the fall and the spring, as were those for the fourth, and the ability differences of students at different times of year were taken into account in analyzing results. Finally, after months of close, intricate work, items were selected, two forms of tests at each level were made up, and the work of standardization began. That means that to establish norms, the tests were administered to a total of 77,413 students for the third edition. The target number for the fourth is 84,000. These students are spread across all fifty states; they are randomly selected within a mixture of regions, district enrollments, and community socioeconomic status to give a full range. The students take the tests in the fall and again in the spring. Another 25,210 students were tested in the fall for the third edition (37,000 is the target number for the fourth) in what are called Equating Studies, in order to have data to compare levels and forms, as well as editions. All sorts of varied statistical analysis follows, more charts and graphs are generated, and then nationwide norms are established, so that givers of the test can determine where their students fall in comparison with thousands of other students across America.

So, when I give the test to any student or group of students at any of the levels, I can find out where each test-taker falls in relation to the rest of those who take the test and also to other students across the country. I can get norms for the fall and the spring, I can get percentile ranks and stanines, and I can also get grade equivalent scores for students who are taking levels of the test that are not the same as their level in school. Most of the time, that will be because the student has difficulties and reads below his grade level, but there are schools that have such high-achieving students that they have to give levels above the grade to get an accurate view of how the students in a particular class are doing.

The fourth edition of the Gates-MacGinitie will have two new coauthors in addition to the MacGinities: Katherine Maria and Lois Dreyer. Dreyer was a teacher of mine at Teachers College; she is now an associate professor at Southern Connecticut State University and the director of the reading center there. Katherine Maria is a comprehension expert who is a full professor at the College of New Rochelle. The two were selected by the MacGinities after a thorough search that winnowed down the long list of interested reading professionals until six were invited to critique the third edition and to participate in an all-day seminar devoted to discussing issues of reading and reading assessment. Comments Kay Hughes, the MacGinities' editor at Riverside Press, "The primary reason for the success of the Gates-MacGinitie is that the tests have always been so well done. We looked hard for people who would have voices of their own, but who we were sure would maintain the high standards the MacGinities have always kept." The grueling selection process might have been a tipoff as to what would be involved in test authorship, but I would doubt anyone could imagine the amount of work involved until actually doing it. "Just" creating the drawings for the tests keeps an artist busy for a full year. Dreyer and Maria will have worked for five years before they're done; they will have written approximately fifteen hundred test items, and that's only part of their job.

Of course, there are people who feel that all standardized tests are the work of the devil, that we should not quantify children, that we should not rank-order them, that we should not put them under the pressure of such testing. I'm afraid I can't agree, although I sometimes rue the fact that children do have to take so many tests. I'd sooner get rid of the weekly quizzes, monthly tests, and twice-yearly exams that proliferate during the school year, though, and have teachers use other measures for assessing how their students are doing. But determining who needs what kind of instruction or any extra help requires the kind of information these tests give. Also, at schools it is important to have both personal observation of the child and these utterly unbiased measures, to support or contradict what the teachers are experiencing. The first indications of difficulties are often obvious only when the child has to deal with the demands of school, so it is more often than not the school's job to make the parents aware of concerns. Most parents' first reaction to the thought that there is something not going just right with their offspring is fear and denial, mixed with a dollop of guilt, so the results of a cool measure can assist school officials in their efforts to help parents come to terms with what is going on and what needs to be done.

Following is a list of questions that should be asked of any clinician who is going to test you or your mother or your cousin or your child. Rule number one is: Do not be afraid to ask questions, any questions that are on your mind, and do not let the examiner or the situation intimidate you into silence. Think about it. Any professional who is unwilling to take the time to talk with you and provide answers for you may also be unwilling to take the necessary time with your child or with both of you when it's time to discuss the results of all the testing.

You must, of course, ask about cost, about whether the examiner offers a sliding scale of fees, and about insurance—sometimes an evaluation is covered and sometimes it is not. You might also want to know how much experience the evaluator has, and if it is "not much," how much supervision there will be and by whom it will be provided. Then, assuming you are confident about the credentials of the person or people involved,

1. Ask whether the examiner plans to provide a written report. Even the best evaluation, without a written report, is useless, because you have nothing to refer to, to give to teachers and/or tutors, or to keep for future reference.

2. Ask how long it will take to get an appointment, and then ask how long the testing will take. You need to know how much of a time commitment you and/or your child will have to make. Also, if you have a child who can sustain attention and energy for only an hour or two, you don't want to set up three- or four-hour sessions.

3. Ask how long it will take from the end of the testing to the conference you will have with the examiner. Also, make sure that at that conference, you will be given the written report to take away with you.

4. Ask about the extent of recommendations. You do not want to go to someone who will simply say that tutoring is recommended. You want names and telephone numbers of possible tutors, and you want specific recommendations for the tutor and classroom teacher to follow.

5. If you or anyone involved is interested in receiving the psychological tests, make sure that the person who is giving the WISC can and does give what are called "projectives," those measures that look at the person's emotional and psychological functioning. Not every psychologist does, and parents of a child I work with spent two thousand dollars on an evaluation and then had to find someone else to give the psychological tests.

CHAPTER SIX

Education and Dyslexia

The Role of the School

FOR A FEW years I concentrated my working hours on seeing students in my private practice and teaching reading remediation at Teachers College. I spent three days every week in New York City, seeing mostly young children, and four days in northwestern Connecticut, seeing mostly teenagers. This was also an education for me, because I spent time in both places at many different schools, some private, some public. In New York, I started my workday at 7:00 A.M., with a student at my home office; after a cup of tea, I was off, traveling from one location to another, seeing students in their schools, and arriving home in time to greet a couple more after school, finishing around 6:00 P.M.

At one private boys' academy, where I saw three students in a row, I regularly had a brief wait between the first and second of the three. This gave me a chance to watch the boys in situations I would not have otherwise seen, and it also gave me an opportunity to talk with their teachers, to better understand how their classwork was going. Sitting for a while with the two second-grade teachers while they supervised the boys at lunch was always enlightening. One of the teachers was very experienced, and so skilled she had her fairly rambunctious group devouring their food and eating out of her hand at the same time. One day, when there was a bit more noise than she thought was reasonable, she stood up, clasped her hands together as though in prayer, gave them her beatific smile, and in her best Australian-laced accent, sought their attention. "Gen-tle-men, gen-tle-men," she called out. "Could I have all eyes 'ere, please." Pause. Big smile. "Ow, thank you; that's just lovely." Pause to appreciate. "My, my, what a 'andsome lot you are, just look at all of you." Pause to admire. "What a fine group of lads!" Pause. "Now, gentlemen, do you remember the other day when we had five minutes of silence at lunch?" Eager nodding of heads. "Do you remember how much you enjoyed it?" Looks of anticipation spreading around the room. "Why don't we just try that again?" And the next thing you knew, the boys were dining in silence and feeling as though they had just been given a much-wished-for gift. "By the end of the year, they're wise to me," she said at the time, "and I can't get away with it as easily, but in the fall and early winter, they're still susceptible." She was an accomplished teacher, too, as well as an ace manipulator. She managed to encourage even the most reluctant scholar, and every child in her class felt as though she liked him the very best of all.

The woman in charge of the other second grade had a very different style, quiet, low-key, but was equally good, even better for the dyslexic students, because she had a greater understanding of their needs and a greater commitment to the methods that meet those needs. The boys I saw were in her class. They each received in-class language arts instruction, and they also had several-times-a-week work with the reading specialist; I was their tutor, and I saw them for one period each, twice a week, during school hours. I came into their room and "pulled them out," as the saying goes. There is a widely backed theory that says such "pulling out" is not good for children, that it makes them and their weaknesses stand out, that it lowers their self-esteem. I say that many children need to have some individual instruction in a quiet place where they can concentrate, that all the children are aware all the time of everyone's strengths and weaknesses, and that how the children respond to "pulling out" depends entirely on how the adults handle it. In this case, the teacher was totally at ease with the concept, and the boys I worked with were always eager to go. They enjoyed the attention. They could see they were getting stronger, and they were also having some fun in the bargain. Far from thinking less of those who were being tutored, the rest of the boys were jealous; several regularly begged to go out themselves, and one even temporarily imagined some reading difficulties to try to get his forty-five minutes of undivided attention. The children I saw during school hours did not have the endurance to add an additional academic commitment to their schedules after a full day at the lyceum, so they would have profited little from before- or after-school instruction. The folks who ran their school were wise enough to understand that and to make appropriate arrangements. Not many schools can or want to work out scheduling this way. You can't blame them, either; it's very complicated, and in a place like New York, space is always at such a premium that there often isn't room for a nonfaculty member. As a matter of fact, the head of this lower school vacated her office when I arrived to make a place for the boys and me to work.

I saw a somewhat older boy from the same school in the afternoons. He was a young man whose reading and writing problems were combined with very little impulse control and great difficulty sitting still, but he was basically a good kid. Still, it took a wise classroom teacher to appreciate him; he was labor-intensive, and there were always a number of other children needing attention, too. This boy was lucky to have the same person two years in a row, which is not always a blessing. In this case, however, the instructor was a man who had been honing his craft for thirty years, and who seemed as fresh and interested in his work as though he had just begun. He appreciated each of his charges, and he had many interests he shared with them. In addition to their regular subjects, he taught them about his travels, discussed music, theater, and dance with them, showed them the autograph collection he had gathered as a child, and one day proudly exhibited the antique he had just bought his sister for her birthday. He taught them social studies and English, and he had them read wonderful books. Most important, though, by example he taught them curiosity, respect, and kindness, because he was curious, he respected them, was kind to them, and he inspired reciprocation. Said the mother of my student, "He teaches them what they need academically, but he also gives them life lessons." Said her son, "He's soooo interesting, and, you know, even when he gets mad at you, you know he's not *really* mad." What a reassuring feeling for a child who tries the patience of adults, and what a splendid gift for a teacher to give.

I made stops at three public schools as well, two on the West Side, one on the East. They varied in quality amazingly. The one I went to most often was thought to be among the top New York City grammar schools, but it was no place for students with difficulties. I had been there once years before, to observe Paul, my first pupil at the Teachers College clinic. He was in the fourth grade at the time; his classroom was filled with dropouts-in-the-making. Many of the students had learning problems, but the teacher had no training in teaching them. The noise level was deafening. The teacher got the students' attention by picking up a metal box and slamming it down on a metal file cabinet. She was almost at retirement and could hardly wait. She was overwhelmed, and she screamed all the time. It was sad for her and sad for the students. I remember most of all a young girl coming up to her and saying she couldn't find a particular word in the dictionary. The teacher wrote the word on the blackboard, in beautiful Palmer-method script, misspelling it and making it impossible for the girl ever to retrieve it from her *Webster's*. It was a depressing introduction to the place.

Now there I was, three times a week, to tutor a third-grader I had already been working with for a year or so. Previously the boy had come to me in the late afternoons. The new plan was to try to get him when he was fresher and less tired; the hope was for him to make faster progress. A smart, funny, highly verbal child who could speak both English and Italian, he was severely reading disabled, and he and his parents, both of whom were classics professors, were confused and discouraged. It was hard for them, as it often is for parents, to acknowledge their child's difficulties. He had started out in a private school, but when the first-grade teacher, a young, attractive, inexperienced woman, stunned his mother by saying, "It's so sad; he just sits there like a vegetable," his placement was, of course, immediately changed. He wasn't accepted at the private school described earlier, and his options were few. "Well, maybe," his parents thought, "the local public school can help him." They were not the only ones who hoped that would be true, of course; classes at the highly respected institution were crammed full. My student barely survived second grade there and was passed on. His third-grade teacher was a man who was, or at least had been, idealistic; he wanted to train his students well, but he was finding it impossible. Instead of the twelve to fifteen students the private school teacher inspired each day, this man had more than thirty children, and they ranged in ability, attentional capacity, behavior, and interest from alpha to omega. Even their age range covered several years. The teacher was constantly frustrated, and though he tried hard and meant well, he met with very little success. He had maps and art posters all over the walls of his room; he had magazines and newspapers for the children; he even had several pets in cages. He talked about literature; he talked about ecology; he talked about wildlife; and several of the children actually listened. But not all, so there was always the thrum of distracted chatter in the air. Not all were good about cleaning assorted cages when it was their turn, either, so the room always smelled bad. There was a disheartening atmosphere in that classroom, and the youngster I knew was demoralized by it.

My student was also eligible for resource room assistance, which he received several times a week. I went with him to one of his sessions, to meet with his special ed. teacher and see him in action. Action, it turns out, was too strong a word; little active work took place. Passivity and defeat permeated the room and infected the five or six children who were there. The teacher seemed worn-out, uncurious, poorly trained. The students, who were at different levels of achievement and who desperately needed individualized direct, explicit instruction in any number of skills, were given worksheets or workbooks to labor over on their own, with occasional supervision. Mostly they stared into space or fooled around quietly with each other, occasionally looking at the sheet and filling something in.

Each time I came to the school, my young man and I were given work space in a section of the library. It was a big, sunny room; we had a snug corner away from the main action, which should have been ideal. However, when there were students in for library period, there was much talking and joking and almost no reading. When there were no classes, the librarian sat with her friends, sipping coffee and gossiping loudly. It was ironic and not a little depressing that more than once I had to ask her to please lower her voice so that my student could concentrate. One good thing came out of this boy's two years at the highly respected school: his parents came to understand that he needed much more than he was getting, and the next year they enrolled him in a school designed specifically for dyslexics, which teaches all subjects in the ways he was able to learn, and where within a year and a half he was on the honor role.

Another boy I saw was at a "magnet" school, again one thought to be wonderful. Budget cuts had begun to make a mark, though; the selection of reading material in the classroom was meager, and the added enrichments of music and art were beginning to be subtracted once again. At a third public school, I saw two second-grade boys who had a teacher who was smart, creative, and not yet burned out by the system. She had over thirty second-graders and an aide. I'm not exactly sure how much the children learned, but they had a good time, and they loved her. She seemed determined to give them some practical knowledge, even if she couldn't get everyone reading. In the spring, they ran a restaurant in their classroom, and they did it with brio. First they visited assorted restaurants in the city and talked to chefs and maître d's and pizza bakers, collecting menus and tips all along the way. Then they planned their own menus, divided up the chores, and opened up for business every day for two weeks. The kids' clientele consisted of parents and relatives and friends, who made reservations and showed up on time; their "kitchen" consisted of a couple of electric frying pans, a hot plate, and a kettle. They priced the meals (such fare as pancakes, soup, and tuna fish sandwiches), made menus, cooked food, waited on tables, presented bills and made change, cleaned up, and thought they were pros. There was no feeling of defeat in this room; there was excitement and enthusiasm. The only trouble with this school was that it was so popular, it was filled to bursting, as packed as a subway car at rush hour all the time; and with cutbacks in janitorial help, it wasn't the cleanest or nicest-smelling place in the world.

The other child I visited during his "work" hours was laboring away at a top-level, coed private school. When I met him, though, he was on the verge of being tossed out. He was halfway through first grade; he couldn't read; he couldn't pay attention; he couldn't learn, they thought. He was also cursed with hearing and vision deficits and blessed with the best adoptive parents in the universe. He was brilliant, too. His mother and father were determined to do right by their younger son, and they educated themselves thoroughly about how to help him. They discovered what and who he needed, found those people, and then established a highly successful partnership consisting of the school, the psychiatrist who was to determine and monitor medication, the psychologist who dealt with his social issues, and me, the educational therapist. What an experience he was. No one has ever wanted to learn more than he. When we started working together, and he was beginning to develop the skills he needed, it felt sometimes as though I were just opening up his skull and pouring in pitcher after pitcher of words and rules and books. Whatever I could give him, he took hungrily. He learned to read and to write, and he learned to think of himself very differently. The school that was ready to kick him out developed a serious commitment to him over the next six years, and he is now thriving in that very competitive atmosphere. It's not that he doesn't need regular assistance; he does. And it's not that every moment is perfect; it isn't. He could use more assistance from the school; some teachers make him copy from the board, which someone with his vision difficulties should never have to do, and he could have used more individualized instruction in keyboarding and writing. But this is a child who is so smart, he absolutely needs the challenge of the kind of school he attends. He is very happy there and achieving more and more each year, and it is the communication, the cooperation, the sharing of time and information by faculty, family, and support folks that has made it possible for him to triumph over his exceedingly rocky start.

Forming a partnership with the parents, the school, and the teachers of a dyslexic child is of vital importance to the child's success. With a united front, everyone is aware of progress and lack thereof, and of other issues that might affect the child's performance in school and at home. With regular communication, there are fewer surprises for all. Situations are dealt with promptly, and the child receives the best education available, hears the same messages in all areas of his life, and is reassured that his difficulties can be and are being dealt with. If the child is in public school, federal law mandates free "appropriate" education in "the least restrictive environment" for those who are identified as learning (or otherwise) disabled. Partnership between the schools and the families is a key ingredient of the law; the individualized education programs (IEPs) that are required of the teams of special educators at the schools must include the parents' input and approval, and there is a schedule of required periodic reviews of and alterations to the plans as well. The Individuals with Disabilities Education Act (IDEA) of 1990 reauthorized and expanded the funding programs originally established in 1975 under the landmark Education for All Handicapped Children Act (PL 94-142); in 1997 Congress once again reauthorized IDEA. Under this legislation, schools have a legal responsibility to seek out the children who have difficulties, to assess and evaluate them, and to provide the special help they need within quite clear guidelines. The Individuals with Disabilities Education Act makes demands of the schools and provides at least partial funding to meet those demands.

What constitutes "appropriate" and "least restrictive," however, is open to debate and interpretation, as are the guidelines for determining eligibility. It's possible for a child to be found eligible in one state and not in another, sometimes not even in another district in his own state. Terminology used and even jobs involved with special education vary from state to state as well. Appropriate education for dyslexic individuals requires intensive training of the teachers who are in charge, and this, sadly, is all too often lacking. Many people feel that "least restrictive" most often means "in the classroom" for learning disabled and dyslexic students. I suggest that a child who has trouble processing language, reading words, and getting meaning from them might find the quiet of the special educator's office far less restrictive than the distracting, noisy, and commotion-filled classroom.

There are other legal protections for the disabled that are not funded, but that sometimes apply to public school students. Section 504 of the Rehabilitation Act of 1973 and the 1990 Americans with Disabilities Act are civil rights statutes that are designed to protect the disabled from discrimination of many sorts and to provide "reasonable accommodations" in a wide variety of areas—access to public facilities, employment, transportation, etc. Section 504 has been helpful for securing services for children who have been denied them under IDEA.

Private schools are not controlled by IDEA. They do not have a set of laws governing them; they do not have to make up IEPs or contact parents on a schedule that is strict and strictly enforced. That does not mean that it is any less important for parents of dyslexic children to forge a partnership with their private schools, though; in some ways it's even more important just because it is not something that must be done by law. I always urge the parents of the students in my private practice to get involved and stay involved in their children's educations; after all, who cares more? These children need advocates, and they need to be taught how to advocate for themselves as well. Sometimes parents are intimidated by the system; other times they are angry at it. Neither attitude adds anything positive to any situation, so I try to help them leave both at home when they go to a meeting or when they talk to a teacher. That doesn't mean that complaints should not be aired or problems discussed, but putting a teacher or administrator on the defensive will only backfire in the end, and often the child is harmed more than helped by an approach that is too submissive or too aggressive. The assumption must be that a group of adults with a like interest—the education of this child—are meeting to ensure that everyone knows what can be known about the child and that everyone is doing what can be done for the child. It doesn't always work, though. Sometimes parents withhold important information about a child in an attempt to protect the child from being "labeled" or because they are somehow ashamed of what they perceive as weakness and are afraid of admitting it. Sometimes teachers and/or administrators don't really know what to do, are not trained to deal properly with the child's difficulties, and are afraid of admitting that; other times they refuse to see what is there, as in Valerie McCarthy's earliest days at school.

A private rural elementary school that I knew well in those days when I split my time between city and country was a tough place for any child with problems. The school did not do any testing before admitting a child, claiming that it accepted and taught all who came, but then the teachers there did not have a clue about what to do if that child had any difficulties, and they weren't especially interested in finding out, either. I have several children in my private practice who went through this system; a couple of them suffered unconscionably. One was very dyslexic, dysgraphic (trouble writing), and dysnomic (trouble finding names of things), the other dyslexic and ADD. Both were expected to perform at their school with little or no accommodation. Once I asked a teacher of the three-d student if he could please find a way to test the child orally, because he had worked so hard on the material and knew it quite well, but was always hung up by his enormous difficulty writing. To my surprise, the teacher agreed readily. I was delighted. The next time I saw the child, I asked him how it went, was it much easier to be able to give his answers aloud and not have to be bogged down in writing them out. He replied that he had indeed had to write them out. Confused, I sought out the teacher and asked him what had happened, why he hadn't given the child the test orally as he had agreed. He said that indeed he had, that he had given it to him orally and merely asked the child to write the answers. This teacher meant well; he was trying to help, and he thought all he needed to do was make it so the child did not have to read the questions. He didn't even know how to think about what else might make a difference. He was smart and wanted to be a good teacher, but he had absolutely no training and no insight into the obstacles this child faced daily.

The ADD child perplexed his teachers; they didn't like him much, and the feeling was mutual. He was tough to deal with, and they didn't have any strategies; their fuses were short, and, by the time he was in second grade, their patience at an end. The child was scolded and isolated from the others regularly, to no avail. His parents had done everything the school asked them to—they had had the child tested and medicated and they had arranged for remediation—but his teachers saw little progress and were not too keen on shouldering any of the responsibility for the situation. The boy's mother and I went to many meetings; they were all difficult. The teachers only knew how to complain about the child; they had made up their minds about him and were not going to change them. His mother was furious; she felt she was doing all she could, and they were doing very little. In an attempt to help them all deal more effectively with a boy I knew had enormous potential, I suggested that the school try a reward system in which he could amass points for containing himself and for reaching a series of pre-established short- and long-range goals, and at defined intervals earn some agreed-upon privilege with a set number of points—not goodies or candies or prizes, but some classroom honor that the successful kids received regularly and he was usually denied. He needed some positive incentive to change his behavior, I tried to explain, adding that research had proven that this type of accommodation worked very successfully with that kind of child. The teachers couldn't imagine that it would be possible to make such an arrangement without doing it for all the children; the head of the school refused to even try a reward system, saying, "I'm not really into behavior modification." The partnership was impossible. By the time those two students left that school, the dyslexic, dysgraphic, and dysnomic one felt like a real dolt, and the ADD one like a really bad boy.

The public schools in that area are in many ways superior to that particular private one. Teachers are generally well trained; classes are small because the population is low; children are, as a rule, well fed and well taken care of because there is little poverty and fewer societal difficulties than in large cities. There are still plenty of problems, of course, and there is also great variety among the student population (in ability, if not in racial heritage); that is the essence of public education, the source of its greatness and its complications. Inclusion is a lovely idea; we are all part of the same race called human, after all, and it's important for children to get used to being with others who are different from them in a wide variety of ways. It's also terrific for those who once felt excluded to be a part of the main community group. However, inclusion complicates teachers' lives considerably, and usually dilutes the effectiveness of even the best. Those skills, those discussions, those methods that work well for small groups of similar students, particularly dyslexic or other learning disabled students, do not transfer easily to groups of fifteen or twenty-five or thirty-five. At one school, I observed a second-grade classroom with fifteen students and one teacher. She was upbeat, enthusiastic, and kind; she knew her stuff, and she liked children. Among those fifteen students were brilliant kids, brilliant dyslexic kids, average kids, average dyslexic kids, less brilliant kids, ADD kids, nonverbal learning disorder kids, and one who didn't speak. There were no children who needed complicated physical attention; everyone seemed healthy and mobile. There were no serious discipline problems, either, and there was a cadre of special educators who came in and gathered children to take with them or stayed and worked in a corner with them. So, in many ways, it was quite an ideal situation, with professional staffers doing what they were supposed to be doing. Still, there were plenty of times when it was the whole group and the one teacher, and it's a tall order to ask one person to educate such a diverse collection of young minds and somehow give each child what he needs. Not as tall an order as is given big-city teachers who have double the number of students and often triple the number of complications, or is given the medium-sized-city high school math teacher I know who expects forty students—many of whom will be reading on a third- or fourth-grade level—in each of his five freshman and sophomore geometry classes this year, but it is asking for more than can actually be delivered.

I don't know about the second-grade teacher mentioned above, but most elementary school instructors haven't had special ed. training, either, so the students who need individualized instruction usually get it only in periodic doses with the special ed. teachers. That particular school is trying to compensate—and succeeding to some degree—for that in terms of reading and spelling by getting the teachers to use programs in the classroom that are based on the principles of Orton-Gillingham but are adapted for use with larger groups of children. It's a big step in the right direction, but there are many, many schools that have not taken even a small step.

Between those children who need special help and those who would flourish if left alone in a room with a stack of books and no teacher is a range of youngsters who are not impaired enough to qualify for special ed. but who do have learning weaknesses, more subtle than overt, perhaps, such as slower processing or mild dyslexia, those who would greatly benefit from individualized attention but who function sufficiently well, if not up to their capacity—students like Rebecca, who was so smart that no one noticed her dyslexia until it was too late to let her have a successful adolescence. Those are the students who don't receive proper attention, and I'd bet there are more girls among them than boys—well-behaved, somewhat distracted girls who continue, in spite of the women's movement, to mask their problems and think it's somehow their fault that they are not high-achievers. "You know," says one public school special educator, "my dream would be to be able to give each child what that child needs, whether he qualified for special ed. or not, but we just can't. It's all we can do to properly teach those who are eligible." Says another, "We have such a wide variety of children to educate that we simply can't provide the absolute best education for each one. What we can provide is an adequate education."

Private schools do have the freedom to give each child what he needs, and some of them actually do so. Valerie McCarthy found a school that set her on a productive and successful path, and so have many other dyslexic students. At the high school level, it's a bit more complicated, but nowhere have I met a more caring faculty than at the prep school where I saw many students over a few years. Almost every teacher was invested in giving every student a chance to succeed, and the school had quite a complicated population: several dyslexics, quite a few other teenagers with assorted other learning disabilities, and a handful of kids who were at boarding school because of problems at home. I've always said that no one in the universe works harder than independent school teachers; that probably goes double for those at boarding schools. All the instructors of one boy who had a serious combination of learning and emotional problems met regularly, and sometimes actually daily, to coordinate their efforts on his behalf and give him the best chance they could. And this was not a boy whose family was going to build a new library or hockey rink, either; he was just a troubled teenager whom they were trying to help. It was a fascinating group of students: I saw one boy whose dyslexia was discovered at the school (it's a good thing he went there, too, because otherwise he would have been at the same public high school that never identified Rebecca's problem) and who was thoroughly relieved to find out what had been holding him back. His attention and seriousness intensified immediately, and his performance and grades improved accordingly. From the moment he was diagnosed, he seemed to just take off. I saw another who was a postgraduate trying to get his grades up a bit before going to college. He had graduated from a serious, well-regarded high school in the Midwest and had been accepted at the college of his choice, but wanted another year before going off there. It was probably a good idea; he had never lived away from home, and he was able to have this year to get used to being on his own while still having more structure and support than he would get at any college. He was a smart lad, and he was a poignant combination of dyslexic, playboy, and scholar wannabe; sometimes he seemed sophisticated, other times very young and naive. Academically, he often tried hard but just as often goofed off and failed to follow through, so he was never quite able to fulfill his potential. I think the idea of achieving the success he sought actually terrified him, as growing up seemed to. I think of him often and still have a note he left me to confirm an appointment to work on a history paper. It contains a lovely dyslexic Freudian misspelling. "Dear Ms. Hurford: I'll see you at seven o'clock. I hope that's the write time."

One young man I saw at that school was very secure emotionally, and severely dyslexic. Even though he had had much appropriate instruction, he still had trouble decoding; his reading level was way below his grade level, and he was only able to read for about twenty minutes at a time before the words simply fell off the page. This lad had had the best help available, though, and wise parents who knew what he needed, so he was completely intact in spite of his disability. He had been spotted and referred by his teacher when he was in first grade. By the time he was in the second grade, that teacher had become his stepmother. Talk about no escape. She was in the unique position of being able to keep an eye on his case in school and at home. She arranged the right sort and amount of early intervention for him, she knew what the correct next steps would be in terms of his tutoring, she was a fine advocate for him, and, most important, she and his father helped him develop areas of expertise that enabled him to be proud and sure of himself. When I met him, during his junior year, he was tenuous academically, but aware of and at peace with all his own strengths and weaknesses. He was a real outdoorsman, and very handsome, too, so he had a great deal going for him; he was able to compensate extremely well. The girls all swooned when he spoke to them, and the boys were impressed when, even though he couldn't play lacrosse because of his sequencing, memory, and coordination difficulties, he could string lacrosse sticks the way the early Native Americans could. He even had his future career planned: he had every intention of developing his own Outward Bound type of business.

For some students, the best choice is a school especially for dyslexics. These are all private, and they are very expensive, but there are ways of getting some financial aid, and some insurance help as well. These academies vary in quality just as any of the others, of course, but one thing I think they all share is a determination to raise the *amour propre*, or self-love, of their students, as well as their skill level and academic performance. Kildonan is the one founded by Diana King, run by her for many years, and made an important force by her passion. She is retired from there now, devoting her time to training teachers, but she remembers each and every one of the students she taught at Kildonan. She even keeps in touch with several. For years the bulk of her students were teenagers who had struggled and generally failed at other schools. King was their court of last resort. When they arrived at the school, the first thing she said to them was always "Congratulations, you are so lucky to be dyslexic!" "What?" they mostly thought. "Am I hearing right?" Good luck is not something they ever thought they had been blessed with, and it never occurred to them that there was anything at all good about being dyslexic, but she was usually able to convince them (as she did young Tom West) that what she said had merit. An added balm for students at schools like Kildonan has always been the great relief of meeting others just like themselves, who have struggled in the same ways and have had the same pains; adolescents who have felt like freaks or been convinced of their own idiocy can begin to understand that they are not freaks or idiots, just as their new friends are not. Younger students can meet lifetime friends who share their interests and difficulties. Cyprian met his fishing buddy at the Kildonan summer camp; I can't imagine their ever not being close. Of course, the very best thing about these places is that they teach all the subjects every day in ways that enable these students to learn. Every student gets one-on-one tutoring some part of every day. Goals are highly individualized. Teachers break down everything into manageable steps and then build it all back together again, and they teach study skills and cultivate study habits that give their pupils what they need to succeed there and when they return to mainstream schools—which is the goal. No one is supposed to stay at these schools forever.

Schools like Kildonan have had a huge increase in their number of applicants in the past few years, and there are many who blame the current trends in reading instruction for a large chunk of that increase. Over the past decade and a half or so, the teaching of reading changed drastically (and the swing of the pendulum indicates that more change is in the offing). Two positions formed: there were those who believed students learned to read better when they were taught the rules of the language, and those who thought that teaching any phonics was the most insulting degradation perpetrated on America's youth and that students learned to read by reading. Partly the antiphonics people were reacting to the old-fashioned, tedious ways that included out-of-context instruction, constant boring drills, and teachers' slavishly going step by step through what the basal readers told them to do, with little thought and almost no creativity. Partly it looked and sounded great that students were learning to read by reading interesting material. That is, after all, what is supposed to be the result of learning to read. Wow! An easy way. It is so American to look for the fastest, least-demanding solution.

Out went structure; in came the notion that it wasn't hard to teach reading, that expertise was not necessary, that teachers didn't need much training because learning to read was a natural act, as natural as learning to speak. It spread across our country like a virus. Charismatic proponents of a new, more exciting way to teach reading revved people up the way preachers do at revival meetings. Teachers gave up their basal readers, often having been told to do so by their schools' administrators, and in their place put predictable books, trade books, beautifully illustrated books. Out went explicit instruction; any rules of the language to be learned were to be learned only implicitly, were to be absorbed by osmosis through reading and writing. It seemed such a golden idea. The children were much more in charge; reading became spontaneous and more fun. Never mind the fact that there was no research base to support this point of view and that there was plenty of research to show that reading is not a natural act, that it is something that humans have been doing for a relatively short time, and that even though there is a small percentage of the population that does seem to learn to read spontaneously, a far greater number, dyslexic and not, must be taught systematically how to decode our alphabetic language.

Adherents of the new way became more and more rigid about what could and couldn't be included in their classes, and actual teaching took up less and less time. Invented spelling triumphed so completely over traditional that many teachers refused even to answer when a child asked how to spell a word. Discovery learning proliferated, where the students "discover" knowledge with little instruction. Rhetoric flew; the two camps became entrenched, and the "reading wars" raged, with whole language winning more and more skirmishes and battles. Private and public schools committed themselves and their students to the seduction of what seemed much more appealing—and much easier on teachers. Out went the old, boring ways, and in came, what? A mess: unprepared teachers convinced that reading was somehow magical and that there was little they should do besides provide books and some "literary" talk; students who seemed to be just fine as long as they stuck with little predictable books but who had no equipment with which to figure out new and complex words; and rampant reading failure. Under the guise of whole language, actual instruction in reading just about disappeared. Casualties mounted, and more and more students began to fall through what Dyslexia Association stalwart and author Priscilla Vail termed the "hole in whole language." The children who did not need to be taught to read flourished, as they would have flourished under any system; the dyslexics and others who were unable to intuitively master the English language, who needed proper, explicit, direct instruction, did not learn, and that is a big chunk of the student population.

It wasn't very long before standardized scores started falling countrywide, special education referrals began growing, and schools like Windward and Kildonan were deluged with applications. Reading problems had once again reached crisis proportions. In 1996 there was a National Summit on Teacher Preparation, and the same year a group of twenty-five organizations representing regular and special education (two groups who are more often competing for funds than joining hands) launched a nationwide public awareness campaign entitled "Learning to Read, Reading to Learn, Helping Children with Learning Disabilities to Succeed." Information kits were distributed that contained, among other things, ten principles of learning to read, gathered from mounds of research, principles that are effective for everyone and critical for those with dyslexia or other disorders. The ten principles they stated were as follows: create appreciation for the written word; develop awareness of printed language; learn the alphabet; understand the relation of letters and words; understand that language is made up of words, syllables, and phonemes; learn letter sounds; sound out new words; identify words in print accurately and easily; know spelling patterns; and learn to read reflectively.

Finally, in January 1997, *The New York Times* published an editorial applauding the long-term studies conducted by the National Institutes of Health that had followed about 2,500 children for as long as fourteen years. The data from those studies showed that one in five American children has "substantial difficulty" learning to read, that girls are just as affected as boys, and that *literature and phonics practice both* are necessary for impaired and unimpaired children alike. Frighteningly, the NIH studies also found that fewer than 10 percent of teachers are actually properly trained and know how to teach read-ing to those students who don't "get it" automatically.

It was a call to arms. States began to panic, most notably California, where reading scores had plummeted and experts had been brought in to formulate new ways of teaching and new standards for teachers of reading. The California Reading Initiative, drawn up by Louisa C. Moats, director of teacher training at the Greenwood Institute in Putney, Vermont, and others, outlined a statewide plan to address the instruc-tional needs of children in terms of reading and writing, to provide them with the correct combination of skills and access to literature, and to set standards for training those who teach them. Moats has been in the forefront of reform of the education of teachers of reading, writing, and spelling, and she is eloquent on the subject, describing carefully the knowledge of our language required to properly teach reading, the ease with phonology, with sound-symbol patterns, with spelling and writing skills, with vocabulary, and with appropriate reading material that teachers must have and mostly lack. Said Moats in 1994, after publish-ing the results of a survey of teachers that had shown how poorly prepared they were and how little they understood the structure of the language, "Until we recognize that teachers do not naturally acquire the kind of expertise in language structure that is required of them for remediating and preventing reading problems, we will neglect to provide the neces-sary training. . . . Lower-level language mastery is as essential for the lit-eracy teacher as anatomy is for the physician. It is our obligation to enable teachers to acquire it." Until recently hers has been a voice in the wilderness, but there are some signs that that is beginning to change. If so, that will be a great boon for dyslexics, who have been sitting in their classes, hoping for that reading miracle.

The increased demands on teachers that inclusion occasions and the quality of teacher training are two of the major issues that affect the chances of dyslexics (and all other students, of course) in "regular" pub-lic schools. Both have been subjects of concern for more than two decades, and both are still problematic. Public Law 94-142 (1975) pro-vided for mainstreaming, or inclusion, in the regular classroom of handicapped students as long as the students' needs could be met there, in addition to authorizing other services, such as more individu-alized instruction in resource rooms.

Immediately (in January 1976) the National Education Association expressed concern about mainstreaming without proper classroom and teacher preparation and about budget cuts forcing a kind of unintentional inclusion by reducing the number of special education teachers who were most able to provide the necessary support services. The organization issued a seven-point statement listing the requirements it felt essential before it could support mainstreaming. The points addressed planning, funding, necessary modification, and proper preparation of teachers for their new roles. Ten years later, the Office of Special Education and Rehabilitation Services expressed concern over inclusion and the adaptation of regular classrooms for children with special needs. Then, in 1992, with questions unanswered and problems unsolved, and amid major cutbacks in education funding, the National Association of State Boards of Education called for full inclusion, saying, "all means ALL," and called for the greater collaboration among regular teachers and specialists that would make it possible. It's a great call, and a noble idea. Dr. Sylvia Richardson of the University of South Florida in Tampa has found that there is greater collaboration now than ever before, that there are some fine approaches to teaching a class with very varied students, and that some good in-class support services have been developed as well. Dr. Richardson has also found, however, that too many teachers are not equipped with either the techniques or the materials to work with their diverse collection of students. She joins Louisa Moats in calling for the redesign of programs for the education of teachers, and echoes the need for training teachers fully in the structure of the English language—as well as in multisensory methods of teaching—so that they will have the knowledge they need to reach those who have difficulty learning to read and write.

The Dyslexia Association has added its voice to those crying out for better preparation and higher standards for teachers of reading, with a position paper—authored by none other than Louisa Moats, with Susan Brady of Haskins Laboratories and the University of Rhode Island—entitled "Informed Instruction for Reading Success: Foundations for Teacher Preparation." The document provides a synopsis of research results and the implications of those results for instruction, describes the kinds of knowledge teachers must have in order to serve properly all children and especially "at-risk" children and those with dyslexia, and makes suggestions for altering teacher education to ensure the competency of teachers to make their inclusive classrooms exciting places filled with opportunities for all to learn.

Colleges and universities are beginning to listen and to try to rid their teacher training programs of what Sylvia Richardson calls mumpsimus, "a tradition or custom obstinately adhered to regardless of how unreasonable it might be," according to the *Oxford Dictionary*. It's not an easy task, however; getting rid of mumpsimus requires a great deal of mind changing and program adaptation, in addition to finding personnel who themselves are sufficiently knowledgeable to teach the teachers. It is a start, though: Teachers College, Columbia University, will now require all its M.A. candidates in the learning disabilities program to take an introductory course in multisensory teaching of basic language skills, and Southern Methodist University in Dallas, Texas, has done the same; Fairleigh Dickinson University in New Jersey is offering a thirty-credit Dyslexia Specialist Certificate, which trains its graduates in multisensory structured language instruction; and the University of New Mexico at Albuquerque is offering, through its continuing education division, a series of four courses in language and multisensory teaching that can later be applied toward a master's degree in special education.

There is great consternation around the country about the state of special education in America on the part of educators, parents, administrators, and voters. Numbers of students and costs involved have swelled dramatically in the past several years, as school budgets keep getting cut and cut, and there are some scary proposals afoot about how to deal with the rise, which is forecasted to continue, though at a slower pace. The New York State Board of Regents has proposed giving school districts block grants instead of per-classified-child funds, and limiting special education classes to 12 percent of the total student population. Aiming to eliminate financial incentives for overclassifying students, the proposal actually provides incentives for underclassifying them or declassifying them, because districts are promised that any funds of the block they don't use for special ed. can be applied to regular classes.

Forward-thinking districts and many private schools as well have decided to heed the current emphasis in dyslexia research and to give some priority to measures of intervention before reading becomes an issue and dyslexia is diagnosed. This kind of intervention focuses not on teaching reading earlier and earlier, or even on instructing students in the sounds and symbols that make up our language, but on developing their phonemic awareness, their awareness of the sounds of English words and how to manipulate them. Teaching phonemic awareness and teaching phonics are two distinctly different things, and there is a body of research that says without developed phonemic awareness, students will have a difficult time learning phonics. That doesn't mean that good early childhood teachers are ignoring teaching the letters of the alphabet and what they say; it does mean that they are adding to the mix the kind of instruction that fosters the metacognitive skills that make up what is known as phonological awareness.

More and more kindergarten teachers are following the tenets of the likes of Hyla Rubin and her colleagues, who have done important work in analyzing and treating young children's language analysis abilities. Rubin et al. recommend making playful instruction in awareness of the qualities of our language a regular part of the class day. Clapping out syllables or moving tokens around for each one fosters linguistic awareness in young children. This can be done very naturally when taking attendance, for example, and once the children are able to segment words and names, they can be taught to add or take away syllables or chunks. To help them become more aware of phonemes—the individual sounds in words—teachers can say something silly and get the children to identify what it is and then correct it by adding the right sound. "Would you close the more, please" would get a group of five-year-olds giggling pretty fast, and I would think many of them would be itching to say, "You mean *door,* not *more.*" Rhyming is something else young children love, and research shows the ability to rhyme is an important precursor of the ability to read. Rubin recommends adding rhyming at several points during the day: teachers can model rhymes and talk about the fact that words do rhyme; they can ask children if certain words rhyme—*note* and *boat* and *coat,* for instance—and then get the children to make up words themselves, real or silly, that rhyme.

There are other ways to foster phonological awareness in young children, many of them, and there are specific programs that help teachers know what to do and how to do it. Teachers need to be trained in language structure (it's not something that is intuitive), and they can and must be so that they are able to give the children in their care the foundation they need to go on to develop solid reading and writing skills. Research has shown that language-delayed children who have received phonemic awareness training have made great strides in their abilities to manage the English language. In addition, children love the activities that best nourish this awareness. Wouldn't it be amazing if early in the next century, new studies showed that playing with language and making games of linguistic analysis with young children was one of the main approaches responsible for lowering the numbers and costs of special education referrals around the country? Board of Regents: Listen up.

CHAPTER SEVEN

Remediating Dyslexia

The Joy of Discovery

W HEN I FIRST got into this field, I thought the best part was going to be the detective work, the teasing out of the details that point the way to a diagnosis, the writing up of educational evaluations so that parents and others could understand what they meant, the suggesting of solutions that could turn things around. Those endeavors, I thought, were what added up to the heart of the matter; those were what I thought were the most intellectual, the most challenging, the most interesting aspects of working with people with reading problems. It didn't take me long, though, to yearn to be the one who actually put into effect some of the splendid (I thought) recommendations I was making. I wanted to see if what I imagined could work actually would. I wanted to be the one to try to make the change, to help the person become a reader and to watch the transformation. Just describing and suggesting wasn't enough; turning a nonreader into a reader is a singular experience. I can't imagine anything more fun or more exciting.

After a few years, I bumped into an old friend from my days at *Life* magazine. I excitedly described my work, throwing in what I thought were a few especially charming *bons mots* from my students. She looked at me, totally baffled, and asked, "But don't you get bored?" I was speechless for a moment, and then it dawned on me. She couldn't understand how anyone wouldn't be bored being around children or working with elementary material much of the time; she thought I had slid right down to the bottom of the success ladder. People have such prejudice against teaching that I knew she could never understand how endlessly fascinating this work is, even though it lacks "glamour" in the traditional sense.

So I never tried to explain to her the captivating places I now have access to—the brains of the people I work with (and bits of their hearts, as well). Could there possibly be any destination more interesting and less boring than that? Not to me. And the rewards are constant, literally constant. Even though, or maybe because, there are so many steps backward and to the side, every step forward is a thrill for both teacher and student; every time a new skill unlocks the language in some way, even some tiny way, it's a very big deal. When I was a brand-new reading and learning specialist, I was given a group of five third-graders to work with who ranged from dyslexic to very dyslexic, from learning disabled to *learning disabled.* They were not in a special school; they were the least able of the students in their class at a "regular" school; they had been together in their small group since first grade; they were the rock bottom, and they each knew it and believed it. They were also a great bunch of kids, with sensitive observations, artistic talent, and plenty of guts. School was not a joy for them; they struggled with reading, with writing, and with each other. I determined I would enliven their reading lives. They seemed already a good distance down Keith Stanovich's Matthew Effect track, and I planned to derail that soul-destroying trip, at least temporarily. I succeeded, and we didn't crash and burn—we had a great time.

The group had never read anything meaty, anything really good, and I vowed I would somehow get them through one of my favorite books, *Mr. Popper's Penguins,* the hilarious tale of how a housepainter and armchair explorer copes with the surprise gift he is sent by his idol, Admiral Drake, from Antarctica. The sentence structure of the book was the most sophisticated they had ever encountered, much of the vocabulary was new to them, and many of the ideas were quite old-fashioned. It was the hardest thing they had ever tackled, but they rose to the occasion. I pretaught words and phrases from the book, and we had all sorts of games to help them master the material. We broke down words into syllables and put them back together again; I took all their phonics instruction from what they would need to get through the book. We studied penguins, we studied the Antarctic, we studied explorers, they learned the differences between the North and South Poles, and they wrote wonderful stories based on what they were learning. Every day they seemed to get stronger, and every day they became more curious. We had plenty of chuckles, too. The book is filled with opportunity for word play, and they delighted in it. We also had penguin talk contests, and we had penguin walk contests. One day we were reading the part of the book where Mr. Popper lets a blizzard fill his home with ice and snow, and the penguins have a great time sliding around on their stomachs, tobogganing from one end of the living room to the other. The students were confused; they didn't know what it meant to toboggan; some didn't know what a toboggan was. As I explained both to them, one or two nodded their heads in recognition, but one little girl remained puzzled. After a while, she raised her hand and queried, "But . . . I thought . . . tu-bah-gan was to try and get something at a lower price?" I said that indeed it was, but not in this book. She blushed, then grinned, then became a penguin and gave a demonstration of belly tobogganing for the rest of the group. When we finished the book, and I took them to see the impressive penguin exhibit at the Central Park Zoo as a reward for their hard work, that same child checked the whole display, turned to me, and asked seriously, "Where's the rookery?" Those words will remain engraved on my heart forever.

A key statement in the Dyslexia Association definition of the condition is "Although . . . lifelong, individuals with dyslexia frequently respond successfully to timely and appropriate intervention." Do they ever. Sometimes they respond successfully to not-so-timely intervention as well. Look at all Rebecca Tomasini has accomplished, then just think about what her teenage years would have been like if someone had given her the intervention she needed when she was younger. Still, she has triumphed over her disability and its almost devastating side effects. So the moral of the story is that late intervention is better than none, but early intervention is best. And *appropriate* intervention is key. Just because somebody thinks he knows what to do to help a dyslexic become a reader, doesn't mean he does. One of the best things anyone ever said to me was when I was in graduate school, just before my first practicum, my first actual work with a student in the clinic. My tiny and intense professor, Lois Dreyer, took me into her office, closed the door, sat me down, peered into my eyes searingly with her dark brown orbs, and told me I would be a different person when I finished what I was about to begin. Then she asked whether I was ready for that or not. She added that there was nothing in my past education or experience that would be of much value to me, that I had to gather a whole new body of knowledge before I would be any good at this.

She was absolutely correct. I've never felt more inept, more unable to count on what I already knew than when I started working with my first student. I had never before known anyone for whom the language just didn't make sense; I had never before known anyone who couldn't rely on his memory at all; I had never before known anyone who wrote his name completely backward; I had never before known anyone who felt worse about himself and his abilities; and I didn't know what to do about any of it. Nothing I would naturally do or say would make the slightest bit of difference to Paul's survival. I studied and studied, and I worried and worried; eventually I taught him quite a bit, and, by the end of that first encounter (which lasted two years), I had indeed become a completely different person—at least in terms of what I knew. I had learned the minutiae of the rules of the English language and assorted, appropriate techniques for teaching them; I had learned about how to find out what was going wrong for the students I met and what to do about it; and I had learned about the research and the theories behind all the practical information I was gathering.

There is indeed a large body of research to guide those of us who do what I do, and through it all a few themes are constant. One primary motif is that dyslexics need direct, explicit phonics instruction; they cannot learn to read without it. The research has proven it, anecdotal tales have documented it, and still there are those who don't want to believe it. It's true, though. You may not like the notion of a bottom-up-type learning, of building skills from small to big, but it works, and the other way doesn't. It doesn't mean that the instruction is going to be boring, or that the children will not be exposed to rich literature, or that they won't be taught other strategies, or that the reading and spelling instruction will take on a life unto itself. It does mean that they will be given the skills they need, taught in an effective way. The reading disabled cannot learn implicitly; they cannot "get" reading by simply being bathed in written words; and if they are not taught the way that they can learn, we don't give them a decent chance. It's really that simple.

A variation on that theme is that multisensory instruction is important for dyslexics. That, too, is true. It helps enormously to get them on the road to reading. Orton-Gillingham-style instruction is what I use and what I was trained for. It was designed by Dr. Orton and school psychologist Anna Gillingham for one-on-one tutoring, and it emphasizes careful, step-by-step multisensory instruction. Beth Slingerland adapted the O-G principles for classroom use, and many schools, both private and public, have decided to give their students a chance and teach them with the Slingerland method or another adaptation of the O-G ideas. There are those who would argue that seeing, saying, and writing or tracing letters and words, that involving all three senses, doesn't really help learning, but merely increases concentration. I don't accept that point of view; I think that engaging the varied senses has a great deal to do with learning to read, that it utilizes different kinds of learning and memory, including the very powerful muscle memory. But even if it were true that increased concentration was the only benefit from multisensory instruction, that would still be good enough for me. Increased concentration means increased learning, and that is what we are here to promote.

Cyprian was just seven when we started working together; he hadn't received any effective instruction as yet, and he could read very little. He had (and still has, seven years later) a most appealing nature; seven years ago he was sweet, small, and scared. He had almost no stamina when we started, and very little belief in his own capabilities, but he was willing, and eventually he learned to work with the strength of a Trojan.

In the beginning, everything was a struggle for Cyp; nothing made sense or came easily. Hundreds of three- by five-inch index cards later, he had learned the consonant sounds and how to write them. (Phyllis Bertin, my Orton-Gillingham trainer, insists that students are not learning to write letters, that they are learning to write sounds, and she is right.) Cyp learned that there were such things as short vowel sounds, and he, the son of two artists who already had a keen sense of the visual, created pictures representing them. Index cards with the *a*pple, *e*lephant, *i*gloo, *u*mbrella, and *o*ctopus were lined up at his side every session, all session, so that he could always consult them, to see and say the word and visually remind himself of the particular sound/symbol relationship he was seeking. Then he learned to sequence the consonant and vowel sounds into words, left to right. This is often a serious sticking point for dyslexics, but, with a lot of work, Cyp learned how to do it. Next he discovered that *pl* and *gr* and *tw* and *sn* and many other blends do indeed do just that, blend their two sounds together into one, and that he might encounter this odd marriage at the beginning or at the end of a word, also that three of these things called "con-so-nants" (one of the first three-syllable words he learned) also sometimes blend together, as in *shr*imp. After that he found out that sometimes vowels appear together, two at a time, in words, and when that happens, they make just one sound; they say the name of the first of them (such as *ai* says *a*).

Enormous effort went into mastering all of this information, and then the tricky lesson had to be learned; Cyp had to understand the concept of magic *e,* that this sneaky vowel, when put at the end of some words, makes no sound at all, but changes the sound of the vowel before it from short to long. It's a mean trick to pull on someone, but without magic *e* there is no reading. He had to learn to add magic *e* to *mat* and make *mate,* to *kit* and make *kite,* to *us* and make *use;* he had to learn about taking if off and going back to the short vowel sounds; and he had to keep it all straight in his head. He learned many other rules and conquered assorted phonic elements, too, but these were the basics that opened up reading for him. And read he did, every single time we met, and he took home the books we read together to read once again to his parents, which gave him additional practice with material I knew he could handle. Step by step, building block by building block, Cyp learned to read, to become reasonably fluent, and to understand what he was reading. To strengthen his memory for sounds and words, Cyp memorized many poems as well, starting with "There was a little girl . . ." and increasing in length and complexity. It was all done slowly, incrementally, multisensorily, and everything was repeated and repeated so that he could "overlearn" it. That is another important concept, overlearning. Dyslexic students can't be taught something once and be expected to have learned it and to remember it. Their memories are not so reliable, particularly for words and sounds, so they have to be taught and retaught until they show they have mastered what they are learning. They need to practice, practice, practice, and then practice again before they can get to Carnegie Hall.

Reading and spelling, or decoding and encoding, are two sides of the same coin. Teaching them at the same time helps students make better sense of the language. Having them write what they are learning solidifies the knowledge. Writing words and sentences encompassing the new sounds requires taking them in, mulling them around, thinking them through, and reproducing them on paper. And after they have written it all down, looking at and reading those words and sentences reinforces the learning even more. Every session I teach beginning readers starts with some multisensory phonics instruction, including dictation. First we review the most recently learned sound, and the student reads the words, phrases, and sentences incorporating that sound; then we add another to the repertoire, first looking at it, then saying it, then reading words, phrases, and sentences using that sound; then we stand up and write swooping, swirling letters of the new sound in the air to establish the pattern and engage the large muscles of the arm. Only after all that does pencil meet paper, and the student writes what I dictate: words, phrases, and sentences with the new sound. Most every student finds the dictation the hardest part of the lesson, because that is when it all has to be pulled together. When it can be done reliably, though, I feel much surer that something has been learned.

The order in which letters and sounds are learned is important, too, because there is only one goal to teaching decoding skills: reading. Even when a child knows just a few letters and sounds, that child must read connected text using them. Therefore, the first building blocks must be chosen carefully so that they make up words, and must be taught as quickly as possible so that the student starts reading and writing those words. Sight words, the words that don't follow the phonetic rules, must be taught each session from the very beginning as well. Then, using the combination of sounds and words, the child must read. That is why there are such books as *Mac and Tab*, a very early phonic reader, and the *Bob Books*. Once it is possible to read words, phrases, and connected text, dyslexics must do so as often as possible; they need to read, reread, and read some more. Nothing makes reading easier and readers stronger than reading. I tell my students that they need to work those reading muscles just as much as they need to develop their muscles for soccer, to build them by using them.

At the same time that Cyp was learning the rules of the English language, rules that would eventually enable him to "break the code" and sound out those Latin- and Greek-based words that he did not know, he was also learning sight words, those mostly Anglo-Saxon concoctions that follow no rules and that must be memorized: words like *said,* and *the,* and *they* and *there,* and *would, could,* and *should,* and on and on. There is a method of teaching sight words that was developed at Teachers College that is foolproof. A drastic claim, but it's true. I have used it with little kids, middle kids, older kids, and adults. No one has been immune. It's called the Bryant Ld-Efficient Method of Sight Word Training, and it alone makes the gazillion dollars of tuition I paid to get my master's degree worth the money. There is a real system to this. Words are introduced on individual index cards, no more than five to seven at a time; they are taught and then drilled until recognized quickly and correctly three times, with immediate removal of those mastered to reduce what is known in the ed. game as "response competition." Then the words are taught again in phrases, then in sentences, and only after all that in connected prose. It sounds tedious, but it isn't. Anyone who is being taught by it realizes that it works, that they actually remember and recognize the words when next they meet them; even the most ADD types can concentrate on this one, believe me. With this method, Cyp built a body of sight words that he could read when he saw them again, and he learned phrases that he would read later in the book. Until he got used to the idea, each time he met one among the pages, he was surprised; it seemed like magic to him, the idea that he actually knew blocks of words from the book before he saw them there. His eyes would light up; he would stop, look at me, look at the book, point to the phrase, and silently ask me if I could believe that what I had just taught him he was actually finding in the text. Nothing before that had made much sense to him; now he had his first ideas about learning and his own ability to learn.

As he mastered and amassed them, Cyp also filed his words in alphabetical order in his special word box, which was decorated with new stickers each session. The boxes filled up and mounted up, making a colorful display of knowledge gained and rewards earned. He filled his work folders with pages and decorated them with stickers, too. The boxes and folders became visual symbols of effort, triumph, and pride. Often we would take a few minutes to look through them, review what was in them, and comment on how much he had accomplished, how far he had come.

Games are important for kids, too. A lot of mileage can be wrought from a few well-planned games. One regular for me is Concentration; some call it Memory; I now call it the Mercy Game. You've probably played it in one guise or another. In my version, index cards with words on them are facedown on the table; my opponent and I turn over two at a time and try to remember what is where so we can make matches. I pick the words and make up the game; I use it to give practice recognizing new or confusing words I want the child to learn and discriminating among those that look alike (such as *thought, through,* and *though*) or sound alike (such as *to, too,* and *two,* and *there, their,* and *they're*). Playful practice is better than monotonous drill any day, and much more motivating; the game is a cinch to rig, too. I want to make sure that the child wins so that she feels powerful and successful and looks forward to the next game, so I regularly turn over the cards I want her to see, actively expressing my dismay when she matches pair after pair after pair. It's always a great deal of fun for both of us, and I have never had anyone catch on to my tactics. Usually the children are too busy gathering up matches and then excitedly announcing to their mothers, who are arriving to pick them up, "I beat her again. I got seventeen and she only got four. I've won every game!" I used to tell one little girl whose sense of herself was as low as could be imagined that she was just merciless, that she just triumphed and triumphed and showed no mercy at all. She always grinned with pride, and after a year or so of hearing about it, she began to ask if we could play the Mercy Game. A while later, I asked her what she did to be so good at the game, and she replied, "I pay attention, and I concentrate; you always tell me I should!"

Card games are terrific, too, for reinforcing particular skills or rehearsing vocabulary—I have one that has lovely illustrations of animal families, and there are different kinds of games to be played, with the end result of the child learning the name for the male, the female, the baby, and the group of each creature. There are also two board games I wouldn't be without. One is called Sea of Vowels, and it gives practice with word retrieval and the short or long vowel sounds; each player draws a card with a picture on it, identifies the picture, sounds out the vowel, and moves to the corresponding letter on the board, which is designed like a body of water, complete with fish and squid and starfish. Eventually one player or another makes it to the sunken chest spilling over with gold and jewels and other riches. The other board game, for somewhat more advanced players, is White Water Raft Trip, a perilous journey fueled by knowledge of either word opposites or homonyms. This is particularly good because there is quite a bit of reading to do, and I always make my opponent do the work of both of us. Interestingly enough, there is very little balking at the extra effort; winning is worth it, and beating me is sublime.

There are many good verbal games to play, too, like Categories— going back and forth naming foods or sports or movies to a rhythm. This is great for organizing thoughts, for expressive language, for word retrieval, even for coordination if a clapping component is added. Another good one is In My Grandmother's Trunk, where you sequentially pack what you'll need for a trip. I also do some listening comprehension exercises for fun. These don't quite qualify as games, but I try to make them seem as much like them as possible. From one of the two *Reading and Thinking* books by Arthur J. Evans, I read a passage of appropriate difficulty, instructing the student to close his eyes and paint a mental picture of what I am reading. Then I ask questions about what I have read, all of which impel the student to draw inferences. The minute he "gets" how to do it, this becomes fun, like playing a guessing game, or putting a puzzle together, and he is beginning to learn to visualize, which can be enormously helpful throughout a dyslexic's academic career. Because they are so good for motivating students, I try to save about ten minutes at the end of most sessions for games. Or I take that time to read to the child a book we have selected from my shelves, one she could not possibly read himself. That is especially important if she is just pooped after working hard or if she is not read to regularly at home. Youngsters need to hear stories and language that are more sophisticated than what they can read themselves. Listening to a parent read increases the child's knowledge, vocabulary, and familiarity with the conventions of the language, and, perhaps most important of all, it turns reading into a special, warm, and happy experience. Parents often underestimate the power of this shared time, though, and permit their busy schedules to crowd it out. So I can offer a substitute. This little pause in the tutoring-session action, this relief of pressure while still learning, gives a break, but a quality break.

Because sequencing is usually an issue for dyslexics, being able to automatically name the letters of the alphabet, the days of the week, the months of the year, and the seasons in their proper orders is something that needs regular attention. This is information that they have to have in their bones, to be able to access it with ease. With some students, five minutes at the beginning of each session is not too much; more than once, I have needed to spend that amount of time for a whole school year before the sequences became solid. Of course, we made games out of it, and it was time well spent. To be able to manipulate the letters of the alphabet properly, one must be able to say what letter is between *m* and *o,* what letter comes before *f,* which one comes after *s,* and so forth, and before, after, between, etc., are tricky concepts to master. One must also know that Sunday is after Saturday and before Monday, that Wednesday is the middle of the week, and that November comes immediately before December and after October. Songs help, and so do associations. Sometimes we work out specialized associations; other times they are built in. For instance, when asking for the months of the year in order, I remind students that this is the month you finish school, go back to school, eat turkey, dress up for Halloween. One boy could never remember the month of April; he always skipped from March to May, so we decided to call it the O'Neill month, for April O'Neill, the heroine of the Ninja Turtle movies.

Of all the devices, gimmicks, ploys, and rewards we use to prod students and motivate them into proficiency, the most important, for little kids, big kids, and absolutely everyone else, is success. Without a single doubt, I know that *nothing* succeeds like success. Nothing at all. Therefore, each tutoring session must be planned to ensure that the student experiences success, that she can do at least something well during that hour, so that she will have a chance to feel competent, so that she will develop a taste for that feeling and want more and more. Also, remember that this group does not enjoy much success in class-work, and remember how much time students spend doing classwork, in school and at home. Their jobs are more time-consuming than many adults' jobs, so there are many hours each day, many days each year, when they feel unsuccessful and inept. The few hours spent in tutoring must start to turn around those feelings, and the only way to do so is with success born of achievement, valid achievement. No condescend-ing feel-good stuff here; it must be the real McCoy to work, and the students all know what is real and what is not.

Cyp discovered things he could do every session, and every session he also read books. Maybe he didn't start with an epic, but if you've never read *The Adventures of Mel and Tess,* don't knock it. These are phonic readers; they come after such tomes as *The Tin Man* and *Ed,* a quite charming little story about Ed the Elephant. Each book rein-forced the sound the youngster was learning to read and write and added new sounds carefully, along with new sight words. The number of books he was able to finish grew and grew—and he had to read everything two times because the research has shown that repeated readings are very important for dyslexics (once for decoding and figur-ing out the words, and once again for discovering what they mean).

There is great hue and cry about making sure that reading materi-als are relevant and interesting to each and every student. What defines relevant and interesting, as far as I can see, is what can be accessed, what can actually be read. If it's too hard, how interesting can it be? The triumph of finishing a book certifies readers. One seven-year-old girl I taught couldn't believe it the first time she read an entire book in one session; she felt very grown-up and very much like a genius. Maybe not a whole lot happens to Mel and Tess, but children can read the books correctly and quite quickly. I've used them with many students; not a single one has been bored, and more than a few have really got-ten into it and eagerly awaited the next adventure.

Another effective text is a first-grade-level book called *Sniff.* It's one of my all-time favorites. It was written in 1937 and is unfortunately now out of print. No student I've taught has ever found it dull. It's about a Scottish terrier named for his devout interest in sniffing and sniffing around, and it is 175 pages long. It has the appeal and the heft of that lofty, far-off goal, the "chapter book." It is a perfectly written book: it introduces words and then repeats and repeats them; it builds in sentence length, going on to the next line and then the next page; it builds in chapter length; it shrinks in text size. It seems easy for a while and then presents a word like *gnaw,* as in "Sniff gnaws a bone," so that the little people can brag about knowing a difficult and arcane word such as *gnaw.* It's just about ideal, but it's not too heavy on plot. The dog arrives home; he eats and drinks and rolls in the grass; he gets a name, a leash, a license, and a new bed. He gets sick, goes to the vet, and gets better; and he turns four months old. At each stage along the way, Mother consults her dog book to find out just what to do for Sniff. And that is just about it. Riveting, you wouldn't call it, and you might have some difficulty finding its relevance as well, although early training in being a good pet owner never hurt anyone, nor does realizing that books have all the answers we need, and that all we must do is look them up.

Now let me tell you about Josh—smart, dyslexic, ADD, and blessed with the best instincts of any child I have ever known. (How many boys pick their favorite baseball player because they respect his hard work? Josh did, Mo Vaughn.) He is a serious boy, but also funny, kind, and earnest. Josh just finished second grade; we see each other in the summer. His first summer with me, after first grade, we started *Sniff* but didn't have enough time to finish it. When Josh arrived for his first session after he had finished second grade, he cried out that he couldn't wait to read more of "Sniffy," so we did. But he was too advanced for the book, I thought, and I wanted him to read something harder, to learn more and push himself a bit. At our second session, I said I had a suggestion, and it was that we stop reading *Sniff* and read something a bit more complicated, because he had learned so much during the school year that I thought he needed a more sophisticated book. He listened, thought about it, and said that it would be okay to read something else, but then what happened to Sniff would always remain a mystery. See what I mean about what is interesting to whom? We reached a compromise; I sent *Sniff* home with Josh so that he could read it to his younger brother, and he and I took on *The Sword in the Tree,* an early-level Arthurian tale by the prolific and brilliant Clyde Robert Bulla. It was perfect for a boy with such a refined sense of fairness; noble knights are right up his alley.

When working with dyslexics, it's important to introduce nonfiction, expository text as early as possible (one can gather up some fine materials that are appropriate for as young as a second-grade-level reader, and there are some sources even for first-graders) and to get them thinking about information, about geography, about happenings and peoples and cultures around the world, so that they can start to build up background knowledge. The earliest subject that seems to pique the interest of new readers is the animal kingdom; few first-, second-, or third-graders can claim no interest in critters. Sports has its place, too. From both of those can grow geography and history. What is key is to turn the child on, light the fire of curiosity, and then help him feed it with books and magazines.

Cyprian's first information turn-on was a book about barn owls, which was illustrated with haunting drawings. He was enchanted; he wanted to learn all he could about them, and he did, by reading many more pages and many more sources than he ever thought he could. With Stephen it was birds in general. When he was in third grade, we took a trip to the library. We selected a number of bird books, he read some of the information aloud to me, I read some aloud to him, and we constructed a research paper that we both are still proud of. With Jonathan it was basketball. The fascination this small, skinny fourth-grader had with the speed and grace of those towering hulks spurred him on to gather clips and promotional material and write a very respectable profile of the Shaq.

It's also important for parents, grandparents, and other caregivers to help the child build up a store of knowledge and to feed curiosity through experiences—cultural, natural, and otherwise. Walks in the woods or park with observing eyes and easy talk about trees and leaves and bark and whatever else presents itself; CDs of all sorts of music played on all sorts of instruments with more talk about what the violin looks like, how the saxophone came into existence; art books with understandable pictures and more talk about colors and the lives of, say, Picasso or van Gogh or Andy Warhol; trips to the firehouse with discussions about equipment and dalmatians, or on trains or ferryboats with descriptions of how they've changed over the years. All the adventures of living should be experienced regularly by these folks who learn so well by seeing and feeling and hearing. It really helps their reading, in more ways than one.

Dyslexics usually have trouble comprehending what they read

not because they have difficulty with understanding in general, but because they have trouble decoding the words. If you can't read the words, or if you use up all your cognitive energies in decoding the words, you won't be able to understand what they are saying. (That is why reading everything twice is so important for struggling beginning readers.) Bringing more varied general understanding to their reading makes recognizing or decoding the actual words easier for dyslexics because they can anticipate them, have some notion of what the words should be. Understanding the text also becomes much easier because they have a framework on which to hang what the words say. An added benefit from increased experience is that they do not have to learn *everything* from the words; they start the books with some already-established knowledge. I have a teenaged student whose parents have been the most committed of any to giving their son chances to learn through doing, and they have done a fabulous job of it. As a family, they listen to live opera on the radio together; they go to plays together; the boy knits sweaters with his mother, raises pigs and grows vegetables with his father, takes dance lessons with his brother, and goes on trips with his grandmother. He has a great deal he can bring to the act of reading.

Reading comprehension requires the homing in on the trees of essential information and avoiding getting lost in the surrounding forest of less important data. This is always a challenge for the dyslexic, but there are ways to help. It's possible to teach skills from a very early age that will enable the student to control the text better, organize his thoughts, and focus more accurately. It can be daunting in the beginning to a young dyslexic who is not used to being in charge. I remember the first *KWL* chart I ever did with Cyprian—it took forever, and he was totally spent at the end. He was in third grade. I gave him a choice of three subjects; I had short passages about each. He selected cheetahs. Before this we had looked at several picture books on the subject (including one called *Cats of Africa*, with photographs by someone I had worked with at *Life*), and he had already learned some facts about these astonishing sprinters. I gave him a four-paragraph article to read, but first I introduced a strategy that I planned he would eventually internalize. We made a list (he talked; I wrote) of everything he already Knew about cheetahs, then a list of what he Wanted to find out about them. When he had decided that the lists were complete, he read the article, looking particularly for the information that would answer his questions. After finishing the reading, we completed the third list, adding what new facts he had *Learned* about cheetahs. *Know-Want* to know-*Learned*. It's a potent exercise. We activated his background knowledge, we created a framework of questions to ask the text, and we reviewed what information he had gleaned, discussing how many of his questions were answered by the passage, how many were not, and what other things he learned for which he had not thought up questions. That was the first time; we made KWL charts time and time again, and they helped.

Passivity is the enemy of the dyslexic, and it lurks around all sorts of corners. If anything, dyslexics need to be more active, more engaged, more aggressive about demanding meaning from text than others, but it's very hard to be active when you feel defeated. Few have the desire, drive, and energy that Josh does. Many feel beaten before they start; they convince themselves that they won't be able to do it, and so it's not really worth the effort. And the resulting passivity is death to reading comprehension. It also feeds on itself. Unfortunately, the same rule holds true for failure that governs success: nothing begets failure as efficiently as failure. Early instruction in comprehension measures like KWLs helps nip this growing malaise; reciprocal teaching is another fine strategy that engenders active reading and improved comprehension. It's the best for turning languid readers into dynamic ones. It requires demonstration by the teacher, what is called "modeling" in the ed. game, and the transfer of skills and control to the student. The relationship is reciprocal; first the teacher teaches, and then the student. It's wonderful for those who are aching to be in charge, much more difficult for those who are exceedingly shy, but it banishes passivity. There are four stages, each of which the student sees modeled by the teacher before being expected to fulfill himself: questioning, summarizing, predicting, and clarifying. It's a great deal like making a KWL chart, only more so; it adds an element of oversight, of management, of what is called metacognition, because each stage is carefully discussed in terms of how it helps readers solve the problems that hinder their comprehension. The goal is to have the student read and understand more clearly and to develop self-monitoring skills. This is another area that is problematic for dyslexics. Often they don't know what they don't know, so it is very important to instill in them the abilities and the mind-set that will make it possible for them to take charge of their own educations.

Many dyslexic youngsters feel they can't take charge of much, that they have little or no control over themselves, their learning, or their lives. To compensate, they sometimes try to wrest control of something or some situation, often in inappropriate ways. To give some measure of choice and practice in exerting authority in an appropriate way within the highly structured environment of a remedial session, I usually recite a list of the tasks we need to accomplish at the outset and ask the child to set the order of attack. That way she can get used to deciding whether to do the most difficult task first and save the most fun for last, or vice versa, whichever suits her style better. Doing this has a certain power and gives the mostly impotent student some voice and a somewhat more vested interest in what we do. There are children who relish this chance to be partially in charge and a bit directive; others are so infused with the feeling that they lack control that it takes them a while to get used to setting the agenda in any way.

Every remedial session should include instruction in writing, in forming letters for the young ones and in composition for young, middle, and older. Correct handwriting practice is easy to include with the dictation, so you can be teaching decoding, spelling, and handwriting all at one time. Print or script, manuscript or cursive, that is the question. Some say that children must learn to write manuscript letters before they learn cursive, or their reading will be impaired, that because they read print letters, they must write print letters, or they will be confused. Diana King would say "Hooey" to that, if she were the type of person who said "Hooey," which she is not. However, she always taught cursive from first grade on, which is when children really start to learn to write at all, and she taught dyslexics exclusively (except when teaching teachers how to teach dyslexics). In addition, she has written some excellent materials on teaching cursive to both right- and left-handed students, so her opinion on the subject carries a great deal of weight. Cursive flows more easily. It is more difficult—though not impossible—to reverse letters when writing cursive, mostly because the letters connect to each other and all go in the same direction, and she would posit that skipping manuscript and starting right off with cursive does not interfere with their reading at all, that they can separate the two functions without getting confused.

Whether you teach cursive or manuscript, if you are tutoring the child and not teaching her in a school, you must choose the method that she is expected to use in school, or you really will confuse her. That settled, the next step is to get her seated properly. Correct posture is important when learning how to write. Feet should be on the floor, both hands should be available—one to do the writing and the other to hold the paper—and properly lined paper should be used. The correct spacing of the lines is important, wider for younger students, with a narrowing of width as they get older, and there must be the middle dotted line so that the student has guidelines to help her learn how to form correctly sized, spaced, and proportioned letters of either variety. If you are teaching cursive, and the student has trouble with the correct slant, fold under a corner and line up the crease with the desk; this will slant the paper, either to the right or left depending on which hand is being used to write, and make life much easier. If the student holds the pencil in anything but what is called a tripod grip—if there is a thumb wrapped over the top, or two fingers on top, or if he uses a death grip, clutching the implement as though it were a life raft—bring out the old plastic or rubber pencil grip and slip it on the pencil; it will force him to place his fingers correctly. If he moans and groans about how he can't possibly write that way, scare him with tales of taking class notes in high school and the mortal pain he will experience if he doesn't develop a more efficient way of writing.

Teaching how to write stories, essays, and reports is a more complicated matter. One powerful tool I use with young students comes under the heading of language experience. The student dictates the story, poem, or whatever to me, and I enter it into my computer in nice eighteen-point Palatino type and print it on my lovely laser printer. Freed from the act of getting the words down on paper in some recognizable form, students produce much more sophisticated work, because they are relying on their speaking abilities, which are way ahead of their reading or writing abilities. Sometimes I sit at the keyboard while the student is composing; other times I take it down as dictation and type it up when the session is over. I make this choice individually; sometimes the act of watching me type is too distracting, and the student can't produce the most interesting results. What this does for kids is make them realize that even though they have trouble reading, and even though they can't sit down and write out much of a story at all, they can actually create much more and much better than they ever thought they could. There is an added bonus as well. After I have typed up the story/poem/essay, I give it to the student to read. At first he is stunned and claims that he can't possibly read it; it's too hard. However, because he is reading his own words, because he has true ownership of what he is reading, suddenly he can read material that is much more advanced than he could otherwise. The experience gives a strong boost to his sense of himself, and it gives his reading abilities and fluency a nudge, too.

The amount of direction and guidance I give during this exercise varies considerably. Sometimes I see if someone has something she wants to write about; other times I present a picture, or a wordless book, and the student writes a story based on what she sees. Sometimes I suggest an experience the child has just had—a trip, perhaps—and that becomes what we write about. Often poetry is the order of the day, and we create a book with eight or nine poems, an artistic cover, and no rhyming permitted. While I take down the dictation, I guide the speaker if things aren't making sense, or if the sequence of events is getting murky. When writer's block sets in, I read back what has been written so far, and the author usually gets unstuck. Sometimes these students are as lyrical as can be. Once I was taking down poems that a third-grade boy was dictating. He was doing one about snow; he became the snow and talked about what he would do, where he would fall. When he had a little trouble going on, I asked him, "What would you cover up if you were the snow?" and his next line was "If I were the snow, I would cover up bad luck."

That is a great way to start, but it is only a start. Dyslexics need real, systematic instruction in how to write, and they need lots of preparatory teaching as well. They need to understand grammar well enough to use it properly, though they certainly don't need to be able to spit back rules or tell anyone the uses of a gerund. They need to be able to construct proper sentences, simple and complex, with correct punctuation. (Concocting wacky stories using the game MadLibs is a great exercise for coaching students in the basic parts of speech and how to use them. And it's fun. A few minutes every third session or so can be a real aid in solidifying nouns, verbs, etc.) Then they need to be able to write topic sentences, to vary their sentences, to support their topic, and to conclude a paragraph. Mastering the five-sentence paragraph (topic, three supporting, concluding) is something they must pursue vigorously, and they can do so. I had a twelve-year-old student once who was severely dyslexic; she had had real trouble learning to read and to write, but she was very, very smart, and extremely tenacious, and in time she became the queen of the topic sentence, and the empress of the five-sentence paragraph. Mastering one paragraph is a great incentive to go on to the next and the next and the next, and this young lady was determined to do so. Because of her hard work, she also learned to write quite successful, well-reasoned essays and reports. It doesn't happen quickly, though. It takes a long time; it takes much demonstration, many different-colored markers, and other visual aids. But there are good published materials to help, particularly those written by Diana King. She has two levels of Writing Skills books, both invaluable, and a very comprehensive manual especially for teenaged dyslexics entitled *Writing Skills for the Adolescent.* Writing—creative writing, essay writing, book report writing, letter writing, and journal writing—is where technology can make a huge difference. Many dyslexics are freed enormously when they get to the computer.

Telling time is an important concept for dyslexics to master, whether they have digital watches or not, and a difficult one; the circular concept of time-telling can be dizzying, and a proper grasp of such notions as before and after can remain elusive. It needs to be fostered regularly, systematically, until mastered. Dyslexics also need to learn how to use words to make sense of the world, to develop reasoning skills. They need to understand that the order of the words in a sentence makes a difference to the meaning, that small words can affect meaning quite drastically, that facts are different from opinions and how to tell the two apart. They need to be able to find the relationships in analogies and to construct their own. To do that, they need to be able to put things in categories, which also helps in determining what is the most important part of a passage and what are the vital and supporting details. Here those old word games will prove to have been helpful by starting the student thinking along grouping lines and about what goes with what. They need to learn how to go from part to whole and back again, or they will never be able to create an outline or its visual equivalent, a semantic map.

There are some outstanding printed materials, written by Joanne Carlisle, that target the development of these skills. She has written a series of workbooklike volumes that require writing; the first time I met her, I told her that I had the best luck using them orally with students so that we could concentrate on thinking and not get bogged down with forming letters, and she said she thought that was an ideal usage. I use her materials with a variety of students, but I have never enjoyed them any more than when I used them with Stephen. He was seven when we started together. He is a complicated boy, very smart, and he hated that he couldn't do things as well as the others. He felt so bad about himself that he was having a great deal of trouble getting along with his class-mates—of which there were only four—and his teachers had already designated him the troublemaker. Having been so labeled, he tried his best to live up to the designation. The world was too much for Stephen at that time; he was not a happy boy. When we started together, he was what psychologists would call well defended. He didn't want to let me in at all. Even so, tutoring sessions constitute quite an intimate rela-tionship, with just the two of us and my focus completely on the child, so I was hard to avoid. After a while, Stephen started to trust me, to realize he *could* do much more than he thought, given the right oppor-tunity, to enjoy himself a bit, to soften a little. Then there was the turn-ing point, the day when we sat at our worktable—at the right angle to each other that I prefer—and I felt his feet resting on mine. What a sweet moment! That was the beginning of what I think is still a won-derful relationship, six years later. Anyhow, Stephen always loved the work with the Carlisle materials—they were challenging, they were interesting, and they made him think without making him write. We would change where we sat, go to another room, sit on other chairs, and he would try to do all the exercises perfectly. Often he succeeded, which made him feel smart and able and mighty cool.

Just a small note. Even with the materials I find invaluable, I never use the entire book or workbook. I always pick and choose the parts that will work best with each child. It would never do just to barrel through page after page, and I'm sure the authors would agree with me.

Learning to follow directions, written and verbal, is one of the most important study skills any student can develop, and it's exceedingly important for dyslexics to make sure they understand the directions before beginning any project, test, or homework. I tackle this instruction in a few different ways. First I terrorize the student by telling the tale of my friend who was majoring in French in college and doing beautifully. At final exam time, she was overconfident; she finished early and thought she had done beautifully. Trouble was, she hadn't followed the directions properly and had translated the wrong passages. She flunked and had to repeat the course. That scares all ages and can be referred to long after the fear is forgotten: "Remember my friend? Now, you don't want that to happen to you."

In those same reasoning books, Joanne Carlisle has designed some nice direction-following exercises. They're complicated, they often require some minor drawing, and they're fun. They're particularly valuable, I think, for the student who hasn't yet developed the patience to insist on understanding before going forward, who prefers to just forge ahead and hope for the best, because they have to be done fairly slowly and very carefully. Students must learn to follow directions that they read and directions that they hear, so their listening skills must be developed. There are a number of ways to work on listening comprehension: read a passage to a child who has been told in advance some questions he will have to answer and have him raise his hand each time he hears an answer; give directions that have a flaw and train the student to find it; things like that. With young ones it's always fun to give a several-step list of things to do—scratch your nose, pull on your ear, walk to the door, touch it, come back, and give me a big smile—and see if they can do it. This is fun and good brain food, and three or four periodic run-throughs make a change in the proceedings while strengthening some key skills.

Changes in the proceedings are essential, and not just to keep things interesting, although that is important, too. Dyslexics overload if given too much at once. They need breaks; they need variety; they need to catch their breath even more than nondyslexics do. The tutor has to watch carefully and balance the content so that the student is stretched as much as possible, but not too far. I have seen a student overload only once in my life, but it's an extraordinary experience. You know how awful it is when your computer gets zapped by an electrical surge, and everything on your hard drive disappears? Well, this is almost the same. Not only does overloading make further learning impossible, but it wipes the slate clean of what has already been learned. It happened with Paul, my first student at the Teachers College clinic. There was no advance warning. I just took him one step too far, asked him to digest one bit of information too much. Suddenly he could do nothing, and he was completely exhausted; he seemed dazed. Everything we had done that session was lost, and we had to start over again the next time. Ever since then, I have been careful to plan the work for each remediation session so that we can stop every fifteen minutes or so and change gears.

After fifteen minutes of phonics, sight words, and dictation, we go to the book and read for fifteen minutes or more; what comes next varies but involves writing of some kind, then some reasoning or study skills, depending upon what the student really needs. Sometimes we concentrate on memorizing some poetry; sometimes we do assorted comprehension activities, or some basic math, like money changing, for those who are having difficulty. In between all this work, work, work, we pause for jumping jacks or some such kinesthetic activity for just a few seconds of refreshment. Sometimes it's just standing up and stretching, but jumping jacks are my favorite. They really clear the head and get the blood going—for both of us. I used to love to do them with Sebastian, who was studying karate and knew how to shout out the numbers, one through ten, in Japanese as we flailed around. For a while, Sebastian and Stephen spent a few minutes every third or fourth session dictating letters to each other, which I wrote in a special notebook and read to each of them. They were the same age but completely different types, with completely different ways of living, and it was fun and useful getting them to explain themselves to each other. They became pen pals of a sort. They enjoyed it, too, and when one Christmas vacation I arranged to take them both to lunch, it seemed more like a reunion of old friends than two ten-year-olds meeting for the first time.

Speaking of refreshment, that is another important part of any remediation session, particularly if work is taking place after school. Children arrive at my office starving—particularly any who are on medication for ADD, because they generally don't eat much lunch—so I always have a refrigerator filled with healthful kinds of snacks that they also like, good cookies, fruit, cheese, crackers, milk, and juice or Gatorade. Those years that I spent just three days in New York, my refrigerator was mighty odd looking. I rarely had "real" food; we ate out those nights, so it was filled with snacks, a kid's dream-come-true. Never underestimate the power of food as a motivator, though; Sebastian always knew that extra commitment to work earned an extra Apple Crumblie, his favorite snack. When the student arrives after a full day of school, I make a little time—only five minutes or so—for chatting and munching and catching up on what happened since last we met before we start to work. Then the food is removed, and there is no snacking during work time. The two activities are utterly separate. I think it's important for the children to develop good study habits, serious concentration, and respect for the task at hand, so food is gone, gum is thrown out, baseball caps are removed, toys are put away. I make time for all of these, but not at the same time that we work. One little girl has a brief show-and-tell before we get to work every time we meet. She always comes rushing in, saying breathlessly, "I have something to show you!" I enjoy looking at whatever it is as much as she enjoys showing it, and she is totally used to the idea of sharing whatever it is we are sharing, and then putting it away and getting down to work. A place and time for all things. Just as there should be a brief time at the beginning of each session for the child to say what is uppermost in his mind, every session should end with some token of appreciation for hard work well done. Stickers, baseball cards, whatever is more appealing to the child, give tangible evidence of progress.

Sessions for older students (and even adults) follow a similar philosophy but a different sort of rhythm. Jumping jacks, stickers, and dictated letters and poetry are out. Still, if they have not had good Orton-style instruction in the rules of the language, they need it. If they are adults who have not learned to read at literacy programs because of their disability, the tutor needs to give them the structure they need in ways they can accept it. If they are parents, sometimes teaching them to read children's books so they can read to their own children gives enough incentive to use these elementary titles. The tutor has to be very flexible, though, and really address the needs of the individual. If a person needs to learn to read manuals or other kinds of materials for his job, that is what the focus should be, and the method of instruction should be adapted accordingly. Adults' oral language capabilities and knowledge and experience of the world will be very different from youngsters' also, and those strengths should be used to aid their instruction. Sometimes there are keys that can unlock abilities that the adults don't even fathom they have; it's the tutor's job to find those keys if they exist.

If the older students had enough good early instruction to know the basics, then work on syllabication and roots and affixes comes next, especially if they are still having some decoding and spelling difficulties (which they probably are), and reading comprehension and writing become the main areas for attack. There are many approaches to improving comprehension; it is hoped that the somewhat older students have had some reciprocal teaching and some organizing instruction like KWLs by the time they are in, say, fourth grade. If not, that is where I would start. A method known as SQRRR—survey, question, read, recite, review—rears its head with older students. It's a means of creating a framework for understanding difficult material and for increasing the active involvement of the student. It's particularly good for textbook reading, for history or science. It seems tedious at first to most young scholars, because they are used to jumping in and just starting to read without thinking about it, whereas SQRRR demands that they look over the selection first, at the bold print, at the questions at the end, at the first sentences of paragraphs, at charts and graphs, etc., and formulate some questions about what they're going to read and then try to answer them during the reading. It sounds as if it would add hours to any assignment, but in fact it decreases the time spent because it is spent more efficiently. Instead of reading a chapter four or five times, following the SQRRR steps makes it possible to get meaning in one better systematized go-through.

Once I taught a class of ninth-grade study skills. The twice-weekly course was not optional; it began in January, and it was for students who had bumped into difficulties in the fall. Imagine how thrilled they were to add a new class to what they felt was already an overloaded schedule; imagine how hard they wanted to work after they discovered they were not to receive grades in the class. They were straight about it, though, saying that they just couldn't work as hard in this class as they had to in ones that counted for their records. I had to respect that. I explained SQRRR to them; we took out their history books and did some of their homework using the technique. The next session, we did the same thing. One student kept her head on her desk or stared hauntingly into space most of the time, but seemed actually to be listening, though not actively engaged. Some of the dozen or so other students saw the merit in the method, adopted it, and said it helped them. That seemed to fan the flame of interest in my tired friend, who promised me she would really give it a try at home, and more than once. A few weeks later, she came running up to me in the hall, excited and more energetic than I had ever seen her. "It works!" she exclaimed, and showed me the B+ she had received on her most recent quiz as proof.

Summarizing is another important skill for dyslexics. It can be taught from the very beginning, but older students usually need more practice, plus they have to be able to summarize quite dense material. Rebecca learned to summarize paragraph by paragraph and write a sentence or two for each. It made a huge difference to her comprehension of some very difficult critical writing, and it helped her contain the material and not feel as though she were drowning in a sea of commentary she couldn't understand.

Rewriting is an idea that has little currency with dyslexics, but one that they must learn to live with, if not love. Often it is such a chore for them to get the words down on paper in the first place that the notion of going through them and changing them is the least-appealing assignment they can imagine. Also, it is often difficult for them to figure out how to improve a piece of writing, to know what it needs. Here again I tell a tale—this time of Ernest Hemingway, who wrote twenty-nine endings to one of his novels before settling on just one. This example of doing it again and again by someone who actually was able to change the way Americans wrote impresses them. And then I teach them what to look for, how to look for it, and how to manage all the elements. They learn to proofread several times and not try to look for everything in one read; they learn to assess the sense and completeness of what they have and then to check the grammar, paragraphing, and punctuation; and they learn to read one time from last word to first to check for spelling, even after using Spellcheck.

Lest this sound like all these elements can be easily put together to form a nice, neat little whole, let me assure you they can't. One of the most constant facts of dyslexics is change: some days they can work to unexpected lengths and triumphs; other days getting small amounts of work accomplished is all they can manage. But progress comes, sometimes in bits, sometimes in lurches, but it comes. I worked with a young woman named Lauren all through her high school years. We became very close, and I had great joy in watching her develop as a student and as a person. When we started together, she had enormous difficulty writing, and some residual trouble with reading. Motivation was also an issue. She took a measure of pleasure in being considered somewhat sassy and naughty by her teachers; she had a genuine fear of being thought of as a Goody Two-Shoes. At heart, though, she was always a fine person, kind, loyal, and caring, but she needed some time to work through the events of adolescence. She finished high school last June; we worked together on her last papers. The difference between those and the work of just a year before was astounding; she had come very far. She was able to take charge of the material, to be confident about her point of view and her ability to support it, and to turn some lovely phrases with no assistance. We basically organized what she needed, made outlines together, and she did the rest. At her graduation, I almost burst with pleasure and pride; she was so beautiful and so together, it made my heart sing.

CHAPTER EIGHT

Technology and the Dyslexic

Computers Can Help

I WAS A REPORTER at *Sports Illustrated* in the seventies, when the magazine made its first commitment to computers. In those days, everyone used typewriters when working in the office, but portable computers—they bore no resemblance to laptops, they were so big and heavy—were newly available, and they made life much easier for the strong-armed technophiles among us who were regularly on the road, attending games and writing to very tight deadlines. There were some editors, though, who thought the ease of producing words with the new technology actually interfered with some of their writers' prose, that the speed with which it had become possible to change words or phrases and even move about blocks of text made for less thoughtful construction of articles.

Two decades later, there are still some editors who continue to value computer-generated articles less than more slowly crafted paragraphs, but very, very few. Now, at the turn of the twenty-first century, *Sports Illustrated* writers and reporters regularly use laptops, and the magazine is even designed and printed by computer. Business people, doctors, housewives, actors, and students all use PC's all the time now as well; the machines have become facts of life in most of our homes and offices. There is, however, an ongoing debate about their real value in schools, particularly in the lower grades. Many say that computers motivate children and prepare them for high-tech futures, and that it's almost never too early to start youngsters on the road to computer literacy. It's true that careers and futures are getting more and more high-tech; a U.S. government report estimated that by the year 2000, 60 percent of the nation's jobs will require computer skills. It's also true that children take to computers much more naturally than many adults do; in response, elementary schools have been computerizing at a frantic pace. Rich philanthropists have donated major money—at one school the gift was to be spent within the very few years that the donor's grandson was enrolled—businesses have provided hardware and software for schools, and districts around the country have found caches of cash with which to join the technological bandwagon and be up and cruising on the Internet. This commitment to the future unfortunately has often come at the expense of programs of the past—arts programs, athletics, and field trips. Has the money been worth it? The results have so far been very mixed.

Even very young children take to computers readily, easily, and happily. What they gain is not clear, however. The quality of the games they play and what they learn from them is in serious question. And there are some who say that the only skill developed by becoming adept at getting around a computer screen is that required of an air-traffic controller. Still, some teachers are joyous about the work produced by their students with the aid of the computer; other educators worry about the substitution of computer time at young ages for more three-dimensional, hands-on types of instruction. There are teachers who rave about the fluency with which their students write on the computer; others find that the speed and the use of "cut and paste" permits their students to move thoughts around at will without worrying about linking them properly (shades of those *Sports Illustrated* editors). Several fourth-grade teachers I know have found their students' writing output on the computer to be thinner in content and shorter in length than what they had previously produced by hand, and so are minimizing the time they spend on the computer in favor of more attention paid to learning organization of thoughts and the rich vocabulary needed to express them. Their distress about their students' messy handwriting has also prompted them to substitute penmanship for some of the time spent on keyboarding practice. They feel the keyboarding can wait for a year, but that the poor handwriting will be locked in if not addressed immediately.

Most agree that the best results from computer use have come in the high school grades, particularly when students are fluent at using the computer as a word processor. And the one group that has consistently shown benefits from computer use is the learning disabled population, 85 percent of whom are dyslexic. The computer is certainly one of the dyslexic's closest allies; the benefits of using a computer for a dyslexic student are varied and sometimes surprising. Students can use computers to help show what they really know and how they can really think, which can be so much more difficult when handwriting is required. Organization of thoughts, words, and entire papers is much easier with computers; designing graphics on computers is a very dyslexic-friendly task, and the Net offers reams of research opportunities for skilled surfers. Dyslexic students improve their communication skills drastically when they begin to use computers, and even professionals use computers to compensate for their dyslexia-based difficulties in diverse and creative ways, many even finding the cyberworld an inviting place to spend some career time.

The Forman School is a grades-nine-through-twelve college preparatory academy especially for language-based learning disabled students in Litchfield, Connecticut. Says Tom Hunt, chairman of the Language Training Department, "We have some classic, textbook dyslexic students here, but we also have some who can decode words okay but who have trouble remembering, who have trouble taking notes because of their grapho-motor difficulties, and who have great trouble with organization." Forman has had a computer lab for writing since 1986; it was begun under the aegis of technology guru and Dyslexia Association regular Richard Wanderman. Tim Shaw is the current director of the almost-always-filled lab; he says it was the Mac and its GUI, Graphical User Interface, that made the difference for Forman's pupils and for other LD students. Before Macs and GUI, there were IBMs with DOS and strange commands and other things in odd language to remember and type—and that was just to get started using the darn things. Suddenly, with Macs, there were ways to access the word processing without having to remember arcane commands. There were pictures, icons. Just click on this icon or that icon, and start working. The previously intimidated became bold and inventive.

Once Forman's students were up and running with their Macs, says Shaw, "They really took to using computers for writing. You know, putting something down on paper was so arduous, and it seemed so permanent. The words seemed so permanent, and their mistakes seemed so permanent. With the computer they were not. It was easy to correct and correct." Shaw says that the printer was important, too. "Their papers started looking classy and professional," he says, adding, "and then they started thinking, 'My paper can *look* so good, I want it to *be* really good.' " There was a surprising bonus for Shaw and others at Forman once their students became regular computer users. They were delighted to find that the teens' reading and handwriting also showed improvement. After puzzling over possible causes for some time, they figured it out. "Feedback is so important," says Shaw, "and often letters look different every time an LD student writes them. So, seeing that the p stays the same each time he enters it into the computer, not having to go through that effort of re-creating it each time, gives regular feedback, and soon that student is solidifying the concept of p and other letters in his head. The visual feedback from the computer helps our students learn the physical makeup of the letters."

Julia Bolus is a poet who teaches creative writing at Forman. Her life is words. She is constantly working on her own, she teaches others to write theirs, and on weekends she assists playwright Arthur Miller with his. Bolus is tiny, attractive, and youthful, with long brown hair and huge brown eyes. Her fully packed schedule never seems to distress her. She never gives the appearance of being rushed; rather, she seems to have time for all. Her voice is as small as she is, soft and gentle. On the telephone, she seems somewhat vague, maybe a little distracted. In person she has the directness, rigor, and intelligent intensity that she brings to her poetry—and to her teaching.

Bolus achieves wonders with her students at Forman, most of whom are there as a last chance, most of whom have experienced constant academic failure, particularly failure with writing. Mostly they also tower over her, but neither she nor they seem to notice. Under her guidance and with her inspiration, these students who had previously found the act of writing something close to impossible create and actually make books—covers, text, and all—and they publish a literary magazine with well-crafted and touching stories and poems. They also keep daily journals on the computer, with her encouragement. These journals are places for them to set down their own thoughts—for themselves, though, not for her or for anyone else. She reads them only when she is invited to do so. Often she has the students turn down the brightness levels of their screens when they are working on their journals, so that they can have complete privacy as they compose, and so that they are also not reading what they are writing and getting preoccupied with editing, with finding mistakes, misspellings, and miswordings. She finds the darkened screen often helps a student get more in touch with what he wants to say and frees him to get the words down on paper more easily. Bolus finds that computers really make the difference for her students; they make it possible for them to produce more writing and better writing than they could possibly do without them. "It's so much more interesting for them when they use the computers," she says, "and less painful. So they are able to put more into it. Also," she adds, "the multimedia presentations they can prepare with the computer can be so complex and intriguing that they draw their peers and other teachers into their subject, thereby getting instant positive feedback for their hard work."

In his 1995 book, *Being Digital*, Nicholas Negroponte, professor of media technology at MIT, *Wired* magazine columnist, and dyslexic, says, "Computing is not about computers anymore. It is about living." He goes on to discuss, among many other issues, the ease with which youngsters adapt to computers, using an experiment in Dakar, Senegal, where children who had no technology in their lives took to the machines with ease and sophistication, to prove his point. As to children with learning difficulties, Negroponte claims, "We may be a society with far fewer learning-disabled children and far more teaching-disabled environments than currently perceived. The computer changes this by making us more able to reach children with different learning and cognitive styles." He goes on to say, "Ten years from now, teenagers are more likely to enjoy a much richer panorama of options because the pursuit of intellectual achievement will not be tilted so much in favor of the bookworm, but instead cater to a wider range of cognitive styles, learning patterns and expressive behaviors."

Thomas G. West, writer, president of the Visualization Research Institute in Washington, D.C., and dyslexic, would tend to agree. He posits in lectures and in his book, *In the Mind's Eye*, that the skills mix of brains like his may indeed be the profile of the future. In the post-literate world he imagines, the dyslexic will be the champ. "According to West," says the book's jacket, "new developments in computer technology herald a significant shift toward the increased use of visual approaches to information analysis throughout our economy, in time affecting the fundamental nature of both education and work; he goes so far as to predict that creative visual thinkers, aided by computers, will be at the forefront of innovation in a dramatically changing society." In other words, every day we get closer to a world where the technology available will be ideal for the dyslexic brain, and the dyslexic brain will be ideal for the technology.

Tom West, son of Ron West and Elaine West Mitchell, isn't sure his or any other dyslexic brain is the brain of the future, but, he says, "I am sure it was the brain of the past, when everything was spatially or visually oriented, and there was no written language to confuse the issue." Tom is excited that somebody is writing about the possibilities for people whose brains work the way his does. He has learned to be proud of how his brain is wired, and he has always known that he could credit many of his strengths, as well as his language weaknesses, to his dyslexia, that some of his strongest abilities are directly attributable to it, like being able to think in three dimensions and to visualize completed complex mechanical models in his head with very little effort. Never mind that the two men have the same name; young mechanical engineer Tom West thinks author Tom West could easily be on the right track.

Cyprian, now in the ninth grade, is a big fan of Nicholas Negroponte's. (Cyp is not a reader for pleasure, because reading is not a pleasure—Negroponte says the same about himself—but he has read parts of *Being Digital* and thinks it's really cool.) A while ago, Cyp went with his parents to a talk Negroponte gave; he was one of very few children among the hundreds in attendance, and he was very enthusiastic about what he heard. It was as though Negroponte were speaking directly to him. Usually quite shy, the youngster greatly surprised his mother and father by raising his hand and asking the professor intelligent, on-target questions.

Whatever the future holds in terms of dyslexics and technology, whether they really will inherit the world and find that theirs are the best and most valued skills, is still unknown. Right now, though, there is clear evidence that teaching dyslexic students as early as feasible— third, fourth, or fifth grade—to correctly and easily use a keyboard, thereby putting them in charge of the computer as word processor, enhances their academic possibilities dramatically. Computers can't ruin or actually create writers, but they can make a big difference for those who have trouble wielding a pen or pencil in addition to getting their thoughts down coherently.

Says West family patriarch Ron, "The PC was my savior. Handwriting was never very difficult for me, but composing was a nightmare. The PC eased my way and allowed me to separate the creation process from creativity. With it I can worry about my thoughts first and then go back and work through the process."

Dyslexics should be able to take the computer as word processor for granted just as easily as the nearsighted and farsighted among us take eyeglasses for granted. It is important, though, that they know their way around the keyboard, that they are taught to touch-type so that they do not have to waste energy in hunting and pecking, in constantly thinking about each letter of each word and where the letters are. Knowing one's way around a keyboard is not an easy matter for dyslexics, however. Ever wonder about the logic behind the keyboard we use? Why it is so scrambled? Well, the simple reason is that early typewriters were very slow, much slower than human hands. Soon people were able to type faster than the typewriter could handle the input, and keys began to jam. So now we have this crazy-quilt lettering designed to slow the user down: *a s d f-j k l ;*—and that is only the home row. Just what a dyslexic needs to try to commit to memory! Enter Diana Hanbury King. We have already looked at the materials King has designed to teach dyslexics how to express themselves in writing. In addition to these invaluable aids, she has created an alphabetic system for learning to touch-type. It's so logical and makes so much sense that I think everyone should learn to type her way. It's also fast; students as young as nine or ten—the optimal developmental age to begin keyboarding—can learn where the letters are in one or two sessions. One starts with naming the fingers—pointer, middle, ring, pinkie, and thumb—and wiggling them around, then learns the placement of the first seven letters of the alphabet—all of which are for the left hand. Saying each letter aloud—"*a*, reach for *b*" (which one must)—while typing it and looking at the screen permits the information to enter the brain through the eyes, fingers, and ears all at once (there is that multisensory teaching again) and to work its way into the muscle memory of the student. With short, regular practice, the computer as word processor becomes a reality for any dyslexic, and, with assured control over the keyboard and the entering of material, the student is put in charge of the technology, a most important point, particularly for those who have used various sorts of "tutoring" programs, which tend to keep the computer in charge.

Computer use can contribute its fair share to the slide into that dreaded condition to which dyslexics are so susceptible, learned helplessness. If a child is sent to the computer all the time to be taught various skills for reading, that computer takes on a power that it should not be granted. It becomes the teacher and not just the tool on which to practice. The student can begin to think that the machine knows more than he does. Every student must be taught and reminded regularly that the machine is merely another device to make our lives easier, that he is the master of the machine and not the other way around. Too great a dependency on a computer is just as great a danger as too great a dependency on a parent, teacher, or tutor. It all adds up to that kind of helplessness that is not real, is not necessary, but can easily become entrenched: learned helplessness. Even older students can be over-reliant on the computer's capabilities, especially Spellcheck. Generally, spell-checking is essential for dyslexics, and a good computer Spellcheck is one of their greatest aids, helping them deal with one of their greatest challenges. Even it can be a trap, though. I have worked with more than one teenager who surrendered to his spelling weaknesses, who decided not to worry at all about spelling, not to try to get any word anywhere near correct, saying only, "Don't worry; Spellcheck will take care of it," as though Spellcheck were some powerful, mystical Aztec god of encoding. As we know, however, Spellcheck won't take care of it; it may be a great aid, but it is no god, and it is not perfect. The word being typed in must be somewhere in the vicinity of the desired word, or the computer can't check it. Too many of those wild configurations of letters, and the author ends up with gobbledygook, with or without Spellcheck.

Another example of students becoming too dependent on comput-

ers is the speed with which they grab papers out of the printer and
hand them right to the teacher, unread. They trust the technology
too much, and lose their command over it. They turn in papers with
spelling mistakes, grammar mistakes, missing lines, sections printed
twice—any number of errors that they might have spotted and corrected had they read what was belching out of the Deskwriter. I work
hard at convincing all my students to read every single paper they have
just printed three times before handing it in to any teacher—one reading for sense; one for grammar, punctuation, and paragraphing; and a
third time backward, from last word to first, isolating each word and
removing the context, for spelling; and I don't accept any paper from
any student in any school, fourth grade and above, that hasn't been
proofread just that way. It may sound tough, but every child, and most
particularly every dyslexic child, must be encouraged to take charge of
what he is doing and to take responsibility for it, to become self-reliant,
and not to rely on anyone or anything else too much.

Computers have made a huge difference in teenaged Cyprian's life,
particularly his academic life, though he loves the games as well. Cyp has
been quite computer literate since he was in fifth grade; he now has a
room at home especially to do his homework in and work on his computer; it's his "office." He can be found in that room, in front of that screen
almost more often than he can be found in front of that other flickering
screen, and even more often than he can be found fishing, his favorite
activity. Cyp has a very difficult time wielding a pen or pencil; it takes him
a long while to write things out. He finds the effort of writing by hand
exhausting, and when he is finished, he has a hard time reading what he
has written. Cyp learned the King method of keyboarding, and writing
is much easier for him and much less of a hindrance now. He knows very
well that the computer is a tool to make his life easier, and he takes full
advantage of the technology. He takes his laptop to school every day and
uses it for any writing chores—notes in history, writing about his reading in English, a science quiz—and at home he does his research on the
Internet or on CD-ROM encyclopedias, and looks up words in his computer's dictionary and thesaurus. His has all kinds of software to help him
make graphs and visual accompaniments to his papers, and his word processing software corrects frequent misspellings like *teh* automatically and
alerts him with a beep to words typed twice and other oft-made mistakes.

Says Cyp about his commitment to computers, "They make such a huge difference. Taking notes, for example. If I try to take notes in class, I have to struggle to keep up, and I have to look up at the teacher, then down at my notes, up at the board, down at my notes, up and down, up and down, constantly. It's enough to make me dizzy. With the computer, and because I can touch-type, I only have to look at the teacher or the board."

Mike Larkin, now in his early forties, found computers when he was a teenager, and has been devoted to them ever since, personally and professionally. In his home, he has laptops and PowerBooks and handheld Newtons and scanners and laser printers; he has a kitchen computer that controls the alarm system, that stores and dials telephone numbers, that turns lights and appliances on and off, and has the coffee ready for him when he gets up. His wristwatch even plugs into his computer. Professionally, he has installed computer systems and headed up computer service teams; he has designed computer graphics. He has worked at Hewlett-Packard, at Apple, and at Sega, and he has had his own computer consulting company. Granted, he did grow up in San Francisco and by high school was living in what soon was to be known as Silicon Valley, but it was Larkin's dyslexia that was the link between him and the new technology.

As a child, Mike was smart and verbal. He was blessed with intense powers of attention and a great memory. Everything he heard in his classes he could understand, store, and give back to his teachers verbally. But he couldn't read, and he couldn't write.

For years his teachers were puzzled. They gave him extra help, but it never worked. They didn't know about dyslexia and how to teach dyslexics, and they kept trying to teach him in the same way that they taught in their classrooms. Mike couldn't learn that way. He confounded them. They knew he was smart; they knew he did well in class discussions and that he was learning some of the material; and they liked him because he was good-looking, well dressed, well spoken, polite, funny, and charming. But his grades were poor, his tests disastrous, and his ability to deal with the written word nonexistent. No one knew what to do with him or about him. He was as confused as they were, and the only thing that kept him from feeling just ghastly about himself was that he was always very popular, was always a member of any group that the others kids wanted to join. There is that compensation again. Then his parents split up, and the cherished only child became the object of a very acrimonious custody battle—the end result of which was young Michael's being sent to a military boarding school at the tender age of twelve, where he stayed for four years, until anti–Vietnam War and antimilitary pressures (in addition to some internal scandals) caused the San Rafael Military Academy to fold. "Imagine," he says. "There it was, the Summer of Love in San Francisco—and there I was, in military school!"

When he first got to San Rafael, Mike was the most miserable preadolescent cadet imaginable, but after he realized that he had no choice—that he was there to stay and that he had better learn to survive—his intelligence and natural charm took over, and he quickly learned how to work the system to his advantage. Once again he became a member of the cool and hip; only this time it was the drill team, a group particularly favored by those in command. He took pride in the much snappier, parade-ready uniform he wore as a part of the team, and he greatly preferred being a member of an elite group of twelve to an ordinary group of fifty.

His next big move was when he discovered that the section to do best at inspections was put in charge of the coveted Coke machine. That bit of knowledge made him compulsive about dust and spit-shines. Power over access to Coca-Cola was power indeed in the intense teenaged quasi-military caste system, and Mike sought that dominance avidly and asserted it ingeniously. Everyone solicited him and his favors, and just about everyone also liked him; they didn't have to fake it. He was an amiable cadet, and he had and still has an agile sense of humor. By the middle of eighth grade, Mike was also six feet tall, having grown six and a half inches in that one school year, and he was a jock in addition to a member of the drill team—he ran on the cross-country team. He was "squared away"; he was liked by all the adults, and he was popular with his fellow cadets.

He was unable to do much about his lousy academic performance, however, because he still couldn't read or write. "Think about it," he says. "I was thirteen years old, and I didn't even read comic books. The only reason I could get by in school at all was that whatever the teacher said I got. I couldn't read the texts, I couldn't take notes, I couldn't take tests, and I couldn't write papers. What I could do, though, was listen and understand." Mike went to a Catholic college some miles away from the school for some testing and remediation by the nuns there, but, from what he described, it seems that they were doing that old-fashioned kind of training-the-eye-to-move-better-and-faster therapy that has been shown not to work. He read passages with parts of them fuzzed out; he sat in front of film strips of words; he had to re-create on paper images that were flashed in front of his eyes. None of it worked for Mike, either; he still couldn't read. Then, finally, enter Mrs. Hobart, assigned by a desperate head of the school to tutor Mike. At first he and Mrs. Hobart worked two days a week, and she helped him with his homework. Almost immediately she realized that this was not what he needed, and that to survive he would have to have much more. She is no longer alive, and Mike never knew what her training was, only that she had once taught, and that she had a child with some learning issues, but it is clear that Mrs. Hobart knew about dyslexia and knew just what to do for the young cadet. She somehow was able to test him herself and send the results somewhere to be scored and evaluated. They came back, and finally, the mystery was solved. Mike had a diagnosis: dyslexia.

Mrs. Hobart then set about giving him the right sort of remediation. She took him to a bookstore and found books that interested him and gave him reasons to want to read. She increased her time with him to four days a week, for at least two hours at a time. She taught him reams of sight words and how to memorize them; she taught him what the rules of sounding out words were; she taught him how to break words into syllables and how to use his finger to cover up all but one syllable at a time (which he still does); she taught him about prefixes and suffixes; and she had him read aloud to her hour after hour after hour. She taught him to read, and she gave him hope.

She gave Mike's mother hope, too, in the form of a book, *Developmental Language Disability—Adult Accomplishments of Dyslexic Boys,* by Margaret Byrd Rawson. The book describes a longitudinal study of a group of fifty-six boys, dyslexic and non, in one of the first schools to make a concerted effort to identify and remediate reading and writing difficulties; it was published in 1968. In it the author found that "dyslexic boys are not necessarily poor academic and occupational risks . . . in fact . . . [they] may be capable of average or even superior achievement." On the flyleaf of the book, Mrs. Larkin wrote her name and address, then "obtained to aid my son, Michael Larkin, to overcome his dyslexic problems." Mrs. Hobart helped him do just that. After some time of working with her, Mike's grades began to climb, and his view of himself grew along with them. By his last year at San Rafael, he was getting mostly A's and B's in his academic work. In fact, he finished his last semester there with a 4.0 GPA. Then the school closed down; Menlo Academy agreed to take the remaining students, and Mike learned what grade inflation was all about.

Menlo should have been easier in lots of ways. At the military school, the boys' characters were tested all the time, and the rules were many and strictly enforced. The kids had to keep each of their dresser drawers open just enough to catch dust on the tops and become inspection booby traps; they had to polish their brass buttons every day and their shoes every night. They were inspected regularly, almost constantly. At Menlo there were room checks but no inspections, and rooms were considered acceptable if clothes were in the closets and not on the floor. There was no running obstacle courses while carrying heavy guns and bayonets, and there was no rigid, military-style pecking order. These were no great benefits for Mike, though. "It's odd," he says, "but all those military school rules were in some way a comfort for me. They say that boys are either destroyed or made by military schools, and I was determined not to be destroyed. It seemed to me that they gave very clear instructions on how to be perfect in their eyes, and it was possible to follow those instructions and achieve what they wanted. At Menlo I actually missed that structure." Menlo was also much superior to San Rafael academically, and Mike found himself struggling anew. Yes, he could read now, but he still couldn't express himself on paper, and his test-taking skills were minimal. No one thought to give him extra time or any of the other accommodations students get today, so Mike had to go through the tortures of tests and exams. "True-or-false test questions were okay for me," he says, "and I could do some multiple choice and an occasional short answer. But essays were impossible." So were most writing assignments. Mike's A's and B's were turning into C's and D's, and his new confidence was slipping right along with them.

Then the Menlo prep school students were given access to time-sharing on a mainframe computer at nearby Menlo College. "What we had was like a rudimentary word processor," says Mike. "We had a keyboard, a telephone, and a roll of paper." This, however, was before there were such things as word processors, PCs, and sweet software like Word and Works and Claris. First Mike and his classmates played some games with the thing; then they had to learn a computer language, Basic; and then they had to learn how to program it so that they could use it in much the same way we now use our laptops, only more complicated. "It's amazing," he comments. "Learning a second language was always impossible for me. I just couldn't do it. I had tried Spanish, I had tried French, I had tried German, and I had tried Russian. I understood them all conceptually, and I started off each one with a bang, and did just fine as long as the class was limited to listening and talking. Then, as soon as grammar and structure entered the picture, it all became impossible. I learned Basic very easily, though, for a couple of reasons. First, computer languages have small vocabularies—there are not so many words to learn, and they can't be used so many different ways—and second, there is no real grammar or syntax to worry about. These languages should be the dyslexic's foreign tongue of choice," he concludes with a laugh.

Mike had never learned how to type, though, had never been taught. Papers were supposed to be handwritten back then, and it was not felt that boys really needed to learn to type anyhow. After all, they were never going to become secretaries. In his case, not knowing proper keyboarding didn't matter. In this primitive computer programming, Mike found his composing home. The typewriter didn't daunt him; he figured out how to hunt and peck, and it was easy for him to move those numbers about and get the machine to spew out his papers, one page at a time. He could also, of course, read the typed words much more easily than he could decipher his own handwriting. "I always had terrible handwriting on purpose," Mike comments poignantly. "If people couldn't read my handwriting, then they couldn't see my terrible spelling." It took Mike many more hours to write any sort of paper than it would have taken a nondyslexic; that is one of the unfortunate facts of academic life for the afflicted. But he didn't mind, because at last he was turning in written work that bore some resemblance to what he knew and what he wanted to say. "You know," he says, "everything about working with computers made it easier for me to write, but I think the main advantage they gave me was that I could fix and fix and fix my mistakes, and no one was involved but me and the machine. The computer doesn't care and doesn't tell anybody if you make five hundred errors. Then, when you finally show somebody what you've done, what you show is the corrected version. The errors are your own business and no one else's."

Mike's grades at Menlo improved enormously after he became proficient at working with the computer; the experience also gave him a glimpse of what he would choose as a career. When he started at Menlo College, he was unsure of what his major would be—whether business or architecture or engineering—but he was always sure about his fascination with technology. He always knew that whatever he did, he would do it with computers. While in college, he took care of his professor's Mac for him, he designed a network and installed equipment when the school was given a mainframe, and he worked in the computer center every semester. He even got a chance to work a second summer at Hewlett-Packard in a program designed to hire new young people each summer so that many would be able to have the same opportunity, and he convinced them they should keep him on the second year with an eloquent and impassioned letter that he wrote himself with no help. In fact, they were so impressed with his desire and his knowledge that Mike stayed on at H-P for the whole time he was an undergraduate. "During my time there, I spent a week or two at every single process for manufacturing semiconductors," he says. "I learned an enormous amount about the nuts and bolts, from the practical, not theoretical, side." By the time he graduated and he and some techno-chums decided to go into business together, Mike knew all he needed to know about the machines, and he became the director of operations for their time-sharing operation. "It was such fun," he recalls. "I had twenty solutions for every problem. All my experience had been really invaluable."

Nothing and no one stays stationary very long in Silicon Valley, though, and Mike soon found himself in the thick of where it was all happening, at Steve Jobs's Apple Computers, designing animation for the company's training and teaching programs. After several years there, he was lured away to become the manager of technical support at game-making central, Sega, where he had up to twenty-four people working for him at one time. It was exciting, and Mike Larkin was having fun, most of the time. There were difficult aspects, though. "I've always tried to stay away from jobs where there is too much writing," says Larkin, "but I found there were times when I would have liked to make my case for something in writing, when I would have been glad to get my entire argument down on paper rather than having to represent it in person. Also, when I figured out a particular answer to a thorny question, I wanted to write it up so that it could be read clearly by others and followed properly." Mike's forte always was solving sticky problems, though, so he put his logical mind to work and came up with a solution for himself. He hired technical writers to put his thoughts and words to paper. Problems disappear when you can find solutions.

Mike Larkin doesn't have to write academic papers anymore, and he has certainly figured out strategies for getting written what he needs to get written. He still finds putting words down on paper a humbling task, though. "Even if I have to leave a Post-it note for someone, I have to write it three or four times before I can say what I want to say." He doesn't have to do that very often, though. Now Mike works out of his state-of-the-art technologically equipped home, which, of course, also has those other accoutrements that come with the territory in California—citrus trees and a luxurious swimming pool. He is his own boss and his own secretary, and he has no writers at his right hand to get his words down correctly. So, once more, technology to the rescue. E-mail now gives him what his first experience with computers gave him—the time and privacy to compose his own thoughts and correct his own grammar and spelling—and he takes full advantage of all the software available. A particular favorite of his is an interactive spelling and grammar check that looks out for words you have told it to, that checks for spelling, grammar, and punctuation and makes different noises depending on what type of error it is alerting the user to, and that takes over everything in the computer and checks it all. "You can really leave me alone with this one," says Larkin.

Sometimes, though, there is nothing like a reliable, tactile, low-tech book. Mike Larkin carries around with him the same dog-eared pocket dictionary that he has used for twenty-five years, and he con-

sults it constantly. He has even highlighted words he looks up frequently, so he can get to them easily. Even the most modern of us need
our security blankets.

Computers are invaluable for offering varied ways for dyslexic students to get their thoughts down on paper and to be creative with
their writing, with graphics, scanned-in pictures, time lines, and animation. The machines help with organization as well, and offer the possibility of keeping weekly, monthly, and semester calendars right there
on their screens, to consult regularly. Cyprian does that; he finds it
much more accessible than the assignment calendar he used to write in
and then be unable to read what he had written. There are also all sorts
of computer software programs that are of aid especially to dyslexics,
from spelling checks that talk, to grammar checks that do the trick, to
programs that make outlines or maps, the visual sort of outlines that are
more accessible to the reading-impaired. There is even one program
that takes the information you give it, turns it into either an outline or
a map, and then follows your commands and goes back and forth
between the two, one minute looking like an outline and the next turning into a semantic map.

Computers and other machines can do the reading as well, scan-
ning books and reading them aloud while the person follows along with
the words on the screen. They are a bit cumbersome, though, as scan-
ning whole books can be tedious and somewhat iffy, and the programs
generally have synthesized voices, which can be off-putting. Still, seeing and hearing the words at the same time offers a student multisensory reading, which usually improves comprehension, without
incurring the cost of the time of a teacher or tutor. Studies have been
done with this kind of technology, focusing on middle school students
and college students and adults. The results have been somewhat
mixed, but generally they have shown that using these contraptions can
help dyslexics read faster and understand better.

If you are looking for assistance with writing, the software is right
on top of things. In addition to all the standard spelling and grammar
aids, which improve regularly in scope and ease of access, there are
programs that are designed for average consumers and are affordable
and available for your home PC that actually permit one to dictate into

the computer microphone in a normal voice at a normal speed and have the machine type up what is being said and present it on the screen. Like a simultaneous translation, only in one language. This program also allows the user to make corrections from spoken commands, and it learns from its mistakes, storing in its 30,000-word vocabulary memory those utterances used often and deleting those used very little. As I write, this is a brand-new product, so none of my students have used it as yet, but I have several whom I will encourage to get it as soon as they can. I already have them talking their papers and reports into tape recorders and then transcribing what they have taped. The new technology would eliminate the time spent in transcribing; what a find!

There are many other kinds of technology that are helpful to dyslexics, too, in addition to computers. The above-mentioned tape recorders, of course, and calculators are certainly indispensable, but I would guess that is true for the student population at large these days, not just for dyslexics. Digital watches make life easier, but I don't think they should be used until that elusive skill of time-telling is fully established. Otherwise, certain abstract concepts, such as the notion of the circularity of time, will not be understood and digested. Handheld spellers seem to be made for dyslexics, particularly the ones that pronounce the words as well as give definitions, synonyms, antonyms, and so forth.

One of the most valuable systems for dyslexics, though not exactly high-tech, is books on tape. Many, many classics that you or your child must read for English class are available at your local bookstore, and there are some establishments and mail-order houses that specialize in renting audiotapes. Many nondyslexics are hooked on taped books, particularly while riding in the car, and it's no wonder, especially when the work is read by some legendary actor. I remember getting a tape of *Frankenstein* for a student of mine who was never going to be able to get through the book in the time allotted and being totally transfixed myself by the drama Julie Harris added to the tale with her stunning and sympathetic reading. The richest source of books on tapes, though, is Reading for the Blind and Dyslexic. Notice the name change; it came some time ago, when the organization realized that the numbers had changed and that more than half of the people receiving books were getting them because of their reading disabilities, not because of vision problems. Again, it's not exactly high-tech—you receive a distinctive bulky tape recorder from them, which is the only machine that will play their tapes—but RFB&D has over 75,000 recorded volumes, including many, many textbooks in just about all subjects, plus fiction, drama, and poetry in more than just English, and computer and research manuals, and 3,000 new titles are added every year. Subscribing to the service requires an application form, documentation of existing vision problems or dyslexia, and a fee. For many it is money very well spent. Cyprian has used the service for some time now, and he finds the tapes helpful, especially for history.

There is one other source for listening to books, decidedly low-tech, but ever diligent and willing to repeat and repeat the words, and that is Mom. Mothers (and/or fathers) of dyslexics spend many hours helping their children with their homework, and reading the textbooks to them is one of the most beneficial things parents can do. Often there is so much reading of such dry and difficult material that many dyslexic students would never be able to get all the meaning they need out of those words in the time they have to read them. There should be a Mothers of Dyslexics Hall of Fame in honor of all the hours spent getting their children through the volumes they face. Valerie McCarthy's mother would have a special place of honor in such an establishment. Night after night, year after year, she read her daughter's textbooks to her, until Valerie reached eleventh grade and decided that she was going to start working for independence and spend whatever amount of time she needed to do her work on her own.

CHAPTER NINE

Colleges and Careers
for Dyslexics

Options and Futures

REBECCA TOMASINI wanted to go to Smith College from the first day she knew what college was. When she was little, she and her family sometimes drove through Northampton, Massachusetts, and her mother always pointed the campus out to her, rattling off names of some of the famous, important women who had gone there. "I knew," says Rebecca, "that Smith was where the smart and sassy women went. That was the place for me." As a child, Rebecca had every reason to believe she would join that elite group; she was smart, and she was sassy in the nicest meaning of the word. When it was time to apply to colleges, however, Rebecca had become more surly than sassy, and she had no proof that she was smart, although she was still convinced she was. The numbers didn't support her claim, though, not her grades and not her SAT scores. Smith was out of the question. The guidance counselors at her high school wanted Rebecca to forget about college completely; they thought she should go into the army instead, where she would learn the discipline needed to straighten her out. Rebecca had no intention of going into the military; life was hard enough as it was. So she went to a much less distinguished college than Smith, where the women were polite, obedient, traditional, and not the least bit sassy in any sense of the word.

Still Rebecca yearned for Smith. Finally she found the courage and applied, and, to her great surprise, was accepted, in spite of her negative numbers. Her first thought was "There must be some mistake," then "So what quota did I fill?" There was no mistake, and she was admitted under no quota, and in January of what would have been her senior year at the other school, Rebecca found herself starting as a junior at Smith. What was her first impression? "The students were the most overwhelming, most impressive collection of women I have ever met—in all ways," she says. The classes were intimidating as well. "It was hard to follow the discussions, they went so fast," says Rebecca, "and there was so much to read!"

And so much Latin to learn. Rebecca signed up for an intensive, daily course; she wanted Latin, and she needed it. But she couldn't learn it. She failed her first test and then she failed her second; her homework was disappointing as well. Finally, when she failed her third exam, she found written on the top, "Have you ever been tested for that catchall, dyslexia?" Rebecca, who had been well trained in high school to feel guilt and shame about her difficulties, immediately thought, "Oh, no. It's all my fault; I'm not doing the right thing." Her teacher persevered, taking her aside and asking, "Have you been tested yet?" Finally Rebecca could ignore her no longer, so she had herself tested and discovered she was dyslexic. Her Latin teacher began to work with her individually, and she reduced her assignment load as well. "She was just great. If the other students had twenty exercises to do, I had ten," says Rebecca. None of this came under the heading of official accommodations; all of it came under the heading of a caring teacher trying to make life possible for one of her bright, struggling students. Rebecca was even able to cry on this woman's shoulder, then and throughout her time at Smith. "Without Thalia," says Rebecca, "I would have dropped out. But she helped change my thinking from 'Oh, God, I'm so lucky to be here' to 'You know what? They're lucky to have me.' I got a C-plus in her class, not good, and it will follow me, but I didn't fail, and I sure came close to failing."

Walker Harman had his dream, too, and when he finally made it to New York and Marymount Manhattan College, he was relieved. At last he was on his own, at a "regular" school, without a phalanx of specialists and tutors monitoring his every breath. "It was the equivalent of going to another continent," he says. "Finally I was able to thrive." Walker was in a special program at Marymount, but it was very different from his last two years of high school—when all his instruction was one-on-one—or his few months at Landmark, which is a college specifically for the learning disabled. The Marymount program, for an extra $1,200 each semester, entitled him to tutoring and whatever other sorts of advice or intervention with his professors that he needed from the learning center. He wanted so intensely to be independent that he was determined to need as little as possible, and he succeeded.

Almost all his courses were "paper courses," with long term papers counting for a great portion of his grades and little or no in-class writing with its lethal-to-dyslexics time pressure. So, when I was his tutor, we spent most of our time editing the papers. It was important to let Walker decide how he wanted to spend our sessions together; he needed the control. He was well aware of what was essential for him to do well, and he'd certainly had enough experience with one-on-one instruction to know how to get the most out of our meetings. Sometimes we talked about his research or what approach he might take before he began to write, but far more often, he produced a draft on his own, and then we got together. "It was such a relief," he says. "When I had an assignment, instead of sitting down with my mother at the dining room table and talking for hours about how much I couldn't do, I made a pot of coffee, sat down, and wrote the paper. Then I dealt with the problems." The problems, in fact, were few. Walker could think and could organize his thoughts; his weaknesses were the typical smart dyslexic's weaknesses—grammar, paragraphing, spelling, some syntax. Usually vocabulary is added to that mix, but Walker had a well-developed body of words at his disposal. "If I hadn't had the learning center at Marymount," he says, "I think I would have been okay." Then he adds, "You know, it's a bit ironic, but in one way, it would have been good for me to stay at Landmark for a while longer. They teach outlining there until you're blue in the face, and I could have used that. I almost never make them. I know I should, and I mean to, but I am stubborn, and I keep thinking I don't need them. That was okay when I was an undergraduate, and I got A's on all my papers anyhow. Now, in law school, the writing is different. I should make one for every single writing assignment, because how crammed-full your work is with factual information is much more important than how gracefully you turn a phrase."

Walker was a theater major at Marymount; as such, he had to get up in front of his classmates and deliver monologues and scenes, and he frequently had to memorize lines. That is something else we worked on, his committing parts to memory, with me reading the other roles. Walker used a tape recorder as well as the script, and he developed really good techniques and memory powers. He had always thought, always been told, that his memory was weak; after four years of scene after scene, play after play, he became convinced of its strength. "Somehow, when you focus on the good things, the negatives seem less significant," he says, "and they almost truly become less significant."

There was one large difference between Walker and his colleagues in the theater department. After they finished working hard, groups of them went out together, bought some beer, and took long walks in Central Park, sipping and schmoozing. Walker never joined them. He had left his beer-drinking and schmoozing days behind him. He was interested in but one thing, doing well in school, and he was totally committed. "I didn't party in college at all," he comments. "I didn't do anything but study and act. I needed to concentrate, and I kept everybody pretty much at bay so I could keep my focus. That was one really good thing about the learning center. The people my age couldn't understand what was going on in my life, and at the learning center I could express myself without someone thinking that what I said was odd or that I was odd. I could kind of use it as a shrink center, too."

Having a place to go and let down all reserves is very important for dyslexic college students. At this point in their lives, they are finding out more about themselves than even their nondyslexic classmates are. They're taking on more responsibilities than they ever have before, making more decisions, and contending with many more situations, both academic and social, on their own, without the support of their former networks of adults. Their tensions are many, and they need a "safe" ear. Recently, at a conference at New York University, I heard a panel of LD college students discuss their experiences. Commented one, "The learning center helps me with stress and problems; I always have someone there who will listen to me gripe and complain."

The focus and concentration Walker had in college isn't always intact for dyslexic or otherwise LD college students. Like Walker, many have had much more structure, overseeing, and one-on-one assistance than their nondyslexic classmates, but unlike him, they can't always find the self-discipline to replace that supervision by others. Generally, dyslexic students have to put in much more time on their work than others do; they have to work harder and longer to achieve their best. Sometimes great grades offer reward and incentive to keep at it, but more regularly the huge effort results in marks that are something less than fabulous. It can seem so unfair; it can feel as though a mad, exhausting treading of water barely keeps a head afloat, particularly if one's roommate blithely skips along and ends up with a better average. It's hard to realize that this time-and-energy investment is just a fact of life, something that comes with the territory. And the realization doesn't always bring acceptance. Dyslexic students rebel as much as other students do, and sometimes they reject the notion that extra hard work has to be a fact of their lives. After all, it can be very discouraging to be slogging away when others are finished and having fun, particularly when the payoffs are just not there, and the parties are. So, temptation rears its seductive head, and there the young dyslexics are, without mother or father to check up on them, without tutor or teacher to call them on not being prepared, not doing their homework, not getting enough sleep. The siren song of the "fun group" can be just too alluring, and good sense can fly out the window. Commented one of the NYU students, "You have to have that division between partying and work. I didn't have it when I first started at another college, and I flunked out. Now my studies come first, no matter how long they take, and that is just it. That party is simply not worth it, I promise you. Take it from the voice of experience."

Loring Brinkerhoff, a consultant on higher education and disabilities, and the former director of the once-renowned LD program at Boston University, says that the most difficult adjustment for dyslexic and other LD college students is getting used to the freedom and lack of structure that they meet when they get there. Back when they were in high school, their academic schedules were regular and set, and they had tutors or other adults to help them make comprehensive study plans that took into account homework, quizzes, tests, exams, papers, and projects. They always knew what was expected of them and when it was expected. At many schools, they could turn in multiple drafts of papers for guidance and comments, and their teachers were always available for extra help as well. None of that carries over into postsecondary education. College students have to be able to manage their own time, and professors are much less available. Professors are not always so great about handing out syllabi, either, and when they do, they often indicate broad, general thoughts rather than specifically what will be covered, so the students can't always be really sure of what is coming up, which makes planning much harder. And college professors don't teach from the assigned texts, as many high school teachers do; students are supposed to make sense of those on their own, so there is no second chance at comprehending what can be very dense reading. (Commented a dyslexic student from Brown at another panel discussion, "We learn who the organized professors are and try and get them.")

As a rule, college professors are much more interested in the bigger picture than in the smaller pieces that make it up, and they are usually not very interested in learning styles, differences, or difficulties, so there is generally much less monitoring of daily work than there is in high school. It is assumed the students are doing what they need to do, and it is the student's responsibility to monitor himself. There are far fewer quizzes and tests, too, so students who are used to regular comment and feedback about how they are doing can get confused and end up with a somewhat less than realistic view of their standing. In addition, the tests that are given cover a great deal more ground, often from a number of sources, so the student has to be able to master more complex material and be able to relate disparate chunks each to the other. Moreover, there are many more straight lectures, lectures, lectures, and much more library research is required. To top it all off, there is a great deal less class time, a great deal more independent work, and, often, huge numbers of students in each class. It can be pretty overwhelming, and even more so for someone for whom self-motivation and organization are not guiding principles.

Preparation for college must start years before. Brinkerhoff suggests a schedule that begins in eighth grade and builds year by year, with a major concentration on giving the teenager independence and ownership of his own difficulty and turning him into his own advocate with his parents, his teachers, and his friends. Brinkerhoff points out how difficult it is for parents to fully inform their children about how they learn; they want to protect them from what they see as something that could be hurtful. On the other hand, once their little darlings are in college, their professors will challenge them to be able to explain just what their disabilities are, how they relate to that particular course, and why assorted combinations of accommodations will help them deal with it. The more the dyslexic student knows about how he learns, why he learns that way, and what he needs to produce his best performance, the better off he will be, not only in high school and college, but from the moment the diagnosis is made. It is my contention that keeping information from children, even with the best of intentions, creates shame and passivity. They know that you know; they wonder why you aren't telling them, and they decide that there is something so bad about them that it can't be discussed. Interestingly enough, all seven of the panelists at the NYU conference—and they were from a variety of schools—agreed that they wished they had started earlier to come to grips with who they were and how they learned, that they would have much preferred to have their parents and their high schools be more open about their problems. Remarked one, "Dealing with my learning disability in college has helped me realize who I *am* instead of who I am *supposed* to be."

Brinkerhoff also makes the point that it is important for dyslexic teens to try out some of the standard collegiate accommodations while they are still in high school, to see how they can use them and if they make a difference. He also encourages students to take as rigorous a course load as they can, to try out a foreign language in high school rather than in college because there is so much more support available at that time, and to consider whether extra time will be a benefit when taking college entrance exams. He suggests that by the time they are high school sophomores, they become familiar with all the kinds of technology that is available to assist dyslexic students, that they learn all about LD programs and colleges when they are juniors, and that they organize themselves thoroughly with the aid of advisors: that they put together a college interview preparation form to use during campus interviews, that they develop a personal transition file with copies of all their diagnostic information in it in addition to their grades, IEPs, and letters of recommendation. He urges sitting in on classes during campus visits, arranging to meet some dyslexic students as well as the services coordinator, and sending thank-you notes to all immediately after every visit. He even recommends that students find opportunities working or volunteering during the summers that will add variety to their application dossiers.

Even if a student follows Brinkerhoff's plan to the letter, the decision about how "out in the open" to be when applying to college can be delicate and can present the teenager with his first real identity crisis. Some, like Tom West, feel it's key to their experience to be accepted at a school without any mention of the disorder. Others, like Walker Harman, have had their difficulties play such a large part in their lives that not mentioning them would be like negating a portion of themselves. Still others want to make sure they get the accommodations due them under the law or enroll in special programs that provide services for extra fees (as Walker did). Some even focus on their learning difficulties in their application essays, usually discussing how they have come to terms with them. No matter what choice a dyslexic student makes, if he wants any adjustments at all, such as extended time, recorded books or lectures, and a quiet room for tests, he *must* make his disability known to the person in charge of evaluating such requests. He does not need to do so until he is accepted, but then he, not his parents, his grandparents, his tutor, or his karate sensei, must do so.

There are two laws that protect learning and otherwise disabled college students: Section 504 of the 1973 Rehabilitation Act and the 1990 Americans with Disabilities Act (ADA). They are very different from the Individuals with Disabilities Education Act, though, which is the legislation that covers elementary and secondary school students. Under IDEA teachers and others must seek out, find, diagnose, and remediate students in their care who have learning problems. Colleges are under no such obligation; in fact, under the law, they are not even allowed to ask an individual about his disability, in order to protect his privacy. It is entirely up to the student to self-identify and to provide the correct documentation, and then the college must provide "reasonable accommodations" in accordance with Section 504 and ADA; if the student doesn't come forward and seek assistance, the school has no obligation whatever. Parents are not encouraged to get involved with their children's daily college life, either, as they are earlier, and some-times the child has not been properly prepared to become his own advocate; he is not aware enough of his own learning disorder and how it affects him academically to speak for himself. Says attorney Jo Anne Simon, "Very often these kids got to college because their parents pushed; now it's the student who has the civil rights, not the parents. The child is so used to having the parents and the school be responsi-ble that he doesn't understand that he now has the responsibility."

Also unlike IDEA, both 504 and ADA are civil rights statutes; they come with no enticing federal funding. Their purpose is to end discrim-ination against the disabled in all areas of life; their underlying philoso-phy is to mandate equal access to what is being offered and to provide "reasonable accommodations" to make that access possible. They define an individual with a disability as someone who has a "physical or mental impairment which substantially limits a major life activity," and learning is considered a major life activity, so dyslexic students are enti-tled to appropriate and reasonable modifications. What is considered "reasonable" varies considerably from school to school, of course; stan-dard aids give assistance with note taking, with reading and writing, and with tests and exams. Specialized tutoring is not generally considered "reasonable," nor are speech and language therapy, occupational therapy, or counseling, all of which are provided students under IDEA. (Most campuses do have counseling centers, but there will not necessarily be someone at the center who knows about learning issues.) Jo Anne Simon used to be the services provider at Gallaudet College, which is a school for the deaf. No special accommodations were made at the school for people who couldn't hear, even though they certainly qualify under the law and would be entitled to support at most schools. At Gal-laudet, however, they were the "normal" population, and the school needed no special adjustments to teach them; requests for assistance came for other reasons.

Rebecca Tomasini's particular request for accommodation was unusual at Smith, and would probably have been anywhere else, as well. The school had had less experience than many in providing for students with learning problems, but they were happy to grant the standard benefits: extra time for papers and exams, reduced assign-ment lengths, note-takers and tape recorders, although they felt that granting the right to take three courses each semester instead of four would have been going too far. They were even willing to let Rebecca drop Latin and substitute any other course—even physical education—to fill out her credits. Language waivers are common at many colleges. At institutions where there is some knowledge about how difficult it can be for dyslexics to study another language, the administration does not force them to go through the tortures of failing again, and they are usually permitted to substitute a cultural course instead, such as studying French history instead of French. It's a logical way of dealing with the issue, even though it has come under criticism from some, most notably the president of Boston University. Rebecca insisted she not drop the language; she wanted to learn Latin. She knew she would need to have it to get into the graduate programs she planned to seek, and she felt that the school had an obligation to teach her and to figure out a way to help her learn it.

The summer after her first half year at Smith, Rebecca worked with me on reading and writing, with another person on study skills, and with a third on Latin. "By the end of that summer, I had pretty well worked out the grammar," she says. Then she went back to Smith and found herself in a Latin course that was lecture, lecture, lecture. She couldn't do it; she was on the verge of failing again. Her former teacher was supportive; together they explained that the classroom teaching was not working, and that there was no one in the academic tutoring center who had any LD or Latin credentials. They requested that the school go to the outside and find someone who was trained to tutor Rebecca so that she could learn Latin. The school said they couldn't do that. Says Rebecca, "At that point, I went ballistic," and she used her anger positively. She learned about the laws and her rights; she became adamant. She even worked her way right up to the top, to the president of the school. Eventually she triumphed, and by the end of December, Smith had provided her with a tutor, not just someone who was good in Latin, either, but someone who knew about dyslexia and who was able to adapt her teaching to the needs of her students. "She wasn't just good," says Rebecca, "she was passionate." The two worked together twice a week for about an hour at a time, more if needed, for the rest of the winter and the whole spring semester. She read to Rebecca, she taught her new ways to approach vocabulary, she worked with her on the imperfects until they were perfect, and Rebecca ended up writing essays on Latin poetry and getting a B- in the course.

The five colleges in the New England area around Smith had been struggling—and they continue to struggle—with figuring out ways to teach foreign languages to their dyslexic students, instead of offering waivers as their only accommodation, and Rebecca was asked to speak to a conference on dyslexia and second language acquisition. "It was funny," she says. "I was one of three students talking about how we had been affected by trying to learn a second language. I gave about a fifteen-minute spiel, and the response was overwhelming. There I was, after all my battles, with two professors fighting over who would sit next to me at lunch after the talk. Many of them couldn't believe I was dyslexic. In fact, nine and a half out of ten people I meet are surprised I'm dyslexic. It's amazing how little people know about dyslexia."

One college that has had quite a bit of practice dealing with dyslexics is Brown University. It all began with a dean who had a dyslexic child; she decided in 1984 that Brown should have a program, and that program should be public and mainstream and not cost a great deal of money. Brown was one of the first schools to ally with the then Orton Society; now there are about twenty Orton college affiliates in the United States and Canada, which means that on those twenty campuses, there is a student organization that is run by dyslexic students with support from the administration and faculty to supply basic services, like a place to meet, etc., and some mentoring. At Brown the first year the group of five wrote a booklet about dyslexia; now there are about two hundred members of the Students with Alternate Learning Styles organization, most with dyslexia, some with other diagnoses such as ADD, and they are very active in spreading the word about learning problems and in getting the whole community to realize how they affect those who have them.

Still, says Robert Shaw, the dean who oversees the activities of the LD students, "There are faculty members who say accommodations provide an unfair advantage." It's somewhat easier to make adjustments at Brown, though, because the school has a more flexible framework than many: there is no language requirement there, although about three quarters of the LD students try one, and any course can be taken pass/fail. Also, it is possible to take longer than four years to finish at

Brown without paying more tuition. Adding note-takers, extra time for tests, and alternate ways of testing is not the same giant leap it would be at a more rigid institution. Many of the Brown professors are willing to assess their students in ways that don't involve tests or papers, but it is up to the student to design the alternative, to come up with a way of showing what she has learned. One young man who was diagnosed dyslexic after his freshman year was permitted by an enlightened history professor to prepare an oral history with photographs instead of turning in three 15-page papers. Comments one LD student, "Brown is unusual in that it supports all kinds of students." Adds Robert Shaw, "All our professors provide accommodations, but they do so with differing amounts of grace." At other schools, declares Loring Brinkerhoff, "We have a long way to go in educating faculty."

About half of the LD students at Brown were diagnosed after they arrived at the school, just as Rebecca was at Smith. Also like Rebecca, many of them were diagnosed after bumping up against a foreign language. Not all, though. One bright young woman failed her first psychology exam, and her professor was totally puzzled. She said to the student, "I know you understand the material, but you just can't write. It's as though your first language isn't English . . . but we're not sure just what it is."

Signing Public Law 94-142 (the Education for All Handicapped Children Act) into effect meant that more and more dyslexic students would be identified, and during the 1980s, the number of diagnosed students in both public and private schools grew almost geometrically. By the 1990s, these kids were old enough to go to college, and the numbers there began to increase as well. According to statistics compiled by the American Council on Education, 2 percent of college freshmen identified themselves as learning disabled in 1991; the number was up to 3 percent by 1994. Dyslexics had long gone to college, as has been made eminently clear by Bruce Waterfall and others, but now many did so fully aware of and talking about their dyslexia, and asking for accommodations up front. Colleges and universities had to look at themselves and assess what they were doing and what they could do. They had to think about costs and facilities. They had to think about standards, and whether people would try to take advantage of them, and professors had to be convinced to think about their work in terms other than "I am an expert; I present the material; if and how you get it is your own concern."

Naturally, there was a backlash. There has been much talk of lowered standards, of the need for requiring a second or third language, and of growing numbers of students faking conditions just to get the benefits. It got so bad that the incoming president of Boston University, which had a program that had been a model for many other schools (and where there was an extra fee for all the services), charged immense abuse of the system, did away with language and math waivers, and demanded the students provide updated evaluations every three years. He even went so far as to tell as though it were true a story about a student dubbed Somnolent Samantha who, he said, had claimed she had a disability "in the area of auditory processing," which meant she would need copies of lectures notes, a seat in the front of the room, extra time on exams, and a separate room to take them in, and also that she might fall asleep in class and need to be filled in on material she missed while she dozed. But she didn't really exist. University president Jon Westling, who had earlier referred to learning disabled students as "genetic catastrophes," simply made up Somnolent Samantha, manufactured her to support his campaign against the disabled students. His fabrication helped the university lose a lawsuit filed by ten students who felt their civil rights had been trampled. Traditionally the courts have tried to work with organizations found in violation of the laws protecting the disabled, instead of punishing them harshly, so, rather than simply ordering BU to be more flexible about foreign language waivers, U.S. district judge Patti Saris instructed the university to re-evaluate its position on not granting them and to report back to her. In her decision, she also wrote, though, that Westling and his staff had been motivated by bias and "uninformed stereotypes . . . that many students with learning disabilities . . . are lazy fakers" who could perform better "if they try hard enough . . . and that many evaluators are 'snake oil salesmen' who overdiagnose the disability," and she awarded $30,000 in punitive damages to the students. She also found that the university was within its rights to refuse to grant math waivers, but said, contrary to Westling's assertions, that BU did not have one single documented case of a student faking dyslexia or any other disability.

There have been other lawsuits against colleges and universities, but the BU case was a very important one; everyone was watching them because of their numbers (they had approximately 480 students with learning difficulties of one sort or another) and because of their distinguished history in the field. How the university will handle disabled students in the future is unknown at the moment, but the dyslexic community certainly can't view the school in the same sanguine terms once possible. It is no longer the understanding place it once was. Some students transferred out during the long, drawn-out suit, and some who were hoping to attend BU, I'm sure, are planning to study elsewhere. Also, some of the exhaustive guides to colleges and universities have decided to drop the school from their lists of places that accommodate students with learning disorders.

The prejudices that exist at BU are not theirs alone; they permeate the society at large and exist at all levels in schools. In fact, Rebecca remembers that she was once told, "Smith is not equipped to deal with students like you." And if those prejudices are present at the undergraduate level, they are even more entrenched in graduate schools, even graduate schools of education. Oddly enough, though, there are medical schools—where you would think the competition would be the keenest—that are beginning to look at and do something for their dyslexic students. Does dyslexia account for the generally terrible handwriting of doctors?

By the time they graduate from college, dyslexic students have had to learn to identify themselves, to advocate for themselves, to discuss their disorders, and to speak up for what they need to overcome them. But what about after college? Dyslexics can become doctors, lawyers, performers, teachers, moneymen, clergymen, writers, even governors and prime ministers; history has shown us so. But how candid or outspoken should or must they be about their disability, and what can they expect the results of their outspokenness to be? Walker Harman discussed his dyslexia in the essay he wrote for his law school application. There are some, though, including Brown's Robert Shaw, who recommend soft-pedaling the information when trying to get accepted at the graduate school level. Walker was accepted and is doing very well at his studies, but he doesn't intend to include such information on his résumé or on any job applications. He doesn't think it will be necessary; he won't be asking for any accommodations, and, he says, "You should only include positive details on your résumé. The only reason for including anything about learning problems would be to talk about how you've overcome them, and why bother doing that?"

Rebecca was told by the career development office at Smith not to talk about her dyslexia when job hunting, but she did not follow their advice. It almost cost her her first job, too, which, ironically, was working with students with learning difficulties at a school in Greece. A Smith graduate who had a say in the hiring process fought for her, though, and she was hired. During her year in Greece, she saw the same kinds of backward attitudes that had existed at her own high school; one sophomore she worked with was going through exactly what she had endured. She taught him the strategies that have worked for her, and his life improved considerably. Then she teamed up with an educational psychologist, and the two put together a talk that they delivered to faculty, to students, and to parents. "It was so amazing," says Rebecca. "At one conference, we had an audience of three hundred parents. None of them spoke English; we had a translator. We were very well received, but I particularly noticed a mother sitting in the back, crying and crying. I found out later that she was going through exactly what my parents went through."

Rebecca says that she intends to continue telling any prospective employers about her dyslexia because it is such an integral part of her life. It also, she feels, gives her a real advantage over many other candidates. "I know how I think," she says. "I know how to get a task done, and I know how to solve problems. So many people fit right into the education system that they don't have to question; they don't have to learn about themselves. Since the education system didn't fit me, and I didn't fit it, I had to discover just exactly how my brain works. Now I know, and that makes me much more able to use all my capabilities. Besides," she adds, "telling a possible employer about my dyslexia is like trying out my favorite jokes on a new date. If he doesn't understand, there's no point in seeing him again."

CHAPTER TEN

Resources

Organizations, Schools, Publishers

T HERE ARE MANY places to turn to for help with dyslexia, whether for oneself, one's child, or anyone else. First and foremost are the organizations that exist to do just that, to be resources for information, for assistance, and for comfort. Among them the most important is the International Dyslexia Association. The Dyslexia Association is nonprofit, and one merely pays a fee to join. You don't have to be dyslexic; you don't have to provide testing or references. Anyone who has anything at all to do with dyslexia should join. The Association offers much printed matter on the subject— books and pamphlets, and even tapes of lectures. Members also receive a quarterly publication called *Perspectives* and yearly compilations of research papers called *Annals of Dyslexia.*

The Association has branches in most states of the United States and in other countries as well; most send out regular newsletters to their members and make referrals to local professionals for testing or remediation. There is an annual meeting in a different American city each fall, where the leading neuroscientists and others present their most current findings, and where workshops and talks offer educational training in Association-approved techniques and tactics. There are also special gatherings during the three- or four-day conferences for teenagers, parents, or college students. Some chapters have their own annual conferences; the one in New York in the spring draws hundreds of participants each year. To get a membership application, contact the headquarters in Maryland:

>   The International Dyslexia Association
>   Chester Building, Suite 382
>   8600 La Salle Road
>   Baltimore, Maryland 21204
>   TELEPHONE: 410-296-0232

There are many other fine organizations that are helpful, but none that are devoted exclusively to dyslexia. They also include information about other learning disabilities, but, remember, dyslexics make up 85 percent of the LD population. Here is a listing of some of the best:

>   National Center for Learning Disabilities
>   381 Park Avenue South, Suite 1420
>   New York, New York 10016
>   TELEPHONE: 212-545-7510

The NCLD is a nonprofit organization for members that offers much printed information and has an extensive referral service. The NCLD also offers seminars and workshops, sends out newsletters and video kits, and maintains an active presence in Washington, D.C., representing the legal rights of the LD population. Its annual magazine is called *Their World*. Anne Ford is the chairman of the board.

•   •   •

>   The National Institute of Child Health
>   and Human Development
>   National Institutes of Health
>   6100 Executive Boulevard
>   Rockville, Maryland 20852
>   TELEPHONE: 301-496-5733

This is the organization that is funding a great deal of research into dyslexia and other learning disabilities, with G. Reid Lyon overseeing

it. It offers material discussing the latest research and reviews of pertinent literature published about learning disabilities.

· · ·

Learning Disabilities Association of America
4156 Library Road
Pittsburgh, Pennsylvania 15234
TELEPHONE: 412-341-1515

This is another national nonprofit organization that holds an annual
conference for its members and that supplies information over the telephone or in assorted printed publications. The LDA has many state
and local chapters that offer their own workshops, conferences, and
presentations of research.

· · ·

Division for Learning Disabilities of the
    Council on Exceptional Children
1920 Association Drive
Reston, Virginia 22091-1589
TELEPHONE: 703-620-3660 or 800-328-0272

The Council on Exceptional Children is a nonprofit organization
that can be joined. It has seventeen specialized divisions, of which the
Division for Learning Disabilities is one. Both groups hold regular conferences and provide booklets, pamphlets, and other printed material.

· · ·

The Educational Resources Information Center
1920 Association Drive
Reston, Virginia 22091-1589
TELEPHONE: 703-264-9474 or 800-328-0272

This is an information clearinghouse that is offered by the Council
on Exceptional Children and funded by the U.S. government.

· · ·

Council for Learning Disabilities
P.O. Box 40303
Overland Park, Kansas 66204
TELEPHONE: 913-492-8755

This is another national organization that can be joined; it was created to provide help for professionals who work in the field of learning disabilities. *The Journal of Learning Disabilities* is available through the Council for Learning Disabilities.

• • •

National Information Center for Children
and Youth with Disabilities
P.O. Box 1492
Washington, D.C. 20013-1492
TELEPHONE: 800-695-0285

This is a clearinghouse that offers information on disabilities of all sorts, not just learning disabilities, and issues related to them. The center refers parents to services such as early intervention programs, advocacy groups, and parent-to-parent groups. It will provide help in finding local groups concerned with dyslexia.

• • •

Parents' Educational Resource Center
1660 South Amphlett Boulevard, Suite 200
San Mateo, California 94402-2508
TELEPHONE: 415-655-2410

An organization for members that provides information and referrals, the Parents' Educational Resource Center also conducts programs and publishes a quarterly newsletter, *Parent Journal.*

• • •

Association on Higher Education and Disability
P.O. Box 21192
Columbus, Ohio 43221-0192
TELEPHONE: 614-488-4972

This international group publishes a bimonthly newsletter, *Alert,* and provides conferences, workshops, and training programs.

● ● ●

National Association of Private Schools
  for Exceptional Children
1522 K Street, NW, Suite 1032
Washington, D.C. 20005
TELEPHONE: 703-684-6763

This organization provides referrals to people who are trying to find information about private schools for the disabled. It sponsors annual conferences and provides written materials.

● ● ●

Association of Educational Therapists
14852 Ventura Boulevard, Suite 207
Sherman Oaks, California 91403
TELEPHONE: 818-788-3850

This, too, is a national organization that one may join. It provides referrals to local educational therapists—which is the new term for people who used to be called tutors, because tutoring could mean help with homework or other such assistance that requires no special training.

● ● ●

Recording for the Blind and Dyslexic
20 Roszel Road
Princeton, New Jersey 08540
TELEPHONE: 609-452-0606

This organization lends books on tape of all sorts—textbooks, fiction, research manuals, computer manuals. It is exceedingly valuable for students. More than half of RFB&D's subscribers are dyslexic. There is a registration fee, and the tapes must be played on the organization's own recorders. To register, an application must be filled out and signed by a teacher, school psychologist, or other professional in disability services to document the difficulty.

• • •

National Library Service for the Blind
and Physically Handicapped
Library of Congress
Washington, D.C. 20542
TELEPHONE: 202-707-5100 or 800-424-8567

This division of the Library of Congress produces books and magazines in special format and lends recordings of both. To make inquiries about the program, leave your address and telephone number, and you will hear from one of the state libraries nationwide that circulate the materials.

Also, many big hospital complexes have centers that provide full evaluations, and some offer remediation as well. In Chicago there is the Masonic. In New York several offer one or both: St. Luke's, New York Hospital, NYU Medical Center, and Mount Sinai, among them. In Dallas the Scottish Rite Hospital has a renowned program, as does Massachusetts General in Boston. Looking into what your nearest medical center offers can be very fruitful. Colleges and universities often offer services as well, particularly those that train teachers and learning specialists.

Computer software becomes obsolete so quickly, I will mention but a few possibilities. One, ClarisWorks, is a word processing program used by many, particularly Mac users. Claris 4.0 has an outlining capability that is very useful both for teaching and for student use. Another is the program I talked about that makes semantic maps, turns them into outlines, then back into maps, so students can see which works best for them. That program is called Inspiration, and it can be ordered from Inspiration Software, Inc., at 503-297-3004. I don't find many computer games very valuable for helping dyslexics, but there is one I like so much, I even encourage some children to use it. Word Munchers gives practice recognizing particular sounds in words and can reinforce teaching for those children who are able to master it quickly enough to make it fun.

Richard Wanderman, a computer and learning disabilities expert, offers an assortment of software to help with phonics, word parts, confusing words, etc. His company is Poor Richard's Publishing, P.O. Box 1075, Litchfield, Connecticut 06759; telephone: 860-567-4307.

Two publications that provide information about computers and people with learning problems are *The Complete Learning Disabilities Directory*, ed. by Leslie MacKenzie, Grey House Publishing, Inc., Pocket Knife Square, Lakeville, Connecticut 06039; and *Handbook of Microcomputers in Special Education*, ed. by Michael Behrman, College Hill Press, 4284 41st Street, San Diego, California 92105

There are two publishers whose wares are very valuable for dyslexics and for people who teach dyslexics. The first, for books on the subject for the professional and the layman, is

> York Press, Inc.
> P.O. Box 594
> Timonium, Maryland 21094
> TELEPHONE: 800-962-2763

The second, for books and materials that are useful in teaching dyslexics, for Diana Hanbury King's books, for Mel Levine's books, and for Joanne Carlisle's Reading and Thinking Series, is

> Educators Publishing Service
> 31 Smith Place
> Cambridge, Massachusetts 02138-1000
> TELEPHONE: 800-225-5450

There are also a number of private schools for dyslexics. What follows does *not* pretend to be a comprehensive survey; it is an alphabetic listing of the schools I know about. Also, a caveat: All schools can vary from year to year, depending upon who is in charge and who is teaching. These are *not* recommendations, and if you are interested in any of them, you must do your homework and find out as much as you can about them. Talk to school officials; ask about the credentials and experience of the teachers; find out about the difficulties of the other students. Does the school really focus on dyslexics, or are more pupils there for other reasons? Visit the place. Tour it; go to classes; talk to students and faculty. Get the names and numbers of parents who have children at the school and talk to them.

> The Assets School
> One Ohana Nui Way
> Honolulu, Hawaii 96818
> TELEPHONE: 808-423-1356

Assets is a school for "gifted, dyslexics, and gifted/dyslexics," offering individualized Orton-Gillingham instruction for boys and girls in grades kindergarten through twelve. Assets also offers a summer program, testing, parent seminars, and night school for adult dyslexics.

> Brandon Hall School
> 1701 Brandon Hall Drive
> Atlanta, Georgia 30350-3799
> TELEPHONE: 770-394-8177

Brandon Hall is a coeducational day and boys-only boarding school for grades four through postgraduate. Students have dyslexia, ADD, and other learning disabilities.

•   •   •

> Brehm Preparatory School
> 1245 East Grand Avenue
> East Carbondale, Illinois 62901
> TELEPHONE: 618-457-0371

Brehm is a coeducational school for junior high, senior high, and postsecondary school dyslexic students.

•   •   •

> The Briarwood School
> 12207 Whittington Drive
> Houston, Texas 77077-4999
> TELEPHONE: 281-493-1070

•   •   •

Camperdown Academy
501 Howell Road
Greenville, South Carolina 29615
TELEPHONE: 864-244-8899

Camperdown is a coed day school for dyslexic students in grades one through eight.

•   •   •

The Carroll School
Baker Bridge Road
Lincoln, Massachusetts 01773
TELEPHONE: 781-259-8342
FAX: 781-259-8852

Carroll is a coed day school for children in grades one through twelve who have language-based learning disabilities.

•   •   •

The dePaul School, Inc.
1925 Duker Avenue
Louisville, Kentucky 40205
TELEPHONE: 502-459-6131

DePaul is a private, independent, nonsectarian school for dyslexic students.

•   •   •

The Forman School
12 Norfolk Road
P.O. Box 80
Litchfield, Connecticut 06759
TELEPHONE: 860-567-8712

Forman is a day and boarding secondary school for boys and girls who have learning disorders, not necessarily dyslexia.

• • •

The Gow School
Emery Road
South Wales, New York 14139
TELEPHONE: 800-724-0138

Gow is a boarding college preparatory school that accepts boys only in grades seven through postgraduate for the school year, but has summer programs for ages eight through nineteen that are coeducational.

• • •

Greenhills School
P.O. Box 15392
Winston-Salem, North Carolina 27113
TELEPHONE: 910-924-4908

Greenhills is a private day school for dyslexic girls and boys in grades kindergarten through twelve.

• • •

The Greenwood School
Watt Pond Road
Putney, Vermont 05346
TELEPHONE: 802-387-4545

Greenwood offers remedial education for dyslexic boys ages ten to fifteen.

• • •

The Hamilton School at Wheeler
216 Hope Street
Providence, Rhode Island 02906
TELEPHONE: 401-421-8100, ext. 168

Hamilton is a coeducational school for students with language-based learning disabilities in grades one through eight.

•   •   •

The Jemicy School
11 Celadon Road
Owings Mills, Maryland 21117
TELEPHONE: 410-653-2700

Jemicy is a coed day school for average to bright children with dyslexia in grades one through eight.

•   •   •

The Kildonan School
Amenia, New York 12501
TELEPHONE: 914-373-8111

Kildonan accepts boys and girls as day students from second grade through postgraduate, as boarding students from sixth grade through postgraduate. There is also a summer camp at Kildonan, Camp Dunnabeck, where students receive daily tutoring and study halls, and also have regular camp activities and sports.

•   •   •

The Lab School of Washington
4759 Reservoir Road, NW
Washington, D.C. 20007
TELEPHONE: 202-965-6600

Lab is a coed day school for learning disabled in grades kindergarten through twelve.

•   •   •

The Landmark School
Prides Crossing, Massachusetts
TELEPHONE: 508-927-4440

Landmark West School
Encino, California
TELEPHONE: 818-986-5045

Landmark is a day and boarding school for language-based learning disabled boys and girls ages eight to twenty, with daily individual tutorials. Landmark also offers six-week summer programs that include daily tutorials, a college prep program, and marine science and seamanship programs.

•   •   •

Oakland School
Boyd Tavern, Virginia 22947
TELEPHONE: 804-293-9059

Oakland is a coeducational school for children ages eight through seventeen (may enroll through age fourteen) who have reading problems.

•   •   •

The Prentice School
18341 Lassen Drive
Santa Ana, California 92705
TELEPHONE: 714-538-4511

Prentice is a day school for dyslexic boys and girls in grades kindergarten through eight.

Saint Andrew's School
63 Federal Road
Barrington, Rhode Island 02806
TELEPHONE: 401-246-1230

Saint Andrew's is a coeducational day and boarding school for students in grades six through twelve who have language-based learning disabilities or attentional/organizational problems.

•   •   •

The Schenck School, Inc.
282 Mount Paran Road N.W.
Atlanta, Georgia 30321
TELEPHONE: 404-252-2591

Schenck is a day school that was founded in 1959 to educate dyslexic boys and girls in grades one through eight.

• • •

The Summit School
664 East Central Avenue
Edgewater, Maryland 21037
TELEPHONE: 410-798-0005 (Annapolis) or
    410-269-0070 (Baltimore)

Summit is for dyslexic boys and girls in grades one through eight.

• • •

Trident Academy
1455 Wakendaw Road
Mount Pleasant, South Carolina 29464
TELEPHONE: 803-884-7046

Trident is a coeducational school for day and boarding students in kindergarten through postgraduate study.

• • •

The Vanguard School
2249 Highway 27 North
Lake Wales, Florida 33853
TELEPHONE: 813-676-6091

• • •

The Windward School
Windward Avenue
White Plains, New York 10605
TELEPHONE: 914-949-5601

Windward is a coeducational day school for language-based learning disabled students in grades one through twelve.

Bibliography and Other Sources

Of course, the most important sources for this book are the valiant, hardworking, humor-filled people whose stories are its heart, and who all wish, I know, that others will be aided by learning about their experiences. To them my undying admiration and my gratitude.

Other vital sources of information and education, for me and many others, are the annual conferences of the New York branch of the International Dyslexia Association and the annual meetings of the Association. I have attended these for ten years, and this book is greatly influenced by the information I have gathered there and by the people I have heard share their research and their knowledge. To all of them I am deeply grateful.

In addition, the following books and articles were helpful:

Aaron, P. G. "Developmental Dyslexia: Is It Different from Other Forms of Reading Disability?" *Annals of Dyslexia* 37 (1987): 109–125.

———. "Is There a Visual Dyslexia?" *Annals of Dyslexia* 43 (1993): 125–148.

Aaron, P. G.; Kuchta, S.; Grapenthin, C. T. "Is There a Thing Called Dyslexia?" *Annals of Dyslexia* 38 (1988): 33–49.

Begley, Sharon. "How to Build a Baby's Brain." *Newsweek Special Edition,* spring/summer 1997, 28.

Bender, Lauretta, M.D. "Highlights in Pioneering the Understanding of Language Disabilities." *Annals of Dyslexia* 37 (1987): 10–18.

Bentin, Shlomo; Leshem, Haya. "On the Interaction Between Phonological Awareness and Reading Acquisition: It's a Two-Way Street." *Annals of Dyslexia* 43 (1993): 125–1438.

Brady, Susan; Moats, Louisa. "Informed Instruction for Reading Success: Foundation for Teacher Preparation." A position paper of the International Dyslexia Association, May 1997.

Carter, Violet Bonham. *Winston Churchill: An Intimate Portrait.* New York: Harcourt, Brace and Company, 1965.

Chall, Jeanne S. "Reading Development in Adults." *Annals of Dyslexia* 37 (1987): 240–251.

Churchill, The Rt. Hon. Winston S. *A Roving Commission/My Early Life.* New York: Charles Scribner's Sons, 1930.

Cicci, Regina. "Dyslexia: Especially for Parents." *Annals of Dyslexia* 39 (1987): 203–211.

Clark, Diana Brewster; Uhry, Joanna Kellogg. *Dyslexia: Theory and Practice of Remedial Instruction.* Baltimore, Md.: York Press, 1995.

Cohen, Jonathan. "On the Differential Diagnosis of Reading, Attentional, and Depressive Disorders." *Annals of Dyslexia* 44 (1992): 165–184.

Crossen, Cynthia. "Brain Research Hints Why Reading Stumps Many Kids." *Wall Street Journal,* 16 May 1997, 3A.

Dembner, Alice. "Boston University Evaluations Proposals for Learning-Disabled Draw Fire." *Boston Globe,* 14 February 1996, 18.

duChossois, Georgeann; Stein, Elissa. *Choosing the Right College.* New York: New York University, 1992.

Elkind, Jerome; Black, Molly Sandperl; Murray, Carol. "Computer-Based Compensation of Adult Reading Disabilities." *Annals of Dyslexia* 46 (1996): 159–186.

Elkind, Jerome; Cohen, Karen; Murray, Carol. "Using Computer-Based Readers to Improve Reading Comprehension of Students with Dyslexia." *Annals of Dyslexia* 43 (1993): 238–259.

Ellis, William. "The School and the Dyslexic—Mutually Exclusive?" *Annals of Dyslexia* 38 (1986): 276–284.

Galaburda, Albert, M.D. "Response to 'The Many Faces of Dyslexia.' " *Annals of Dyslexia* 36 (1986): 192–195.

———. "The Testosterone Hypothesis: Assessment Since Geschwind and Behan, 1982." *Annals of Dyslexia* 40 (1990): 18–38.

Gardner, Howard. "Beyond the IQ: Education and Human Development." *Harvard Educational Review* 57 (May 1987): 187–193.

———. "The Theory of Multiple Intelligences." *Annals of Dyslexia* 38 (1988): 19–35.

Jansky, Jeannette Jefferson. "Language and the Developing Child: Pivotal Ideas of Katrina de Hirsch." *Annals of Dyslexia* 36 (1986): 196–214.

Jones, Bobbie H. "The Gifted Dyslexic." *Annals of Dyslexia* 36 (1986): 301–317.

Leong, Che Kan. "Developmental Dyslexia Revisited and Projected." *Annals of Dyslexia* 41 (1991): 23–40.

Lewin, Tamar. "College Gets Tougher on Verifying Learning Disabilities of Aid Applications." *New York Times,* 13 February 1990, A16.

———. "Fictitious Learning-Disabled Student Is at Center of Lawsuit Against College." *New York Times,* 8 April 1997, B9.

Lindamood, Phyllis C.; Bell, Nanci; Lindamood, P. "Issues in Phonological Awareness Assessment." *Annals of Dyslexia* 42 (1992): 242–259.

Louganis, Greg, with Eric Marcus. *Breaking the Surface.* New York: Random House, 1995.

Lyon, G. Reid. "Toward a Definition of Dyslexia." *Annals of Dyslexia* 45 (1995): 3–27.

MacGinitie, Walter H. and Ruth K. *Gates-MacGinitie Reading Tests,* 3d ed., Chicago: The Riverside Publishing Company 1989.

MacGinitie, Walter H. and Ruth K.; Dreyer, L.; Maria, K. *Gates-MacGinitie Reading Tests,* 4th ed. Chicago: The Riverside Publishing Company, in press.

Miles, T. R. "Dyslexia: Anomaly or Normal Variation?" *Annals of Dyslexia* 36 (1986): 103–117.

Moats, Louisa Cook. "The Missing Foundation in Teacher Education: Knowledge of the Structure of Spoken and Written Language." *Annals of Dyslexia* 44 (1994): 81–102.

Mossberg, Walter S. "Personal Technology." *Wall Streeet Journal,* 12 June 1997, B1.

Nash, J. Madeleine. "Fertile Minds: A Special Report." *Time,* 3 February 1997, 48–56.

Nealson, Patricia. "Ruling Against BU a Bitter Victory for Ten Learning-Disabled Students." *Boston Globe,* 19 August 1997, B2.

Negroponte, Nicholas. *Being Digital.* New York: Alfred A. Knopf, 1995.

Oppenheimer, Todd. "The Computer Delusion." *Atlantic Monthly,* July 1997, 45–62.

Pfeiffer, MaryBeth. "Special Ed Costs Soar." *Poughkeepsie Journal,* 6 April 1997, 1A.

Pompian, Nancy W.; Thum, Carl P. "Dyslexia/Learning Disabled Students at Dartmouth College." *Annals of Dyslexia* 36 (1986): 276–284.

Rawson, Margaret B. *Developmental Language Disability: Adult Accomplishments of Dyslexic Boys.* Baltimore, Md: The Johns Hopkins Press, 1968.

———. "The Many Faces of Dyslexia." *Annals of Dyslexia* 36 (1986): 187–191.

———. "The Orton Trail: 1896–1986." *Annals of Dyslexia* 37 (1987): 36–48.

Reich, Cary. *The Life of Nelson A. Rockefeller: Worlds to Conquer, 1908–1958.* New York: Doubleday, 1996.

Richardson, Sylvia O. "Coping with Dyslexia in the Regular Classroom: Inclusion or Exclusion?" *Annals of Dyslexia* 46 (1996): 37–48.

Shaywitz, Sally E. "Dyslexia." *Scientific American,* November 1996, 98–104.

Stanovich, K. E. "Matthew Effects in Reading: Some Consequences of Individual Differences in the Acquisition of Literacy." *Reading Research Quarterly* 21 (1986): 360–407.

Stanovich, K. E. "The Right and Wrong Places to Look for the Cognitive Locus of Reading Disability." *Annals of Dyslexia* 38 (1988): 154–177.

Stapes, Brent. "Betrayed in the Classroom." Editorial, *New York Times,* 13 January 1997.

Straughn, Charles T., II. *Lovejoy's College Guide for the Learning Disabled,* 3d ed. New York: Macmillan, 1993.

Trapani, Carol. "Board of Regents Floats Plan to Streamline System." *Poughkeepsie Journal,* 6 April 1997, 3A.

Viall, J. Thomas, ed. *Perspectives,* vol. 22, no. 4. Baltimore, Md.: The Orton Dyslexia Society, 1996.

———. *Perspectives,* vol. 23, no. 1. Baltimore, Md.: The Orton Dyslexia Society, 1997.

———. *Perspectives,* vol. 23, no. 2. Baltimore, Md.: The Orton Dyslexia Society, 1997.

Vogel, Susan A.; Walsh, Patricia C. "Gender Differences in Cognitive Abilities of Learning-Disabled Females and Males." *Annals of Dyslexia* 37 (1987): 142–165.

Warrick, Nicola; Rubin, Hyla; Rowe-Walsh, Sheila. "Phoneme Awareness in Language-Delayed Children: Comparative Studies and Intervention." *Annals of Dyslexia* 43 (1993): 153–173.

West, Thomas G. *In the Mind's Eye.* Buffalo, N.Y.: Prometheus Books, 1991.

Wheeler-Scruggs, Cindy, ed. *Perspectives,* vol. 21, no. 4. Baltimore, Md: The Orton Dyslexia Society, 1995.

———. *Perspectives,* vol. 22, no. 2. Baltimore, Md.: The Orton Dyslexia Society, 1996.

———. *Perspectives,* vol. 22, no. 3. Baltimore, Md.: The Orton Dyslexia Society, 1996.

Index